JUSTICE AND HEALTH CARE

JUSTICE AND HEALTH CARE

SELECTED ESSAYS

ALLEN BUCHANAN

OXFORD
UNIVERSITY PRESS
2009

OXFORD
UNIVERSITY PRESS

Oxford University Press, Inc., publishes works that further
Oxford University's objective of excellence
in research, scholarship, and education.

Oxford New York
Auckland Cape Town Dar es Salaam Hong Kong Karachi
Kuala Lumpur Madrid Melbourne Mexico City Nairobi
New Delhi Shanghai Taipei Toronto

With offices in
Argentina Austria Brazil Chile Czech Republic France Greece
Guatemala Hungary Italy Japan Poland Portugal Singapore
South Korea Switzerland Thailand Turkey Ukraine Vietnam

Published by Oxford University Press, Inc.
198 Madison Avenue, New York, New York 10016
www.oup.com

Library of Congress Cataloging-in-Publication Data
Buchanan, Allen E., 1948–
Justice and health care : selected essays / Allen Buchanan.
p. cm.
Includes bibliographical references and index.
ISBN 978-0-19-539406-1
1. Medical care—Law and legislation—United States.
2. Right to health care—United States. I. Title.
KF3821.B83 2009
344.7303'21—dc22 2009021745

9 8 7 6 5 4 3 2 1

ACKNOWLEDGMENTS

Whatever is valuable in this volume builds on the work of many other bioethicists, but there are four individuals to whom I owe a special debt of gratitude: Dan W. Brock, Baruch Brody, Alexander Capron, and Norman Daniels. I have profited greatly from a long association with Dan, which began even before we served together as Staff Philosophers to the President's Commission on Medical Ethics in 1982–83. He is my model of what a bioethicist should be. I am grateful to Alex Capron for making possible perhaps the most important formative experience in my career in Bioethics. He appointed me to the position of Staff Philosopher, but even more importantly, he was more responsible than any other single person for making the President's Commission a success, both intellectually and politically. In doing so, he created the environment in which I became a bioethicist. Like everyone else who thinks about justice in health care, I have been enlightened by Norman Daniels's probing, systematic, philosophically sophisticated work on the topic. I owe thanks to Baruch Brody, not only because I have learned so much from his work in Bioethics over the years, but also because he first prompted me to think seriously about the relationship between market processes and issues of justice. He commissioned me to write a conference paper which eventually became my book, *Ethics, Efficiency, and the Market*, and this work, in turn, provided a foundation on which to begin to construct my views about justice and health care.

I also want to thank three people who were more directly involved in this project: Kit (Christopher Heath) Wellman, Peter Ohlin, and Molly Wagener. Over the years a number of people had suggested that it might be useful to collect my work on justice and health care, but it was Kit's forceful urging that finally prompted me to move forward with the project. Peter Ohlin and Molly Wagener of Oxford University Press have been both supportive and efficient in shepherding the manuscript through the production process. It has been a pleasure to work with them both.

Finally, I wish to acknowledge the following generous permissions for reprinting the papers that constitute this volume: Blackwell Publishing for "The Right to a 'Decent Minimum' of Health Care" (*Philosophy & Public Affairs* 13(1): 55–78); Jones and Bartlett Publishers, Sudbury, MA, pp. 321–62. www.jbpub.com for

"Health-Care Delivery and Resource Allocation," (*Medical Ethics*, Robert M. Veatch, ed., 321–62, 1997); University of Utah Press for "Public and Private Responsibilities in the U.S. Health Care System" (*Changing to National Health Care*, R. Heufner and M.P. Battin, eds., 1992); Blackwell Publishing for "Privatization and Just Healthcare" (*Bioethics* 9(3): 220–39, 1995); National Academy Press for "Ethical Issues in For-Profit Health Care, " co-authored with Dan W. Brock (*For-Profit Enterprise in Health Care*, Bradford Gray, ed., 224–49, 1986); Duke University Press for "Managed Care: Rationing Without Justice, but Not Unjustly" (*Journal of Health Politics, Law, and Policy*, 23(4): 617–34, 1998); The Johns Hopkins University Press for "Trust in Managed Care Organizations" (*Kennedy Institute Journal of Ethics*, 10(3): 189–212, 2000); Oxford University Press for "Is There a Medical Profession in the House?" R. Spece, D. Shimm, A. Buchanan, eds., 105–36); Oxford University Press for "Specifying the Content of the Human Right to Health Care," co-authored with Kristen Hessler (*Medicine and Social Justice*, R. Rhodes, M. Battin, A. Silvers, eds., 84–101, 2002); and Springer Publishers for "Responsibility for Global Health," co-authored with Matthew Decamp (*Theoretical Medicine and Bioethics* 27(1): 95–114, 2006).

CONTENTS

LIST OF ABBREVIATIONS

AMA	American Medical Association
CBA	Cost–Benefit Analysis
CEA	Cost-Effectiveness Analysis
DRGs	Diagnostic-Related Groupings
GDP	Gross Domestic Product
HMO	Health Maintenance Organization
ICCPR	International Covenant on Civil and Political Rights
IPA	Independent Practice Association
MCO	Managed Care Organizations
TRIPS	Trade-Related Aspects of Intellectual Property
WHO	World Health Organization
WTO	World Trade Organization

JUSTICE AND HEALTH CARE

INTRODUCTION

This volume collects ten essays, written over a period of nearly three decades, on some of the most fundamental issues concerning justice and health care. Although they deal with a wide range of topics, from the nature of the right to health care to the role of physicians in health-care systems, there is a surprising degree of unity among the essays, resulting from the author's growing awareness of the need to move from a consideration of abstract theories of justice to a more empirically informed ethical analysis that takes seriously the fact that health care is complex institutionalized activity.

Because institutions coordinate behavior by creating incentives that would not exist or would be insufficient in their absence, the focus on institutions leads to a consideration of incentives and of the relationship between incentives and moral commitments. The result is an approach to justice and health-care issues that facilitates more productive interaction between the normative analysis of philosophers and the policy work of economists and political scientists. To frame the same point differently: This author approaches issues regarding justice and health care from the distinctive vantage point of a political philosopher, but with the understanding that political philosophy's traditional preoccupation with the justice and legitimacy of institutions must be informed by sound political science and economics.

The essays are not arranged in chronological order. They are sequenced so as to make clear the development of a distinctive line of thinking about justice and health care. That line of thinking begins with a consideration of the nature and grounding of the right to health care, probes the problems of specifying the content of that right and of identifying those agents who are obligated to help ensure that the right thus specified is realized, and then progresses to an examination of the problems that arise when we attempt to implement that right through appropriate institutions. The two final essays of the volume pursue these same issues at the global level.

What lies at the end of this thought-journey is not a theory of just health care, if by a 'theory' one means a neat hierarchy of principles capable of resolving all or most questions about justice in health care. The result is more modest, but, I believe, worthwhile nonetheless: a deeper appreciation of the complexities of thinking systematically, self-critically, and realistically about justice in health care, along with a measure of skepticism toward attempts to identify a single principle or even a small set of principles that will tell us all we need to know.

SYNOPSIS

The Right to a Decent Minimum of Health Care

This essay (originally published in *Philosophy & Public Affairs*, 1984) subjects to critical scrutiny the perennially popular but frustratingly vague notion that the right to health care is not an unlimited right but rather a right to a "decent minimum" of health care. It also offers criticisms of the most developed theory of justice in health care, Norman Daniels's attempt to ground the right to health care in a principle of equal opportunity. This essay articulates criticisms of Daniels's theory and more generally of attempts to apply abstract principles of justice to health care that Daniels himself came to acknowledge some years later. Among the most important of these criticisms are the following: (1) The attempt to derive a right to health care from the right to enjoy the normal opportunity range in a given society may involve a circularity which has unfortunately conservative implications for health-care policy. The array of life-plans which all (or most or many) people in a given society can reasonably pursue or that constitute a tolerable or adequate life in that society will be determined in part by the availability and quality of health care in that society. In other words, the normal opportunity range is itself in part a social artifact—and in some cases a consequence of the injustice of the society's institutions. So if the principle of equality of opportunity requires efforts to ensure that all can enjoy the normal opportunity range for their society, the demands of justice will be unduly constrained by injustice. If instead all are to enjoy the broadest opportunity range available to humans in the most favored circumstances, the principle of equal opportunity will be over-demanding and insensitive to variations in resources across societies. (2) Daniels's view does not guarantee a universal right to a decent minimum, because it is silent on how we are to make difficult allocation decisions under conditions of scarcity. It does not tell us, for example, whether we are to devote all health-care resources to narrowing the distance between the opportunity ranges of the worst off and the normal opportunity range or to divide resources among all who fall short of the normal opportunity range. In fact, nothing in Daniels's view acknowledges that there is a problem of scarcity and hence a need to ration. Depending upon which rationing principles are added to Daniels's view, it may or may not provide a grounding for a right to access to an adequate level—or any level—of care for all. Whether it does will depend upon which rationing principles are added to it, but without such principles, Daniels's principle of equal opportunity falls far short of providing the basis for an account of just health care.

This essay also makes a fundamental distinction that the previous literature had overlooked: between grounding a legal entitlement to health care in a corresponding moral right to health care and grounding it in a plurality of moral considerations, some of which need not be framed in terms of rights, including the need for coordinated, efficient beneficence. The pluralistic basis for a legal entitlement to a decent minimum developed in this essay is not only more in tune with the nature of the historical struggle to include health care among the entitlements provided by the modern welfare state; it also provides a more secure normative basis for such an entitlement than the attempt to ground it in any one moral principle, including Daniels's principle of equal opportunity.

Finally, it is argued that it is mistaken to think that a better theory of justice in health care will fully resolve the vagueness of the notion of a decent minimum of care. Instead, there is an ineliminable role for collective choice, through legitimate political processes. Better theories of justice in health care can provide valuable constraints on how the right to an adequate level of care is to be fleshed out, and sound empirical evidence about the efficacy and cost of various health cares services is indispensable as well, but in the end what is included in the adequate level or decent minimum of care made available to all is not a fact to be discovered but rather a choice to be made.

Health-Care Delivery and Resource Allocation

The preceding essay argued, *inter alia*, that the right to health care is limited. This second essay (*Medical Ethics*, 2nd ed., Robert M. Veatch, ed., 1997) explores an inescapable implication of that claim, namely, that health-care resources must be rationed. Although the focus is on health-care resources, this essay construes the basic problem as that of rationing for the improvement of health very broadly, so as to accommodate not only the allocation of medical services but also of any other resources affecting health status, including those employed for the provision of basic sanitation, food, shelter, and pollution-control.

This essay offers a rigorous analysis of the concept of rationing as applied to health care and health-promoting resources, articulates alternative criteria for evaluating allocations of scarce health-care resources, and identifies the strengths and weaknesses of these criteria. It provides a nontechnical but accurate introduction to key economic concepts and policy tools relevant to allocation, including cost, efficiency, cost–benefit analysis, and cost-effective analysis. It also identifies the dubious normative assumptions that underlie unreflective uses of these economic concepts and analytic tools and makes clear the ineliminable role of moral principles in tackling issues concerning the allocation of health-care resources. Employing real-world rationing scenarios, including the allocation of scarce organs and of chemotherapy, this second essay identifies different levels of decision-making at which rationing decisions are made and explains why rationing principles that may be suitable in one context are inappropriate in another. Both bioethicists who are not trained in economics and economists who have not studied moral philosophy will find this essay valuable.

"Public and Private Responsibilities in the U.S. Health Care System" (*Changing to National Health Care*, R. Heuffner and M.P. Battin, eds., 1992)

The first two essays explored the idea of a right to health care and the problems of rationing that arise once it is acknowledged that this right is limited. The next step in thinking through the implications of a right to health care is to consider the kinds of systems in which the right can be implemented. The previous essay demonstrated the limitations of abstract theorizing about justice in health care; this essay begins the transition from abstract theorizing to grappling with the problem of achieving or approximating justice through the workings of institutions. Once we shift to the problems of institutional implementation, it becomes clear that an account of what health care people are entitled to is only one part of the picture; there is also the issue of responsibility: Who is obligated to do what in order to ensure that all get what they are entitled to? Just as the preceding essay showed that institutions are needed to supply determinate content to the entitlement to health care, this essay makes the case that institutions play an indispensable role in achieving a fair and effective division of responsibilities for realizing that entitlement.

The focus of this essay is on the mixed character of the U.S. health-care system, but the analysis it offers is applicable to other mixed systems as well. Today, almost all health-care systems are mixed in nature: Some health care is provided and/or funded by government and some is privately provided and largely or exclusively privately financed. In the United States and most other developed countries, governments have appealed to competition, in one form or another, to reduce the costs of health care. Private health care insurers report that they experience conflicts between ethical obligations and the pressures of cost-containment. And health-care advocates complain that private insurers are defaulting on their ethical obligations.

This essay steps back from the debate over this conflict to ask: What is being assumed about the role of private health-care insurers and providers in this talk about conflicts between cost-containment and ethical obligations? If the obligation to ensure that all have access to adequate health care is a *societal* obligation, why should we assume that private entities have obligations regarding access for which they can be held accountable?

To answer these questions it is necessary to distinguish two quite different models of the relationship between private entities and government in society that endeavors to ensure that all have adequate access in a mixed system. According to the first model (the government responsibility model), government's role is to fill whatever gaps in access are left by the operation of the private insurance market; there is no assumption that private insurers have any obligations of justice so far as access to health care is concerned, though they may, like other parties, have some "imperfect" duties of beneficence and may voluntarily assume obligations regarding access as well. Private entities have no obligations of justice for which society may rightly hold them accountable (unless the obligations they voluntarily assume take the form of legal contractual obligations). According to the second model (the assigned responsibility model), society, working through government, allocates determinate obligations to both government and private entities—obligations for which they may rightly be held publicly accountable. Under this sort of system, if private insurers fail to fulfill their assigned obligations, they act unjustly and may rightly be subjected to social and even legal sanctions.

The essay shows that the debate over access fails to distinguish between these two models and that this failure facilitates unproductive bickering over who has failed to solve the access problem. The problem is that in the United States we have the worst of both models: If we regard the system as of the first sort, then it is clear that government is not fulfilling the gap-filling role and that government officials are simply diverting attention from this fact by pointing the finger of blame at private insurers; if we regard it as a system of the second sort, then the difficulty is that there has been no societal assignment of determinate obligations to private entities for which they could be reasonably held accountable. While the existing system doesn't satisfy the conditions of either of the two models, different parties tacitly invoke one or the other models to launch accusations about the other. In any mixed system, unless there is a clear public understanding of which of the two models the system is supposed to exemplify, there is a risk that the rhetoric of mutual blaming will undercut progress toward a more just system. It is one thing to say that society, though authoritative political processes, *should* assign determinate obligations regarding access to private entities; it is another, to act as if this had already been done. Acting as if the assignment of determinate obligations for access has already taken place diverts attention from the fact that a necessary condition for doing so has not yet been achieved or even seriously attempted, namely, an authoritative specification of what the adequate level or decent minimum of care to which all are entitled is.

Determinate obligations to provide health care cannot be specified until we know what health care people are entitled to, but even if we know what they are entitled to, we cannot hold any particular party responsible for doing its fair share of securing access until we develop an authoritative assignment of obligations. In the absence of an authoritative assignment of obligations, charges that private insurers are not meeting their obligations are groundless.

"Privatization and Just Healthcare" (*Bioethics*, 1995)

In mixed systems there is a perennial push to increase the reach of the private sector: even countries with extensive government involvement in health care have increasingly encouraged the development of private health-care insurance and provision, mainly in hopes of achieving lower costs in the public system. This essay argues that advocates of privatization tend to rely on an incomplete set of criteria for determining whether a health-care system is just. They fail to include three crucial criteria: the financial costs of ensuring adequate access for all must be distributed fairly, the burdens of rationing must be distributed fairly, and the system must have the capacity for reform and improvement toward a closer approximation of a fully just system. Even if privatization reduces costs and does so without adversely affecting access to care, it may still fail to satisfy these three criteria. So showing that privatization can reduce cost without compromising the quality of care is not enough to make the case for privatization. But the case for privatization is even more seriously incomplete than that: The set of criteria for evaluating health-care systems and hence for evaluating efforts to increase the role of private provision in health-care systems, should be expanded even further to take into account the relationship between the provision of health care, on the one hand, and biomedical education, research, and the efficient utilization of care, on the other. Privatization proposals, if implemented, should not hinder the education and training of appropriate numbers and types of health-care providers, the effective pursuit of high-quality biomedical research, or the cost-effective utilization of the fruits of biomedical research on ways to improve health. Quite apart from the fact that actual, as opposed to ideal, privatization efforts may in some cases reduce the quality of care, especially for vulnerable populations, when the full set of relevant criteria for evaluation are taken into account, the case in favor of privatization looks much weaker. The essay concludes by arguing that advocates of privatization typically hold inconsistent assumptions about the behavior of government officials: They assume that government officials are incapable of running a reasonably efficient public system, while at the same time attributing extraordinary capacities to officials when it comes to regulating the private health-care sector. They also tend to assume, without good reason, that large-scale privatization is compatible with adequate political and financial support for a dwindling public sector. Neither of these assumptions is well supported by the available evidence.

"Ethical Issues in For-Profit Health Care" (with Dan W. Brock, *For-Profit Enterprise in Health Care*, Bradford Gray, ed., 1986)

The preceding essay provided a critical assessment of the case for privatizing health care; this essay continues the discussion of the ethics of privatization by scrutinizing the chief objections against having a health-care system in which for-profit enterprises play a major role. Although it was written at a time when the debate was just beginning, it still provides the most comprehensive, balanced articulation and evaluation of the ethical issues raised by the growth of for-profit health-care enterprises. The essay considers in detail the following allegations commonly made against for-profit health-care enterprises: (1) for-profit health care exacerbates the access problem, (2) for-profits are unfair competition for nonprofits, (3) for-profits treat health care as a commodity rather than as a right, (4) for-profits are obligated to provide uncompensated services because they benefit from public subsidies for medical research and education, (5) for-profits damage the physician–patient relationship, erode trust, create new conflicts of interest, and diminish quality of care, and (6) for-profits undermine medical education. Each allegation is shown to rest on inaccurate or unsubstantiated empirical claims (e.g., about sharp differences in the behavior of for-profit and not-for-profit enterprises), on a simplistic view of the moral issues (e.g., that it is reasonable to expect physicians to consider only what will produce the most net good for the individual patient in each treatment decision), or on flawed economic reasoning (e.g., the failure to see that it is physicians and patients, not for-profit health-care enterprises, who are the primary beneficiaries of public subsidies for medical research and education). The article concludes that it is a mistake to focus on how for-profits worsen or ameliorate access and equally wrong to regard the access problem as resulting from an ethical failure on their part. Instead, the emphasis should be on the need for a coordinated societal response serious injustices in access to health care and how to achieve it.

"Managed Care: Rationing Without Justice, but Not Unjustly"
(*Journal of Health Politics, Law, and Policy*, 1998)

The preceding essay gave reasons to be skeptical about the claims that there is a clear difference in ethical performance between for-profit and not-for-profit health care and that for-profit entities are defaulting on obligations to ensure access to care for all. This essay shifts the focus to the emergence of managed care, an institutional form that transcends the distinction between for-profit and not-for-profit legal status. Managed care is an attempt to contain spiraling health-care costs through limiting the provision of care, chiefly by changing the incentives under which physicians work. Thus, in focusing on the ethics of managed care, this essay continues to develop the implications of the realization that health care must be rationed.

The essay begins with a simple, nonjudgmental characterization of what managed care is. A managed care organization combines health insurance and the delivery of a broad range of integrated health-care services for a population of plan enrollees and finances the services prospectively from a limited budget. Given this characterization, it is obvious that managed care organizations must contain costs. The following cost-containment techniques are commonly associated with managed care: (1) payment limits (e.g., diagnostic-related groupings [DRGs] for Medicare hospital fees); (2) requirement of preauthorization for certain services (e.g., surgeries); (3) the use of primary care physicians as "gatekeepers" to control referral to more costly specialists; (4) so-called deskilling (using less highly trained provider for certain services than was usual in the pre-managed care era); and (5) financial incentives for physicians to limit utilization of care (e.g., year-end bonuses or holdbacks of payments that physicians receive only if they do not exceed specified utilization limits). In addition, managed care increasingly uses data from outcome (efficacy) studies to develop practice guidelines and for the ongoing assessment and refinement of diagnostic and treatment services.

Managed care broadly understood can be provided by for-profit or non-profit entities and through public, private, or mixed systems. For this reason the analysis provided in this essay has application far beyond the particular context of debate about managed care in which it was written. If, as some have recently dared to begin to hope, the United States finally develops a system that achieves universal access to health care, the problem of rationing will, if anything become more acute, and various cost-containment techniques first developed under the rubric of "managed care" will become even more salient and ethically controversial.

Three ethical objections to managed care are frequently heard: (1) by skimming the cream of the patient population (the least sick and hence least expensive to provide care for), managed care organizations (MCOs) fail to discharge their obligations to ensure access, or at least, to not worsen it; (2) MCOs engage in rationing, thereby depriving patients of care to which they are entitled; and (3) by pressuring physicians to ration care, MCOs interfere with physicians' fulfillment of their fiduciary obligation to provide the best care for their patients. This essay argues that all of these three objections are misconceived. The first rests on a false assumption that the health-care system includes a workable division of responsibility regarding access that assigns obligations regarding access to MCOs. The second objection wrongly assumes that we in the United States have taken the first step toward assuring equitable access to care for all, namely, articulating a standard for what counts as an "adequate level" (or "decent minimum") of care to which all are entitled. The third objection tacitly denies the necessity of rationing, by assuming that physicians are to provide that treatment which can be expected to produce the greatest net benefit for the patient, regardless of cost. These three misguided objections obscure the most fundamental ethical flaw of managed care: The fact that it is a part of a larger institutional setting within which no principled connection can be made between the inescapable activity of rationing and the basic requirements of justice. Without systemic institutional reform to identify and establish a level of care to which all are entitled and to provide an authoritative assignment of responsibilities for securing access, it is not possible to hold managed care organizations responsible in the ways that the most prevalent criticisms of managed care try to do.

"Trust in Managed Care" (*Kennedy Institute Journal of Ethics*, 2000)

This essay deepens the analysis of the ethics of managed care begun in the preceding essay and like it operates with a broad characterization of managed care that is applicable across the full spectrum of profit and nonprofit, private and public health-care organizations and systems. Two basic criticisms of managed care are that it erodes patient trust in physicians and subjects physicians to incentives and pressures that compromise her fiduciary obligation to the patient. This essay first distinguishes between status trust and merit trust. Status trust is the trust physicians enjoy simply by virtue of being recognized as physicians; it is trust conferred by being in a certain socially-constructed professional role. In contrast, merit trust in physicians depends upon an estimate of their actual competence and performance.

It is then argued that (1) the current value of status trust in physicians is probably over rated and certainly underdocumented; (2) status trust can be excessive and that excessive status trust is dangerous; (3) erosion of status trust may not be detrimental if accompanied by a well-founded increase in merit trust; and (4) under conditions of managed care the physician's commitment to traditional medical ethics cannot serve as an adequate basis for merit trust, chiefly because traditional medical ethics conceives of the fiduciary obligation of the physician toward the patient in a manner that denies the reality and the necessity of rationing care.

Next, drawing on an analogy between managed care organization and polities, it is argued that (5) the most appropriate basis for merit trust in managed care is the extent to which the organization satisfies five criteria.

- (i) Nondiscrimination—the burden of cost-containment should not fall disproportionately on persons due to their race, ethnicity, gender, or age, or on the basis of other morally arbitrary characteristics.
- (ii) Impartiality—like cases should be treated alike; for example, physicians should not selectively bend of violate utilization limits for friends, colleagues, colleague's family members, etc.
- (iii) Publicity of rules—at least the most important rules defining rationing practices should be publicized to employees and enrollees.
- (iv) Publicity of justifications for rules—the organization should be prepared to provide public justifications for the priorities reflected in the rules that define its rationing practices.
- (v) Accessible, fair, and timely procedures for appeals of denial of coverage, for example, mechanisms for independent review of denial of coverage decisions.

Although some of these organizational virtues (in particular (i) and (ii)) can be characterized in terms of fairness or justice, it is more accurate to see them as collectively constituting a conception of *legitimacy* for managed care organizations. The term "legitimacy," when applied to governments is usually understood to mean "the right to rule." Managed care organizations are not governments, but, like governments, they issue rules and apply carrots and sticks to secure compliance with them and also claim that the rules they issue are authoritative within their domains of operation.

Focusing on legitimacy-making characteristics in determinations of whether a managed care organization is entitled to trust may be more fruitful than focusing on justice or fairness. In circumstances in which there is not only disagreement about what justice requires, but also uncertainty even among theorists of justice, determining whether or not an institution or an organization is legitimate may be crucial for how we ought to act toward it: generally speaking, if an organization is legitimate, then the proper response to its imperfections is to try to reform it, not to reject it outright. In contrast to the recent work of Norman Daniels and James Sabin, then, this essay does not view items (i) through (iv) as constituting a kind of second-best form of fairness or justice; instead, it recognizes that (1) legitimacy is not the same as justice or fairness and that (2) legitimacy is especially important in precisely those circumstances in which there is so much disagreement and uncertainty about what fairness or justice requires. The key point is that we may be able to achieve a consensus on legitimacy-making features even if we cannot agree with others on—or are ourselves uncertain about—what justice or fairness requires. Thus, under current conditions, legitimacy, rather than justice or fairness may be the most appropriate basis for merit trust in the case of managed care organizations.

The next section of the essay explores the conditions needed for robust competition for merit trust among managed care organizations and indicates the kinds of public policies needed to facilitate such competition. Robust competition for merit trust would require that the following conditions be satisfied: (1) consumers have access to information relevant to making reasonable comparative judgments about the legitimacy of competing organizations, (2) consumers have adequate incentives to get such information, and (3) consumers are able to exert effective pressure on private and public purchasers of insurance so that their judgments about the relative legitimacy of competing organizations will influence purchasing decisions.

Finally, it is shown how the account of organization-based merit trust can accommodate the special fiduciary obligation of medical professionals, and can provide a basis for trust in physicians as participants in such organizations, without indulging in the delusion that it is the physician's duty always to provide all care that is expected to be of net benefit to the patient. Instead of attempting to provide each patient with all the care that would be of any net benefit to her (which would be to deny the necessity of rationing), the physician's duty is to function as a "critical cooperator" in a legitimate managed care organization. The analysis of the ethics of managed care in this and the preceding essay explore fundamental issues that will arise in any form of institutionalized health care that takes the problem of rationing seriously; their relevance is not limited to a narrow construal of "managed care."

"Is There a Medical Profession in the House?" (*Conflicts of Interest in Clinical Practice and Research*, R. Spece, D. Schimm, and A. Buchanan, eds., 1995)

As the preceding two essays demonstrate, the problem of conflicts of interest is at the heart of the managed care debate and will arise in one form or another in any health-care system in which physicians are expected to be agents acting on behalf of patients but at the same time are required to cooperate in organizational or system-wide processes for the rationing of care. This essay deepens the preceding two essays' analysis of the relationship between the goals of health-care systems, including equitable access to care, and conflicts of interest, examining more thoroughly alternative conceptions of the role of the physician and the meaning of medical professionalism. The primary aim of this essay is to uncover and critically examine certain highly problematic but rarely articulated assumptions that frame the debate about physicians' conflicts of interest in health care. The most fundamental assumptions are these: (1) the reduction of patients' trust in medical professionals is a bad thing; (2) unless physicians are regarded as professionals, trust in them and the benefits it brings for patients will not exist; (3) there currently is in this country a medical profession, according to a conception of what a medical profession is that makes it desirable that there be such a profession. Together these assumptions comprise what may be called "the myth of professionalism." To explicate and critically assess these assumptions it is necessary to clarify what is meant by a profession in this context and to explain the justification or rationale for having a profession. It is also necessary to distinguish clearly between the existence of a profession and the belief in its existence, but in such as to take into account the fact that for this type of social entity, belief is partly constitutive of the entity itself. The essay argues that each of the three assumptions is dubious and that taken together they places serious constraints on the range of policy options for dealing with problems of conflict of interest in the context of increasing pressures for rationing and growing entrepreneurial activity in health care. In addition, the essay clarifies the relationship between professionalism and trust, critically examining the pervasive but unreflective assumption that trust in health-care providers is impossible unless health-care providers are professionals according to the conventional understanding of professionalism. The conclusion is that uncritical acceptance of the myth of professionalism prevents us from dealing effectively with—and indeed, even from properly understanding—the problem of conflict of interest. The chief methodological implication of this exceptionally provocative (some would say offensive or at least irreverent) article is that debates about justice in health care, especially insofar as they engage the critical problem of conflict of interest, are unwittingly shaped highly dubious assumptions about medical professionalism.

"Specifying the Content of the Human Right to Health Care"
(with Kristen Hessler, *Medicine and Social Justice*, R. Rhodes and M. Battin, eds., 2002)

This essay and the next reflect two important recent shifts in the character of the debate about justice and health care: The recognition that health care is only one factor among many that affect health outcomes and the growing interest in questions of global justice. The essay first makes the case that the right to health care, understood as one important element in a right to resources and conditions for health, is defensible as a human right. Assuming that there is a human right to health care, there is the problem of specifying its content. Several attempts to specify a determinate content for a human right to health care are considered and found wanting. It is then argued that a more fruitful approach is to ask: What should be the primary institutional locus of the process of determining the content of the human right to health care? More specifically, should the task of specification fall primarily to international institutions or to individual states (the Unites States, France, China, etc.)? Drawing on work on the epistemic functions of institutions by both Hessler and Buchanan, the essay concludes that democratic states should enjoy a defeasible presumptive authority to determine the content of the human right to health care as that right is applied in their domestic health-care policies. This essay takes a significant step toward connecting the long-standing debate among bioethicists on the nature of the right to health care and the problem of specifying its content, on the one hand, and the recent efforts by philosophers, international lawyers, and international relations theorists that tries to integrate systematic moral reasoning with institutional analysis in theorizing human rights, on the other.

"Responsibility for Global Health" (with Matthew DeCamp, *Theoretical Medicine and Bioethics*, 2006)

The preceding essay focuses on the nature of the human right to health care, on the problem of determining the content of that right, and on the importance of institutions in solving that problem. This last essay returns to a theme of earlier essays in this volume, but on a global level: the problem of responsibility. What is a fair distribution of responsibilities for reducing unjust inequalities in health status on a global level? More specifically, how is it possible to move from assertions about human rights to health resources, including health care, to the assignment of determinate, concrete responsibilities for realizing such rights? The essay begins by noting the recent emergence of ethical concerns about "global health" and identifies several likely sources of this development, including: (1) the growing recognition that some major risks to health are global in nature and require a global response; (2) the emergence of transnational "epistemic communities" that provide us with more information about the health problems of people in distant lands than ever before; and (3) the fact that human rights discourse and, more generally, the articulation of a cosmopolitan ethical perspective, are beginning to supply a principled normative basis for taking global health seriously as a moral issue.

Next, the essay argues that there is an unfortunate tendency in the global health literature to make uncritical assumptions about who is responsible for global health problems, where being responsible means having some determinate duty to help solve these problems and being liable to be held accountable for failing to discharge it. Unprincipled "duty dumping"—for example, blaming pharmaceutical companies for the lack of access to live-saving drugs in less-developed countries—may have short-term political benefits, but it wrongs those who are improperly held responsible and obscures the need for developing institutions that will achieve a fair distribution of determinate duties. Thus, this essay develops at the global level a theme advanced earlier with respect to domestic health systems: Before the language of obligations for access can gain traction, it is necessary both to specify what all should have access to and to devise an effective and fair, authoritative assignment of responsibilities for access. Unless these two conditions are fulfilled, justice discourse is likely to impede rather than facilitate moral progress.

The essay then makes the case that the responsibilities of States regarding global health are both more determinate and more extensive than is usually assumed. This result is consonant with the preceding essay's argument that there is a human right to health care, given the assumption, common to the human rights literature, that States are the primary addressees or duty-bearers of human rights. Among the most important responsibilities of States are the following: (1) to avoid committing wrongful acts, at home or abroad, that have health-harming effects (including fighting unjust wars and training and equipping the military forces of other States or non-State groups that are likely to use those forces to commit injustices) and (2) to withhold international legal recognition and other forms of political and economic support from States that fail to fulfill their responsibilities regarding the health of their citizens or, through corruption and gross economic mismanagement, deprive them of the resources they could use for securing better health care or healthier living conditions. In brief, if more States did a better job of fulfilling their obligations to refrain from committing injustices and from supporting states that commit injustices, the positive impact on global health would be enormous.

Next, the essay explores some of the roles that non-State actors, both organizations and individuals, can play in reducing global health injustices. In some cases, large-scale non-State actors such as global corporations can improve the health of significant numbers of people simply by fulfilling the least controversial sort of moral obligation: the obligation not to harm innocent people (e.g., by ceasing to dump toxic wastes in rivers or to support dictators who violate the human rights of their own people). It would be a mistake, however, to focus exclusively on the so-called negative obligation not to harm, as the philosopher Thomas Page would have us do. Non-State actors, whether individuals or organizations, are obligated to work with others to help develop institutions that will protect the human rights of all people, including the right to health care and to other conditions needed for health. Amplifying at the global level a theme developed in several of the preceding essays, this final essay emphasizes that achieving justice is not a matter of implementing abstract principles of justice through existing institutions, but instead requires both the development of new institutions to perform the essential task of articulating a determinate content for the human right to health care and the use of existing legitimate political institutions to devise an authoritative assignment of responsibilities for realizing the right thus specified.

1

THE RIGHT TO A DECENT MINIMUM OF HEALTH CARE

Allen Buchanan

THE ASSUMPTION THAT THERE IS A RIGHT TO A DECENT MINIMUM

A consensus that there is (at least) a right to a decent minimum of health care pervades recent policy debates and much of the philosophical literature on health care. Disagreement centers on two issues: Is there a more extensive right than the right to a decent minimum of health care? What is included in the decent minimum to which there is a right?

PRELIMINARY CLARIFICATION OF THE CONCEPT

Different theories of distributive justice may yield different answers both to the question "Is there a right to a decent minimum?" and to the question "What comprises the decent minimum?" The justification a particular theory provides for the claim that there is a right to a decent minimum must at least cohere with the justifications

I would like to thank Mary Anne Bailey, Jules Coleman, Thomas Hill, Jr., Daniel Wikler, and the editors of *Philosophy & Public Affairs* for their perceptive comments on an earlier draft of this essay. I am especially indebted to Deborah Buchanan for her careful and detailed criticisms.

it provides for other right-claims. Moreover, the character of this justification will determine, at least in part, the way in which the decent minimum is specified, since it will include an account of the nature and significance of health-care needs. To the extent that the concept of a decent minimum is theory-dependent, then, it would be naive to assume that a mere analysis of the concept of a decent minimum would tell us whether there is such a right and what its content is. Nonetheless, before we proceed to an examination of various theoretical attempts to ground and specify a right to a decent minimum, a preliminary analysis will be helpful.

Sometimes the notion of a decent minimum is applied not to health care but to health itself, the claim being that everyone is entitled to some minimal level, or welfare floor, of health. I shall not explore this variant of the decent minimum idea because I think its implausibility is obvious. The main difficulty is that assuring any significant level of health for all is simply not within the domain of social control. If the alleged right is understood instead as the right to everything which can be done to achieve some significant level of health for all, then the claim that there is such a right becomes implausible simply because it ignores the fact that in circumstances of scarcity the total social expenditure on health must be constrained by the need to allocate resources for other goods.

Though the concept of a right is complex and controversial, for our purposes a partial sketch will do. To say that a person A has a right to something, X, is first of all to say that A is entitled to X, that X is due to him or her. This is not equivalent to saying that if A were granted X it would be a good thing, even a morally good thing, or that X is desired by or desirable for A. Second, it is usually held that valid right-claims, at least in the case of basic rights, may be backed by sanctions, including coercion if necessary (unless doing so would produce extremely great disutility or grave moral evil), and that (except in such highly exceptional circumstances) failure of an appropriate authority to apply the needed sanctions is itself an injustice. Recent rights-theorists have also emphasized a third feature of rights, or at least of basic rights or rights in the strict sense: valid right-claims "trump" appeals to what would maximize utility, whether it be the utility of the right-holder, or social utility. In other words, if A has a right to X, then the mere fact that infringing A's right would maximize overall utility or even A's utility is not itself a sufficient reason for infringing it.[1] Finally, a universal (or general) right is one which applies to all persons, not just to certain individuals or classes because of their involvement in special actions, relationships, or agreements.

The second feature—enforceability—is of crucial importance for those who assume or argue that there is a universal right to a decent minimum of health care. For, once it is granted that there is such a right and that such a right may be enforced (absent any extremely weighty reason against enforcement), the claim that there is a universal right provides the moral basis for using the coercive power of the state to assure a decent minimum for all. Indeed, the surprising absence of attempts to justify a coercively backed decent minimum policy by arguments that do *not* aim at establishing a universal right suggests the following hypothesis: advocates of a coercively backed decent minimum have operated on the assumption that such a policy must be based on a universal right to a decent minimum. The chief aim of this article is to show that this assumption is false.

I think it is fair to say that many who confidently assume there is a (universal) right to a decent minimum of health care have failed to appreciate the significance of the first feature of our sketch of the concept of a right. It is crucial to observe that the claim that there is a right to a decent minimum is much stronger than the claim that everyone *ought* to have access to such a minimum, or that if they did it would be a good thing, or that any society which is capable, without great sacrifice, of providing a decent minimum but fails to do so is deeply morally defective. None of the latter assertions implies the existence of a right, if this is understood as a moral entitlement which ought to be established by the coercive power of the state if necessary. This simple point finds expression in traditional ethical theories and in our ordinary moral discourse, for a distinction is made between both "ought" judgments that express claims of right and those that express imperatives founded on moral virtues other than justice. In particular, a distinction is drawn between imperatives of justice and imperatives of charity or beneficence or generosity, the assumption usually being that only the former may be enforced.

Further, the difference between "we ought to provide X to A" and "A has a right to X" is *not* a difference between different degrees of strength or constancy in our moral convictions. To the morally virtuous person the imperatives of charity may be as urgent as those of justice. This point has troubling implications for attempts to establish right-claims by the use of what Rawls calls the method of reflective equilibrium. According to this method, we are to appeal to our particular considered moral judgments as provisional data to be accounted for and organized by a smaller set of more general moral principles. The difficulty is that we may be much surer that someone ought not to lack a certain form of health care than we are about whether the ground of this judgment is a principle that structures our sense of justice or our sense of charity or beneficence or generosity. And even if we can show what makes health care, or certain kinds of health care, morally important, this in itself will not show that there is a right to health care, unless the appropriate connection with principles of justice can be made.

THE ATTRACTIONS OF THE IDEA OF A DECENT MINIMUM

There are at least three features widely associated with the idea of a right to a decent minimum which, together with the facile consensus that vagueness promotes, help explain its popularity over competing conceptions of the right to health care. First, it is usually, and quite reasonably, assumed that the idea of a decent minimum is to be understood in a society-relative sense. Surely it is plausible to assume that, as with other rights to goods or services, the content of the right must depend upon the resources available in a given society and perhaps also upon a certain consensus of expectations among its members. So the first advantage of the idea of a decent minimum, as it is usually understood, is that it allows us to adjust the level of services to be provided as a matter of right to relevant social conditions and also allows for the possibility that as a society becomes more affluent the floor provided by the decent minimum should be raised.

Second, the idea of a decent minimum avoids the excesses of what has been called the strong equal access principle, while still acknowledging a substantive universal right. According to the strong equal access principle, everyone has an equal right to the best health-care services available. Aside from the weakness of the justifications offered in support of it, the most implausible feature of the strong equal access principle is that it forces us to choose between two unpalatable alternatives. We can either set the publicly guaranteed level of health care lower than the level that is technically possible or we can set it as high as is technically possible. In the former case, we shall be committed to the uncomfortable conclusion that no matter how many resources have been expended to guarantee equal access to that level, individuals are forbidden to spend any of their resources for services not available to all. Granted that individuals are allowed to spend their after-tax incomes on more frivolous items, why should not they be allowed to spend it on health? If the answer is that they should be so allowed, as long as this does not interfere with the provision of an adequate package of health-care services for everyone, then we have retreated from the strong equal access principle to something very much like the principle of a decent minimum. If, on the other hand, we set the level of services guaranteed for all so high as to eliminate the problem of persons seeking extra care beyond this level, this would produce a huge drain on total resources, foreclosing opportunities for producing important goods other than health care.

So both the recognition that health care must compete with other goods and the conviction that beyond some less than maximal level of publicly guaranteed services individuals should be free to purchase additional services point toward a more limited right than the strong access principle asserts. Thus, the endorsement of a right to a decent minimum may be more of a recognition of the implausibility of the stronger right to equal access than a sign of any definite position on the content of the right to health care.[2]

A third attraction of the idea of a decent minimum is that since the right to health care must be limited in scope (to avoid the consequences of a strong equal access right), it should be limited to the "most basic" services, those normally "adequate" for health, or for a "decent" or "tolerable" life. However, although this aspect of the idea of a decent minimum is useful because it calls attention to the fact that health-care needs are heterogeneous and must be assigned some order of priority, it does not itself provide any basis for determining which are most important.

THE NEED FOR A SUPPORTING THEORY

In spite of these attractions, the concept of a right to a decent minimum of health care is inadequate as a moral basis for a coercively backed decent minimum policy in the absence of a coherent and defensible theory of justice. Indeed, when taken together they do not even imply that there is a right to a decent minimum. Rather, they only support the weaker conditional claim that if there is a right to health care, then it is one that is more limited than a right of strong equal access, and is one whose content depends upon available resources and some scheme of priorities which shows certain health-care services to be more basic than others. It appears, then, that a theoretical grounding for the right to a decent minimum of health care is indispensable.

ARGUMENTS FOR A UNIVERSAL RIGHT TO A DECENT MINIMUM

Elsewhere I have explored what I believe to be the main approaches to justifying and specifying a (universal) right to a decent minimum of health care: utilitarian arguments (for a derivative right), Rawlsian ideal contract arguments, and an argument from equality of opportunity developed by Norman Daniels.[3] Here I can only briefly summarize my reasons for concluding that none of these approaches is adequate.

Utilitarian Arguments. The chief difficulty with utilitarian arguments is that they are not capable of providing a secure foundation for a right to a decent minimum for *everyone.* Consider, for example, the class of Down's syndrome newborns. These retarded individuals, who often suffer from various physical defects as well, require a large expenditure of social resources over a lifetime. And relative to these costs the contribution these individuals make to social utility is not large, at least as far as we must work with a conception of contribution that is in some way quantifiable. If this is so, then Utilitarianism will justify excluding these infants from even the most minimal health care provided to others as a matter of right.

It is important to see that individuals in this class are capable of various enjoyments and would greatly benefit from the services from which they are excluded. Thus, Utilitarianism may require that, even for the most basic services, what is guaranteed for one individual may not be available to another, even though their needs are equal and both would benefit greatly from the service.

My purpose in developing this example is not to show conclusively that there are no circumstances or no likely circumstances in which Utilitarianism would support a (derivative) universal right to a decent minimum of health care. Instead I have only shown that, granted certain plausible factual assumptions which may in fact be satisfied in our society at this time, there is good reason to doubt that Utilitarianism provides a secure foundation for such a right.

Rawls's Ideal Contract Theory. There are well-known objections to Rawls's ideal contract view as a general theory of rights. It has often been noted that the parties' choice of the difference principle depends upon the implausible assumption that they are extremely, indeed infinitely, averse to risk. Further, Nozick and others have challenged the intuitions about fairness on the basis of which Rawls constructs the original position and have also offered examples to show that the difference principle requires redistributions that are intuitively unfair to the better off. Instead of rehearsing these familiar issues, I will concentrate on a different question: Even if these general objections can be met, does Rawls's theory provide the basis for a substantive right to a decent minimum of health care? If Rawls's theory supports a right to health care, it must be derivative upon the basic rights laid down by the principle of greatest equal liberty, the principle of equality of fair opportunity, or the difference principle. And if there is to be such a derivative right to health care, then health care must either be among the primary goods covered by the three principles or it must be importantly connected with some of those goods. Now at least some forms of health care (such as broad services for prevention and health maintenance, including mental health) seem to bear the earmarks of Rawlsian primary goods: they facilitate the effective pursuit of ends in general and may also enhance our ability to criticize and revise our conceptions of the good. Nonetheless, Rawls does not explicitly list health care among the social primary goods included under the three principles.

Let us suppose that health care is either itself a primary good covered by the difference principle or that health care may be purchased with income or some other form of wealth which is included under the difference principle. In the former case, depending upon various empirical conditions, it might turn out that the best way to satisfy the difference principle is to establish a state-enforced right to health care. But whether maximizing the prospects of the worst off will require such a right and what the content of the right will be depends upon what weight is to be assigned to health care relative to other primary goods included under the difference principle. Similarly, a weighting must also be assigned if we are to determine whether the share of wealth one receives under the difference principle would be sufficient both for health-care needs and for other ends. Until we have some solution to the weighting problem, Rawls's theory can shed only limited light upon the question of priority relations between health care and other goods and among various forms of health care.

It is important to see that the informational constraints imposed by Rawls's "veil of ignorance" preclude a solution to the problem of weighting health care against other primary goods because the answer will depend upon facts about the particular conditions of the society in which the notions in question are to be applied. At best Rawls's hypothetical contractors would choose a kind of *place-holder* for a principle establishing a right to a decent minimum of health care, on the assumption that the content of the right can only be filled out at later stages of agreement in the light of specific information about their particular society.

However, nothing in Rawls's conception of rational decision suggests that once the relevant, concrete information is available, rational persons will agree on a single assignment of weights to the primary goods. It follows that Rawls's theory does not itself supply content for the notion of a right to a decent minimum of health care: instead, at best, it lays down a very abstract structure within which this content will be worked out through the democratic political processes specified by the list of equal basic liberties. Given this, Rawls's theory advances us very little beyond the broad intuitive consensus that there is a universal right to a decent minimum of health care.

Daniels's Argument from Equality of Opportunity. Partly in response to some of the difficulties noted in the previous section, Norman Daniels has developed an alternative Rawlsian approach to the right to health care. Instead of basing the right to health care on an intuitive but ill-defined notion of a decent minimum, Daniels founds a universal right to health care on a stronger, more inclusive version of Rawls's principle of fair equality of opportunity.

Daniels approaches the right to health care by utilizing the idea of "the normal opportunity range" for a given society. This is "the array of life-plans reasonable to pursue within given conditions obtaining in a society." Daniels suggests that we can best understand the distinctive nature and importance of health care if we see that it promotes, restores, or provides surrogates for "normal species functioning," and that normal species functioning is an important contributor to an individual's attainment of the normal opportunity range for his society.[4] The principle from which health-care rights are derived according to Daniels may be stated as follows:

D: Social resources are to be allocated so as to ensure that everyone can attain the normal opportunity range for his or her society.

The success of Daniels's approach depends both upon the plausibility of the overarching principle of equality of opportunity (D) and on the plausibility of the implications of this principle for health-care entitlements. Though he has not yet committed himself unequivocally on this issue, Daniels seems to believe that principle D implies that there is a right to health care that exceeds what is usually thought of as a right to a decent minimum. Daniels emphasizes that the connection between normal species functioning and opportunity and the idea that health care is to be understood as whatever promotes, restores, or replaces normal species functioning achieves two important goals of a theory of health care: it gives us a way of ranking various health-care services as to their relative importance for normal species functioning and provides a principled way of defining the class of health-care needs which does not limit them to *medical* needs as defined by the current health-care delivery system.

A natural objection to Daniels's view is that even if one reason why health care is important is that it contributes significantly to attainment of the normal opportunity range, this is surely not the only reason, or in many cases not the most basic one. After all, health care often relieves suffering, prevents unwanted death, or enhances one's capacity for enjoying what everyone is able to do, even when it does not extend one's range of opportunities. Though I think this criticism has considerable force, I believe there are other, more telling objections.

The first difficulty is the definition of "normal opportunity range." The phrase "the array of life-plans reasonable to pursue" is ambiguous. For *whom* must a life-plan be reasonable to pursue if it is to be included in the normal opportunity range? If to be included a plan must be reasonable for *everyone* to pursue, regardless of his or her physical abilities, skills, and talents, then the list will be so modest that it is doubtful that it could provide content for a substantive universal right to health care of the sort Daniels wants. If, on the other hand, inclusion in the normal opportunity range requires only that the plan be such that it is reasonable for someone or other to pursue it, then D becomes astonishingly strong, since it will include life-plans requiring exceptional talents and rare characteristics.

On this strong interpretation, Daniels's principle of equality of opportunity is vulnerable to the same objection that leads to the rejection of the strong equal access principle. Granted the gap between most individuals' actual opportunity ranges and the array of plans it is reasonable for some individuals to pursue, and granted the almost limitless possibility for technology and other services which can help narrow the gap, a conscientious commitment to D would create an enormous drain on resources. To say that everyone has a right to whatever arrangements are necessary to insure that it is reasonable for him to aspire to become a neurosurgeon, a first-class logician, an accomplished pianist, or the spouse of a movie star seems excessive to say the least.

It is important to see that this objection cannot be met by replying that the right to health care is only a right to the resources required to achieve normal species functioning for all. For even if it could be shown that this goal is much more modest than that of achieving the normal opportunity range (on the strong interpretation) for all, this would be beside the point. In Daniels's view the basic consideration is the attainment of equality with respect to the normal opportunity range—normal species functioning is only important as one factor among others that contribute to it. So my objection is to the basic principle of justice Daniels proposes.

Finally, if neither the strong nor the weak interpretation is acceptable, Daniels might suggest that the normal opportunity range is that of life-plans which constitute a normal or tolerable or adequate or decent life in the society in question. This strategy, however, is one which Daniels should be reluctant to embrace, since he introduced the notion of a normal opportunity range in the first place to avoid the unilluminating move of "specifying" the notion of a decent minimum by reference to equally uninformative notions such as that of an adequate or tolerable life.

A second difficulty is that if we eschew the strong interpretation, the attempt to derive a right to health care from the right to enjoy the normal opportunity range for one's own society may involve a sort of circularity which has unfortunately conservative implications for health-care policy. The array of life-plans which all (or most or many) people in a given society can reasonably pursue or that constitute a tolerable or normal or adequate life in that society will be determined in part by the availability and quality of health care in that society. In other words, the normal opportunity range is itself in part a social artifact. Thus in a society with very poor health-care services the normal opportunity range is correspondingly narrow, even if the society were in fact affluent enough to afford a wider range of services which would allow a wider normal opportunity range. Consequently, a principle which requires only that resources be allocated so as to assure that everyone attains the normal opportunity range would be inadequate in situations in which the normal opportunity range was unacceptably narrow due to a failure to allocate sufficient resources for health care. This suggests that Daniels's principle requiring equal opportunity must be supplemented with a principle requiring *maximization* of the opportunity range, or at least that the opportunity range is to be maximized up to some limit. After all, the importance of health care on Daniels's account is that it facilitates opportunity, and anyone who is concerned with opportunity rather than with equality for its own sake will desire arrangements which require more than mere equality of opportunity if opportunities are few but can be expanded.

Now a principle requiring equality of opportunity relative to a given opportunity range and a principle requiring maximization of the opportunity range (or maximization up to some limit) may conflict with one another. But if this is so, then some way of balancing the demands of these two principles must be found. In a society in which there were no legal barriers to opportunity and none based on racial or sexual discrimination, it is not obvious that either justice or rational self-interest would require, as Daniels seems to assume, the choice of a system that guarantees equality with respect to the opportunity range rather than a system that allows some inequalities but a wider opportunity range. If the latter alternative is appropriate, then we are again pushed in the direction of the vague but intuitively plausible notion of a decent minimum: this time the notion of a decent minimum opportunity range to which the requirement of equality applies.

A third and somewhat surprising feature of Daniels's position, and one which many will view as objectionable, is that it appears that principle D does *not* guarantee a *universal* right to a decent minimum of health care. For D is silent on how we are to make difficult and basic allocation decisions: it does not tell us whether we are to devote all resources to narrowing the distance between the opportunity ranges of the worst off and the normal opportunity range or to divide resources among all who fall short of the normal opportunity range. Indeed, nothing in D even acknowledges that there is a problem of scarcity.

Whether or not D will require some minimal set of health-care services for *all* will depend upon which additional principles we adopt to cope with priority problems in the face of scarcity. If our first priority is to narrow the gap between the worst off and the normal opportunity range, then, depending upon how badly off the worst off are and depending upon the total amount of resources available, there may be nothing left for even minimal services for those who do not fall within the worst-off class. As in the case of Utilitarianism, whether there is a universal right to a decent minimum will depend upon the facts about the society in question. But in Daniels's scheme it will also depend upon what additional principles of distributive justice are used to supplement the principle of equality of opportunity when the commitment to such a strong principle collides with the realities of scarcity.

If, on the other hand, the commitment to raising the opportunity range of the worst off is to be limited by a principle stating that everyone has a right to some set of services even if there are others who are farther from the normal opportunity range, then, unless this universal right-claim can be nonarbitrarily specified and supported, it appears that we have again ushered in the idea of a decent minimum. And contrary to what Daniels says, his principle of equality of opportunity is a supplement, rather than a replacement for it.

A CHANGE OF STRATEGY

So far I have considered several proposed principles or theories of justice and seen, rather surprisingly, that they do not provide a firm basis for the claim that there is a universal right to a decent minimum of health care or else that they encounter serious difficulties in supplying a practical specification of the content of that right. These deflationary results would be welcomed by a libertarian, who would explain them by the hypothesis that *there is no right to a decent minimum*. Further, a sophisticated libertarian would explain the pervasiveness of the (false) belief that there is a right to a decent minimum by the hypothesis that those who hold this belief have mistaken the moral imperatives of beneficence or charity for those of justice.

I shall argue, however, that even if the libertarian were right thus far there is still a sound justification for an enforced principle guaranteeing a decent minimum of health care to everyone. The alternative strategy I wish to explore is pluralistic. My suggestion is that the combined weight of arguments from special (as opposed to universal) rights to health care, harm-prevention, prudential arguments of the sort used to justify public health measures, and two arguments that show that effective charity shares features of public goods (in the technical sense) is sufficient to do the work of an alleged universal right to a decent minimum of health care.

Arguments from Special Rights. The right-claim we have been examining (and find unsupported) has been a *universal* right-claim: one that attributes the same right to all persons. *Special* right-claims, in contrast, restrict the right in question to certain individuals or groups.

There are at least three types of arguments that can be given for special rights to health care. First, there are arguments from the requirements of rectifying past or present institutional injustices. It can be argued, for example, that American blacks and native Americans are entitled to a certain core set of health-care services owing to their history of unjust treatment by government or other social institutions, on the grounds that these injustices have directly or indirectly had detrimental effects on the health of the groups in question. Second, there are arguments from the requirements of compensation to those who have suffered unjust harm or who have been unjustly exposed to health risks by the assignable actions of private individuals or corporations—for instance, those who have suffered neurological damage from the effects of chemical pollutants.

Third, a strong moral case can be made for special rights to health care for those who have undergone exceptional sacrifices for the good of society as a whole—in particular those whose health has been adversely affected through military service. The most obvious candidates for such compensatory special rights are soldiers wounded in combat.

Arguments from the Prevention of Harm. The content of the right to a decent minimum is typically understood as being more extensive than those traditional public health services that are usually justified on the grounds that they are required to protect the citizenry from certain harms arising from the interactions of persons living together in large numbers. Yet such services have been a major factor—if not *the* major factor—in reducing morbidity and mortality rates. Examples include sanitation and immunization. The moral justification of such measures, which constitute an important element in a decent minimum of health care, rests upon the widely accepted Harm (Prevention) Principle, not upon a right to health care.

The Harm Prevention argument for traditional public health services, however, may be elaborated in a way that brings them closer to arguments for a universal right to health care. With some plausibility one might contend that once the case has been made for expending public resources on public health measures, there is a moral (and perhaps Constitutional) obligation to achieve some standard of *equal protection* from the harms these measures are designed to prevent. Such an argument, if it could be made out, would imply that the availability of basic public health services should not vary greatly across different racial, ethnic, or geographic groups within the country.

Prudential Arguments. Prudent arguments for health-care services typically emphasize benefits rather than the prevention of harm. It has often been argued, in particular, that the availability of certain basic forms of health care make for a more productive labor force or improve the fitness of the citizenry for national defense. This type of argument, too, does not assume that individuals have moral rights (whether special or universal) to the services in question.

It seems very likely that the combined scope of the various special health-care rights discussed earlier, when taken together with harm prevention and prudential arguments for basic health services and an argument from equal protection through public health measures, would do a great deal toward satisfying the health-care needs which those who advocate a universal right to a decent minimum are most concerned about. In other words, once the strength of a more pluralistic approach is appreciated, we may come to question the popular dogma that policy initiatives designed to achieve a decent minimum of health care for all must be grounded in a universal moral right to a decent minimum. This suggestion is worth considering because it again brings home the importance of the methodological difficulty encountered earlier. Even if, for instance, there is wide consensus on the considered judgment that the lower health prospects of inner city blacks are not only morally unacceptable but an injustice, it does not follow that this injustice consists of the infringement of a universal right to a decent minimum of health care. Instead, the injustice might lie in the failure to rectify past injustices or in the failure to achieve public health arrangements that meet a reasonable standard of equal protection for all.

Two Arguments for Enforced Beneficence. The pluralistic moral case for a legal entitlement to a decent minimum of health care (in the absence of a universal moral right) may be strengthened further by non-rights-based arguments from the principle of beneficence.[5] The possibility of making out such arguments depends upon the assumption that some principles may be justifiably enforced even if they are not principles specifying valid right-claims. There is at least one widely recognized class of such principles requiring contribution to the production of "public goods" in the technical sense (e.g., tax laws requiring contribution to national defense). It is characteristic of public goods that each individual has an incentive to withhold his contribution to the collective goal even though the net result is that the goal will not be achieved. Enforcement of a principle requiring all individuals to contribute to the goal is necessary to overcome the individual's incentive to withhold contribution by imposing penalties for his own failure to contribute and by assuring him that others will contribute. There is a special subclass of principles whose enforcement is justified not only by the need to overcome the individual's incentive to withhold compliance with the principle but also to ensure that individuals' efforts are appropriately *coordinated*. For example, enforcing the rule of the road to drive only on the right not only ensures a joint effort toward the goal of safe driving but also coordinates individuals' efforts so as to make the attainment of that goal possible. Indeed, in the case of the "rule of the road" a certain kind of coordinated joint effort is the public good whose attainment justifies enforcement. But regardless of whether the production of a public good requires the solution of a coordination problem or not, there may be no *right* that is the correlative of the coercively backed obligation specified by the principle. There are two arguments for enforced beneficence, and they each depend upon both the idea of coordination and on certain aspects of the concept of a public good.

Both arguments begin with an assumption reasonable libertarians accept: there is a basic moral obligation of charity or beneficence to those in need. In a society that has the resources and technical knowledge to improve health or at least to ameliorate important health defects, the application of this requirement of beneficence includes the provision of resources for at least certain forms of health care. If we are sincere, we will be concerned with the efficacy of our charitable or beneficent impulses. It is all well and good for the libertarian to say that voluntary giving *can* replace the existing array of government entitlement programs, but this *possibility* will be cold comfort to the needy if, for any of several reasons, voluntary giving falters.

Social critics on the left often argue that in a highly competitive acquisitive society such as ours it is naive to think that the sense of beneficence will win out over the urgent promptings of self-interest. One need not argue, however, that voluntary giving fails from weakness of the will. Instead one can argue that even if each individual recognizes a moral duty to contribute to the aid of others and is motivationally capable of acting on that duty, some important forms of beneficence will not be forthcoming because each individual will rationally conclude that he should not contribute.

Many important forms of health care, especially those involving large-scale capital investment for technology, cannot be provided except through the contributions of large numbers of persons. This is also true of the most important forms of medical research. But if so, then the beneficent individual will not be able to act effectively, in isolation. What is needed is a coordinated joint effort.

First Argument. There are many ways in which I might help others in need. Granted the importance of health, providing a decent minimum of health care for all, through large-scale collective efforts, will be a more important form of beneficence than the various charitable acts A, B, and C, which I might perform *independently*, that is, whose success does not depend upon the contributions of others. Nonetheless, if I am rationally beneficent I will reason as follows: either enough others will contribute to the decent minimum project to achieve this goal, even if I do not contribute to it; or not enough others will contribute to achieve a decent minimum, even if I do contribute. In either case, my contribution will be wasted. In other words, granted the scale of the investment required and the virtually negligible size of my own contribution, I can disregard the minute possibility that my contribution might make the difference between success and failure. But if so, then the rationally beneficent thing for me to do is not to waste my contribution on the project of ensuring a decent minimum but instead to undertake an independent act of beneficence; A, B, or C—where I know my efforts will be needed and efficacious. But if everyone, or even many people, reason in this way, then what we each recognize as the most effective form of beneficence will not come about. Enforcement of a principle requiring contributions to ensuring a decent minimum is needed.

The first argument is of the same form as standard public goods arguments for enforced contributions to national defense, energy conservation, and many other goods, with this exception. In standard public goods arguments, it is usually assumed that the individual's incentive for not contributing is self-interest and that it is in his interest not to contribute because he will be able to partake of the good, if it is produced, even if he does not contribute. In the case at hand, however, the individual's incentive for not contributing to the joint effort is not self-interest, but rather his desire to maximize the good he can do for others with a given amount of his resources. Thus if he contributes but the goal of achieving a decent minimum for all would have been achieved without his contribution, then he has still failed to use his resources in a maximally beneficent way relative to the options of either contributing or not to the joint project, even though the goal of achieving a decent minimum is attained. The rationally beneficent thing to do, then, is not to contribute, even though the result of everyone's acting in a rationally beneficent way will be a relatively ineffective patchwork of small-scale individual acts of beneficence rather than a large-scale, coordinated effort.

Second Argument. I believe that ensuring a decent minimum of health care for all is more important than projects A, B, or C, and I am willing to contribute to the decent minimum project, but only if I have assurance that enough others will contribute to achieve the threshold of investment necessary for success. Unless I have this assurance, I will conclude that it is less than rational—and perhaps even morally irresponsible—to contribute my resources to the decent minimum project. For my contribution will be wasted if not enough others contribute. If I lack assurance of sufficient contributions by others, the rationally beneficent thing for me to do is to expend my "beneficence budget" on some less-than-optimal project

A, B, or C, whose success does not depend on the contribution of others. But without enforcement, I cannot be assured that enough others will contribute, and if others reason as I do, then what we all believe to be the most effective form of beneficence will not be forthcoming. Others may fail to contribute either because the promptings of self-interest overpower their sense of beneficence, or because they reason as I did in the First Argument, or for some other reason.

Both arguments conclude that an enforced decent minimum principle is needed to achieve coordinated joint effort. However, there is this difference. The Second Argument focuses on the *assurance problem*, while the first does not. In the Second Argument all that is needed is the assumption that rational beneficence requires assurance that enough others will contribute. In the First Argument the individual's reason for not contributing is not that he lacks assurance that enough others will contribute, but rather that it is better for him not to contribute regardless of whether others do or not.

Neither argument depends on an assumption of conflict between the individual's moral motivation of beneficence and his inclination of self-interest. Instead the difficulty is that in the absence of enforcement, individuals who strive to make their beneficence most effective will thereby fail to benefit the needy as much as they might.

A standard response to those paradoxes of rationality known as public goods problems is to introduce a coercive mechanism which attaches penalties to non-contribution and thereby provides each individual with the assurance that enough others will reciprocate so that his contribution will not be wasted and an effective incentive for him to contribute even if he has reason to believe that enough others will contribute to achieve the goal without his contribution. My suggestion is that the same type of argument that is widely accepted as a justification for enforced principles requiring contributions toward familiar public goods provides support for a coercively backed principle specifying a certain list of health programs for the needy and requiring those who possess the needed resources to contribute to the establishment of such programs, even if the needy have no *right* to the services those programs provide. Such an arrangement would serve a dual function: it would coordinate charitable efforts by focusing them on one set of services among the indefinitely large constellation of possible expressions of beneficence, and it would ensure that the decision to allocate resources to these services will become effective.

OBJECTIONS AND REPLIES

It might be objected that these two arguments rest upon either of two unacceptable premises: (1) that if something is a moral principle (or at least a basic moral principle) then it may be given the status of a law and enforced by the state, or

(2) that it is the role of the state to insure that its citizens are morally virtuous. If the enforced beneficence arguments rested on either of these very general premises they would be implausible, because both (1) and (2) have unacceptable implications for individual liberty. But the enforced beneficence arguments do not assume that any moral principle, or any basic moral principle, may be enforced; nor do they assume that the state is in general the guardian of our morals. Instead, they only contend that one important moral principle may be enforced if, in the absence of enforcement, familiar problems of coordinated joint action would arise. Further, it seems most plausible to regard the conclusion of the enforced beneficence arguments as defeasible: if political conditions were such that the establishment of the required enforcement mechanism would contribute to a dangerous concentration of government power, then the lesser of evils might be to forgo a solution to the coordination and assurance problems.

However, it is unpersuasive to argue that—at least in the United States at this time—a compulsory contribution scheme constitutes an unacceptable threat to liberty by endowing the government with uncontrollable powers. Moreover, some of the most significant dangers which make a general policy of the "enforcement of morals" unacceptable simply do not apply with any force to the case at hand. In particular, opponents of the enforcement of morals usually rightly point out that such policy would destroy the conditions required for individual autonomy, privacy, and for the flourishing of intimate personal relationships. This is certainly true for the enforcement of many moral principles, especially principles of sexual or religious morality, but it is not at all convincing in the case of arrangements to enforce the moral duty of charity or beneficence. Nor is it obvious that enforced beneficence should be rejected because it will inevitably lead to the enforcement of those moral principles which are more closely connected with autonomy, privacy, and intimate personal relationships.

A more interesting objection is that the enforced beneficence arguments rest on a misunderstanding of the nature of the duty of beneficence: beneficence is traditionally understood as an imperfect duty not just in the sense that the amount of aid one renders is a matter of choice but also in the sense that the choice of recipients is also discretionary. In other words, beneficence only requires that one render aid to some who are needy, not to all. But if so, then the enforced beneficence argument is vulnerable to the same objection I leveled earlier at Utilitarianism: it does not provide a firm moral foundation for a guaranteed minimum for *all*.

At this point, it is important to approach the traditional concept of beneficence more critically than is usually done. Three points must be emphasized. First, some support must be given for the view that beneficence is discretionary with respect to the choice of recipients of aid. It is not enough to offer this assumption as an analytic truth which follows from the concept of the duty of beneficence. Even if the boundaries of the traditional concept could be so clearly delineated, the question of whether it is permissible to choose to aid A and not to aid B (when A's and B's needs are identical) is a moral question. And depending on the answer we arrive at, we may find it appropriate to revise the traditional concept. Second, the more plausible accounts of why the benefactor may be selective seem to be pragmatic rather than conceptual or moral. Third, these pragmatic considerations seem to have less weight when beneficence is viewed—as it is in the enforced beneficence arguments—as a collective, rather than an individual, enterprise.

Even if we could say with confidence that the traditional concept of beneficence includes the idea that the benefactor may be selective, we should ask why this is so. If one examines the *grounds* for the duty of beneficence, either in commonsense morality or in ethical theory, it seems that these are so general that the conclusion they support is that there is a duty to aid the needy—anyone in need, not just some, if one is able to do so.

For example, in the Second Part of *The Foundations of the Metaphysics of Morals*, Kant offers an argument for the conclusion that one ought to help those in need, at least if one can do so without excessive costs to oneself. Kant's claim is that one cannot consistently will the universalization of a maxim of not aiding others in need because to do so would be to deprive oneself of aid from others: a world in which everyone acted on this maxim of nonbeneficence would be one in which one could not count on being helped by others. Now it appears that the same argument would rule out a maxim of helping another in need only if one chooses to: in a world of discretionary benefactors one could not count on aid. Thus one would expect Kant to reject a formulation of the duty of beneficence that allows the benefactor to choose which of the needy he will help (independently of any consideration of the degree or importance of their need). However, Kant does not draw this conclusion. Though he provides an argument that supports the conclusion that we ought to help whoever is in need, Kant does not challenge the traditional view that the duty of beneficence allows the benefactor to exercise discretion in deciding whom to aid.

Similarly, at the level of commonsense morality, the considerations that underlie the duty of beneficence seem very general. One ought to help those in need because they are our fellow human beings in need—not because of any further special characteristics they happen to possess or because of any special preferences we have. Yet here, too, as in Kant's theory, it is usually said that there is much latitude in discharging the duty of beneficence. One may choose to help some and not help others.

How can the very general character of the ground of the duty of beneficence be reconciled with the assumption that the benefactor may exercise discretion? The explanation, I suggest, lies not in moral theory or in an analysis of the concept of beneficence, but in an appreciation of two facts about the circumstances in which individual—opposed to collective—beneficence often occurs. The first is that an individual's resources are so limited that either he will not be able to render significant aid to anyone unless he is selective or he will be able to do so only at excessive cost. The second is that in many cases the individual has more control over his beneficent efforts, and hence more assurance of their success, if he renders aid directly to those close at hand. (One may refrain from contributing to the aid of those far away simply because one is aware that there are numerous opportunities for diverting and diluting one's contribution before it reaches the intended recipient.) It may also be that some of those who accept uncritically the traditional view that beneficence is wholly discretionary as to the choice of beneficiaries do so because of a rather simplistic and overly optimistic assumption: namely, that if each of us freely chooses some beneficiary or other, everyone, or virtually everyone in need, will receive some aid. This assumption ignores the problem of coordinating individual acts of beneficence emphasized in the two arguments mentioned earlier.

Each of these reasons can, in particular circumstances, justify a policy of selective beneficence. However, in conditions in which a collective effort can provide a minimum of care for all who can need it, without excessive costs to the benefactors, the very same general considerations that ground the duty of beneficence support a nonselective policy.

It is true that two perplexing questions remain unanswered. What counts as excessive costs? And should a guaranteed decent minimum policy aim only at the needy who dwells within the borders of a particular nation-state? Neither of these problems, however, is peculiar to the enforced beneficence arguments; they afflict rights-based approaches as well. Further, while the various moral justifications offered to support the alleged right to a decent minimum are also general in that they apply to human beings as such, the reasons for restricting the enforcement of rights to the national level, when they are good reasons, are as pragmatic as those that explain the assumption that benefactors may be selective. Even if these pragmatic considerations support a restriction of the class of those who are to be aided (or those whose rights are to be protected by our government), they do not justify the much stronger claim that beneficence (or the protection of rights) is essentially discretionary. I conclude, then, that the idea that beneficence allows discretion in the selection of recipients does not itself constitute a telling objection to the enforced beneficence argument for a decent minimum of health care. Instead, it seems more accurate to conclude that the enforced beneficence arguments force us to get clearer about what is central to the concept of beneficence and what is a practical concession to the difficulties of being beneficent in an imperfect world.

A libertarian might raise the potentially more serious objection that the enforced beneficence argument fails to recognize a fundamental qualification. While acknowledging that there may be some rules of social coordination or some principles specifying moral obligations or obligations to contribute to public goods that may be enforced, even in the absence of corresponding rights, the libertarian will point out that enforcing them is permissible *only if* doing so does not violate important moral rights.

I agree wholeheartedly with this qualification. However, if the qualification is to become a sound criticism of the enforced beneficence arguments, the libertarian must discharge two difficult tasks, the second of which no one has yet successfully executed. First, he must clearly specify *which* basic moral rights would be violated by any attempt to enforce the principle of beneficence as it is applied to health care. Second, he must provide a coherent and plausible *justification* for the claim that *these* basic moral rights do exist. To rule out in principle an enforceable duty of beneficence the libertarian would have to specify and justify either a virtually unlimited general right against interference or coercion or a virtually unlimited right to private property. The great obstacle to doing either is that he must avoid begging the question by appealing to intuitions that his nonlibertarian opponent does not share. In the absence of a sound theoretical justification for such rights, the burden of proof is on the libertarian to substantiate the claim that the enforcement in question violates important moral rights.

We have now come full circle. At the outset, I noted that the burden of proof is on those who claim that there is universal right to a decent minimum of health care. I then argued that various attempts to provide theoretical support for the claim that there is such a right are inadequate. If we abandon the quest for a justification for the claim that there is a universal right, however, we should not conclude that the libertarian view triumphs by default. The non-rights-based, enforced beneficence arguments shift a similar burden of proof onto the libertarian.

If the approach I have outlined succeeds, it provides a way of avoiding both the burden of justifying the claim that there is a universal right to health care and the equally onerous burden of justifying a virtually unlimited right to private property or against coercion. Surprising as it may seem, an answer to the question of whether society ought to guarantee certain health-care services for all does *not* depend upon our ability to adjudicate decisively between libertarian and welfarist theories of basic rights.

I would like to conclude by observing that the non-rights-based, enforced beneficence approach has interesting implications for the issue of how we are to specify the content of the decent minimum. We have seen that while the type of rights-based argument determines the sorts of considerations which are to guide the specification of content, little can be said about the specification prior to the outcome of political processes or extensive empirical research. This conclusion will be disturbing if one assumes that the guaranteed minimum is a matter of right, since we often tend to think of rights as rather sharply defined. However, the traditional notion of duties of charity or beneficence is that they are "imperfect duties": by their very nature they are not precisely delineated.

Now those who favor the non-rights-based approach can argue that the difficulty encountered by rights-based approaches in specifying the content of an alleged right to a decent minimum provides indirect support for the position that there is no right to a decent minimum but only an enforceable duty of beneficence or charity to contribute to the attainment of a decent minimum. In other words, the advocate of the enforced beneficence approach can warmly welcome the lack of a principled specification as a vindication of his view rather than accept it begrudgingly as an embarrassing theoretical lacuna. The idea would be that we must frankly acknowledge that the character and scope of the list of services included in the decent minimum is a matter of collective choice. All that is necessary is that there be some fair procedure for reaching a social decision on which set of services to provide.

2

HEALTH-CARE DELIVERY AND RESOURCE ALLOCATION

Allen Buchanan

Increasingly, medical ethics involves decisions concerning the allocation of health-care resources and the institutional arrangements for making those decisions. The key concepts of health-care resource allocation and cost need to be defined because they shape the moral and policy discussion. This chapter considers different criteria for evaluating allocation of health-care resources. Two types of models of allocation are examined: efficiency models and ethical models.

In efficiency models of allocation, utility maximization, cost–benefit analysis, and cost effectiveness are the standards for judgment. Efficiency criteria are not by themselves sufficient for evaluating allocations; ethical criteria are also necessary. Two case studies, which present issues involved in rationing chemotherapy and the allocation of human heart for transplantation, illustrate the differences in the two approaches.

Broader issues relating to the ethics of resource allocation are also presented. Among these are the problem of access to health care and controversies over rival specifications of the right to health care, including utilitarian, egalitarian, equality of opportunity, and "decent minimum" views. In addition, it is argued that a comprehensive conception of just health care must address the question of how the cost of providing access for all to an adequate level of care is to be distributed fairly.

Originally published in *Medical Ethics*, 2nd. Ed. Robert M. Veatch, ed. (Sudbum, MA: Jones & Bartlett, 1997).

Recently, attention has shifted to include beneficence as well as justice. Issues central to approaches that emphasize beneficence include the nature of societal obligation, the free-rider problem, the assurance problem, and the enforcement of obligations. Although many strategies have been offered for making ethical evaluations of health-care resource allocation, none, so far, is fully adequate or uniquely attractive.

Virtually every significant problem in medical ethics includes ethical issues concerning the allocation of scarce resources or is shaped by allocation decisions that are subject to ethical evaluation. For example, in deciding whether to prolong the life of a severely disabled newborn, when doing so will involve great financial burdens (for her parents, the hospital, and the public coffers), the decision-maker—whether it be a parent, a court-appointed legal guardian, the physician, or a hospital administrator—is in effect choosing to allocate scarce resources to this particular baby rather than to someone else or something else. Unless previous allocation decisions had been made to channel resources into neonatal research and into the construction of the neonatal intensive care units in which the results of research were applied, then the need for the allocation decision that will determine this particular baby's fate would never have arisen.

This chapter is a critical survey of several major views on the ethical evaluation of decisions concerning the allocation of health-care resources, and the institutional arrangements established for making those decisions.

PRELIMINARY ANALYSIS OF KEY CONCEPTS

Health-Care Resources

In the most inclusive sense, health-care resources are any goods or services that can reasonably be expected to have a positive effect on health. Thus, health-care resources include, but are not restricted to, medical resources. Furthermore, health-care goods and services are not limited to those that are produced by persons ordinarily recognized as health-care professionals, such as physicians and nurses. Health-care resources are not just medical drugs, procedures, and treatments; they are also the many resources used for pollution control, shelter, and food required for normal growth and functioning.

Allocation

To *allocate* is to distribute resources among alternative uses. Allocation in this broad sense does not presuppose an allocator (an individual or a group) who deliberately distributes the available resources. Thus, a competitive market allocates social resources through the interactions of individual exchangers, each of whom makes allocation decisions concerning only his or her own resources in the pursuit of his or her own particular ends. Allowing a market for the buying and selling of organs, for example, is just as much an allocation decision as the adoption of an explicit rationing policy that allocates organs according to a criterion of social contribution or personal desert.

Even when an allocation of resources results directly from a social (rather than an individual) decision, the allocation is often a by-product of the pursuit of other goals (rather than an intended result). For example, a law stating that nurse–midwives must be supervised by physicians if their services are to be reimbursed by third-party payers has an allocational effect. It transfers income from nurse–midwives to physicians because the physicians charge nurse–midwives for the service of supervision, and it restricts the available number of practicing nurse–midwives to those who are able to secure such supervision. Similarly, a decision to pump millions of dollars of public funds into cancer centers affects the allocation of physicians among specialty training programs. If more money is available for residencies in oncology than for primary-care residencies, more medical students may become oncologists and fewer may become primary-care specialists. In neither of these examples is it necessary that any decision be aimed at the allocational effect in question. Allocations are subject to ethical assessment, however, regardless of whether they are the objects of explicit allocation decisions.

Cost

In the sense most pertinent to reasoning about allocation, the cost of something may be defined as the value of the most preferred alternative. Suppose that one has to decide how to spend one's weekly entertainment budget. In the order one prefers them, alternatives are (1) seeing the ballet; (2) attending a football game; and (3) going out to dinner. Because one's budget is limited, if the ballet is chosen, one loses the opportunity to attend the game and dine out. Since the game is the next most preferred alternative, its value is the cost of one's decision to see the ballet. In this sense, all costs arc "opportunity costs." Given that resources—including time—are limited, deciding to use a resource for one purpose forecloses opportunities for alternative uses.

TYPES OF ALLOCATIONS

Discussions of allocation often utilize a distinction between macro- and microallocation. This distinction is, however, of limited use, and can be misleading unless its relative nature is clearly recognized. A decision by the U.S. Congress to allocate *N* billion dollars for medicare and *N* + *m* billion for national defense is perhaps the paradigm of a macroallocation decision. A microallocation decision would be, for example, a decision made by a particular physician when she decides to use the one available bed in her burn unit for Mr. Jones rather than for Ms. Smith. There are, of course, many types of allocation decisions that are smaller scale than the former but larger scale than the latter.

In response to this complexity, it is tempting to say that whether an allocation is "micro" or "macro" is determined by the *level* of decision-making authority or the level of available resources to be distributed. Talk of levels, however, is misleading to the extent that it encourages the fiction that there is an overall system, of a hierarchical character, within which decisions are interconnected in some principle way. Whether any existing society is this highly structured in its mechanism for allocation may be a matter of controversy, but it is fair to say that the United States, perhaps more so than many industrialized countries, currently lacks anything that could realistically be called an allocation system with regard to health-care resources.

It is perhaps more useful to begin with a classification of fundamental types of allocation problems that leaves open the question of what sort of allocational system, hierarchical or otherwise, will be needed to solve them. James F. Childress offers the following list:

1. What resources (time, energy, money, etc.) should be put into health care and into other social goods such as education, defense, eliminating poverty, and improving the environment?
2. Within the area of health (once we have determined its budget), how much time, energy, money, etc., should we allocate for prevention and how much for rescue and crisis medicine?
3. Within either preventive care or rescue medicine, who (if anyone) should receive resources such as vaccines or artificial hearts when we cannot meet everyone's needs? (Childress 1982)

CRITERIA FOR EVALUATING ALLOCATIONS

Existing, predicted, or proposed allocations may be evaluated on grounds of efficiency, ethics, or both. It is unfortunate that discussions of the ethics of health-care resource allocation typically ignore the efficiency evaluations that dominate the work of real-world policy makers and policy analysts, who in turn often convey the impression that by exclusively employing efficiency criteria they are approaching allocation issues in a nonethical or value-neutral way. Both approaches are mistaken.

Allocation decision processes may also be evaluated ethically and for efficiency. A decision process may be inefficient due to excessive expenditures of material resources (e.g., equipment for information gathering and processing), time, or human resources, or because the cost of the social conflict the process engenders is excessive. Even if an allocation decision is itself ethically unassailable, the process by which it is reached may be challenged from an ethical standpoint for procedural unfairness or on grounds that the decision-maker lacked appropriate authority. For example, an adequate ethical evaluation of an allocation decision may require an assessment of the procedural fairness of the decision-making process (from which that allocation issued) because there is no consensus among reasonable persons as to whether the allocation, considered by itself, is ethically acceptable.

Efficiency Criteria

The dominant conception of efficiency among economists is that of *pareto optimality*. A state of a system is pareto optimal if there is no feasible alternative state in which at least one person would be better off and no one would be worse off (Buchanan 1985, pp. 4–13). A move from a state that is not pareto optimal to one that is pareto optimal is a pareto improvement, and the latter state is pareto superior to the former.

Many economists and policy analysts find the paretian conception of efficiency attractive. One important reason for its appeal is that it avoids what many consider insurmountable obstacles to making the interpersonal utility comparisons that would be required if the principle of utility, a criterion of utility maximization, were employed instead. According to the *principle of utility*, allocational states are to be ranked according to how much net, overall utility they produce. The net, overall utility of a particular allocation is calculated by summing up the net utility for each individual affected. The net utility for each individual is the sum of the benefits that allocation produces for him or her, minus the costs ("disbenefits") to him or her. An allocation maximizes utility if the net, overall utility it produces is at least as great as, if not greater than, the net, overall utility produced by each of the feasible alternative allocations.

To determine whether an allocation maximizes utility, it is necessary to sum up utilities and disutilities (or costs and benefits) for different individuals, and the interpersonal utility comparisons require that we be able to locate every person's state of well-being along a single numerical scale. The obstacle to achieving this is that there does not appear to be a nonarbitrary method for selecting a common zero point or baseline from which different individuals' utilities could be measured, nor a way to determine a common unit of measurement. Even if a utility scale could be constructed for each individual by recording the choices he or she makes among various options, this seems to provide no basis for relating the respective utility scales to one another in a way that allows the needed aggregation (Brock 1973, pp. 245–49; Sartorius 1975).

To ascertain whether an allocation is pareto optimal (or to determine whether a change from one allocation to another would be a pareto improvement), however, it is not necessary to make interpersonal utility comparisons. All that is required is that each person's well-being under a particular allocation be comparable to his or her own well-being under alternative feasible allocations.

Although an allocation may be pareto optimal and still not maximize utility, a move from one allocation to another that constitutes a pareto improvement at least entails an increase in utility because at least one person's utility increases and no one's decreases. Consequently, use of the paretian concept of efficiency can be seen as a kind of second-best alternative to the utility-maximization criterion.

If the paretian conception of efficiency is seen in this way, relying on it as the exclusive or primary standard for evaluating allocations is no more plausible than a similar reliance on utility maximization would be, if the problem of interpersonal utility comparisons were solved. But there are strong objections to the principle of utility, quite apart from the difficulty of interpersonal comparisons.

First of all, it would be a mistake to view the principle of utility simply as a principle of collective rationality that is an uncontroversial extension of the principle of individual rationality prevalent in economic theory. The latter simply defines efficiency as taking the least costly, most effective means to one's end, that is, as individual utility maximization. Some who assume that utility maximization would be the appropriate criterion for evaluating allocation (were it not for the problem of interpersonal comparisons) and who view pareto optimality as a second-best approximation, may be under the impression that the principle of utility is an uncontroversial extension of the principle of individual utility maximization. This, however, is an error. First, if it is assumed that what is rational for an individual is to maximize his or her own utility, whether it is rational for anyone to seek the maximization of overall utility depends on whether, as a matter of contingent fact, the decision is the best way for him or her to maximize his or her own utility. Clearly there are many instances in the real world in which maximizing one's own utility and maximizing overall utility diverge. Whenever they diverge, the economic definition of rationality as individual utility maximization undermines, rather than supports, the claim that overall utility maximization is the rational standard for evaluating allocations.

Second, the principle of utility fares no better if it is understood not as the principle of individual rationality extended to society, but as an ethical principle.

To assume that the principle of utility is the appropriate standard for evaluating allocations is to make the ethically controversial assumption that society is to be viewed as an apparatus for maximizing overall utility. Such a view of society may be incompatible with according proper respect to individual persons, who ought not to be regarded merely as contributors to ends that are not their own (Buchanan 1985). A particular allocation, or a complete social system, might maximize overall utility and yet be grossly unfair or unjust, which would violate the most fundamental rights of some individuals. Rawls and others have observed that a system in which some persons were slaves would in fact maximize overall utility, as long as the gains to the masters exceeded the losses to the slaves (Rawls 1971). That the criterion of utility maximization would not only allow but indeed require such a system, if it did in fact produce the most utility, is taken by many to be a telling objection to utilitarianism.

This extreme example illustrates the more general objection that opponents of utilitarianism often raise—that evaluating social arrangements, including allocations, simply according to their tendency to maximize overall utility neglects fairness as a fundamental ethical value. Similarly, utilitarianism has frequently been criticized for ignoring another key ethical value: personal desert. That one individual deserves some good, but another does not, is never itself a reason for the utilitarian to allocate the good to the former person; all that matters is how much utility can be gained.

Ethical objections also apply to attempt to evaluate allocations using the paretian criteria for efficiency. An allocation may be pareto optimal, yet grossly unjust or unfair (e.g., it may be impossible to improve the condition of some of the slaves without worsening the condition of some of the slave holders). Similarly, the pursuit of pareto improvements recognizes no role for personal desert as such—all that matters is whether a change can be made that improves the condition of some without worsening the condition of any, regardless of who deserves the benefits conferred.

It follows that policy analysts who evaluate allocations solely by the standard economic (i.e., paretian) criterion of efficiency are either mistakenly assuming that they have avoided controversial ethical issues or are offering a fundamentally incomplete evaluation that must be supplemented by ethical criteria. If the paretian standard of efficiency is employed as the sole criterion for evaluating allocations, what is required is nothing short of a full-scale defense of utilitarianism, which, as we have just seen, is a very controversial ethical theory.

If, on the other hand, the paretian standard is offered not as the sole criterion for evaluation, but as one standard among others, including those that embody ethical values such as justice, fairness, and personal desert, what is needed is a theory, a systematic account, of how much weight should be given to efficiency relative to the other standards of assessment.

Cost–Benefit and Cost-Effectiveness Analyses

In part because the direct and unrestricted use of the utility-maximization criterion requires staggering amounts of information about the consequences of all feasible alternatives, and in part because in the more vexing policy decisions none of the feasible alternatives is likely to be pareto optimal (typically there will be losers as well as winners, no matter what is done), policy analysts have developed other efficiency criteria. The most widely discussed of these are cost–benefit analysis (CBA) and cost-effectiveness analysis (CEA), which M. C. Weinstein and W. B. Stason concisely define and contrast as follows.

> The key distinction is that a benefit-cost [or cost-benefit] analysis must value all outcomes in economic (e.g., dollar) terms, including lives or years of life and morbidity, whereas a cost-effectiveness analysis serves to place priorities on alternative expenditures without requiring that the dollar value of life and health be assessed. (Weinstein and Stason 1977)

The preceding definition restricts CBA to a comparison of the health benefits of a particular allocational decision with the costs of implementing that decision. If this restriction were lifted, so that all costs and benefits of a particular decision were compared with all costs and benefits of each feasible alternative, CBA would be identical with the use of the utility-maximization criterion. Although CBA in the sense defined by Weinstein and Stason is narrower than utility maximization because it only compares health benefits with costs, it nonetheless, in principle, allows quite diverse programs to be ranked. For example, CBA purports to tell whether a program to educate teenage females about prenatal care would produce a greater ratio of health benefits (for pregnant teenagers and the children they bear) to financial costs of the program than the ratio of health benefits (for persons with hypertension) to the costs of a hypertension screening program. According to CBA, resources are to be allocated to those uses that have the highest health benefit–cost ratios.

As should be apparent, the chief objections to utility maximization apply with equal force to CBA. Even in the narrow sense, CBA requires interpersonal utility comparisons because the cost–benefit ratio for a given allocation is determined by subtracting the total financial cost from the sum of all the health benefits to all persons affected. Similarly, the most obvious ethical objections to utility maximization apply to CBA, even when restricted to health benefits—neither criterion for allocation takes into account fairness or personal desert.

There are, in addition, special difficulties with the methods that cost–benefit analysts have proposed for assigning a dollar value to lives saved or to life-years gained as a result of the alternative allocations whose cost–benefit ratios are to be compared. The two most common methods are: (1) future earnings (or human capital) and (2) willingness to pay.

According to the former, the monetary value of each individual's life, for purposes of calculating a cost–benefit ratio, is his or her total expected lifetime income. Critics of the future-earnings approach point out that it places a higher value (on average) on the lives of men than on the lives of women. The difficulty is not simply that women who work in the home typically receive no reported wages for their labor—this could be remedied by calculating the market value of their domestic services and counting it as income. The real problem is that even when women receive income for their services, they often receive lower pay than men do for performing comparable work. Hence, to value women's lives for purposes of determining allocations of health-care resources according to their expected future earnings simply compounds the unfairness of an already unfair social system.

As we have already seen, to allocate resources strictly according to which allocation has the highest overall benefit–cost ratio is to assume that utilitarianism is the correct ethical theory. Even if this controversial assumption is left unchallenged, however, future earnings are an inadequate measure of the value of human life for purposes of calculating overall utility because the effect an individual's life (or the loss of it) has on overall utility is not equivalent to his or her future earnings. For one thing, an individual's earnings represent (at best) the utility his or her services produce for those who pay for them, not the total utility—or disutility—produced by his or her rendering of those services. In other words, the future-earnings approach does not take into account the effects of "externalities," whether positive or negative, on overall costs or overall benefits. An *externality* is a spillover, or neighborhood effect, or third-party effect of an exchange. For example, air pollution from a chemical plant is an externality (a negative one in that it results in harm to people, wildlife, and plants), a cost that is not reflected in the exchange between the chemical plant and its customers. Even if an individual's future earnings were an adequate approximation of his or her contribution to social utility, it can still be objected that it is unethical to view society as a kind of grand machine for producing ever more utility and human beings as cogs in the machine ("factors of production" in a productive enterprise).

Quite apart from its ethical defects, the future-earnings approach is flawed as an account of how people actually value not only their own lives but the lives of others as well. The value a parent places on her child—and the loss she feels at the child's death—typically has little to do with what the child's lifetime income would have been had he or she survived. Similarly, the value an individual places on his own life typically reflects the value he places on the future experiences and activities he will be deprived of, not the loss of future earnings. The future-earnings approach, then, is not only ethically deficient, but descriptively inaccurate.

The second method assigns value to a life or to prolongation of a life according to the amount of money the person whose life it is would pay to avoid the loss of his life (or to reduce the risk of losing it) or to prolong it for some specified period. The chief attraction of the willingness-to-pay approach is that it is subject-centered—the value assigned to a life is determined by the preferences of the individual him- or herself, not by others. Unfortunately, however, willingness to pay does not avoid the ethical objection raised earlier against future earnings. It, too, systematically reproduces whatever injustices in the distribution of wealth already exist, because how much a person is willing to pay to avoid death or reduce the risk of death depends on how great his or her resources are. If the current distribution of wealth is unjust or unfair, relying on the willingness-to-pay approach to make allocation decisions is unfair and unjust.

Although the forgoing problems are extremely serious, it would be a mistake to conclude that CBA has nothing of value to bring to decision-making concerning the allocation of health-care resources. Understood in the most general way, CBA is an indispensable procedure for overall practical reasoning, not just for matters of resource allocation. In its broadest outlines, it is simply the attempt to make the gains and losses of alternative courses of action explicit and, to the extent that this is possible, to make them sufficiently commensurate with one another so that at least an approximation of a maximizing strategy can be formulated. Any theory of practical reasoning that recognizes that there is a plurality of goods, that at least some gains are not costless, and that values are at least sometimes roughly commensurate, utilizes CBA in this generic sense, and this includes non-utilitarian ethical theories.

In the latter, moral values that represent constraints on overall utility maximization can be reflected in the weights that are assigned to different gains and losses. For example, an ethical theory that rejects utilitarianism and takes certain individual rights as fundamental, but that recognizes that rights may conflict, might nevertheless find it illuminating to use a cost–benefit procedure, in the broadest sense, to arrive at reasonable trade-offs between basic rights when they conflict.

The preceding objections to CBA are not to be understood, then, as a rejection of all practical reasoning that attempts to weigh losses against gains and in some sense maximize gains. Instead, they are criticisms of attempts to use specific maximizing techniques that either ignore or beg important ethical questions about the proper scope of maximizing reasoning and the appropriate weight that different values (for instance, fairness versus efficiency) ought to be given when a maximizing procedure is appropriate.

There are two quite different ways to construe the ethical objections to both the future-earnings and the willingness-to-pay approaches. One is to argue that even if one or both adequately captures the economic value of life, attending only to the economic value of life is an insufficient basis for calculating overall benefit, even if we accept the principle that we are to maximize overall benefit in making allocation decisions. In this first view, future earnings and willingness to pay are incomplete measures of the value of lives, where value is objective and commensurate in the way required for a maximizing calculation. On the second reading, a critic of these two approaches can admit that one or both of them adequately captures the economic value of lives and that the only objective and commensurate sense of value is economic, yet also maintain that there are ethical considerations (e.g., of fairness) that place limits on the extent to which the value of a person's life (in this objective and commensurate sense) ought to determine his or her share of resources. For the first view, the charge is that willingness to pay and future earnings are inadequate measures of the value of lives; for the second, it is that maximizing value is not the sole consideration in allocating resources.

Unlike CBA, CEA does not require that health benefits, including lives saved or prolonged, be measured by the same units (dollars) as the costs of the allocation of resources that provides those benefits. All that is necessary is that all the health benefits expected from a particular allocation be measured by a common unit, usually "quality-adjusted life-years," and that all costs be measured by a common unit (dollars). CEA allows a ranking of alternative programs for producing a given level of health benefits according to the dollar costs of each for producing the desired effect.

There are two major limitations on the usefulness of CEA. The first, needless to say, is the difficulty of formulating a reasonable, objective concept of quality of life for determining the unit of benefit measurement, the quality-adjusted life-year. Perhaps the chief issue is the extent to which the quality of an individual's life (or of a life-year) is to be understood in a subjective fashion, that is, according to his or her own estimate, or objectively.

The second is simply a variant of the major ethical objection to CBA and to utilitarian approaches more generally—CEA itself recognizes no ethical concerns about how benefits are distributed, except so far as the distribution affects the total benefit produced. In other words, to determine allocations exclusively according to CEA is to beg fundamental allocation questions. CEA might indicate, for example, that a program that establishes mobile coronary care units produces more health benefits for the money than does a liver transplant program, but it cannot indicate what proportion of total social resources should be allocated to health care and what proportion to education or defense. This is a serious limitation because, at the present time, there are many who believe that the health-care sector has been draining a disproportionate share of social resources away from other areas.

ETHICAL CRITERIA

The Need for Ethical Criteria

We have seen that efficiency criteria are not by themselves sufficient for evaluating allocations; ethical criteria are also necessary. Often, allocation decisions, especially those toward the "micro" end of the continuum, are made in a much less systematic way than advocates of CBA or CEA would prefer. But here, too, the need for ethical and efficiency criteria is apparent. Two examples are discussed briefly below: The allocation of human hearts for transplantation and the selective use of cancer chemotherapy. For the former, the ethically controversial nature of the process is apparent—there are not enough transplantable human hearts for everyone who needs one, problematic choices are being made, and the effects of these decisions, if not the decision-making processes themselves, are often exposed to public scrutiny by the harsh glare of the media. For the latter, the usual situation is *not* one in which a limited quantity of a cancer drug is available to a physician and he or she must decide which patients will get it. Nevertheless, ethically controversial decisions are made daily as to which patients will receive certain cancer drugs and in some cases it is clear that the high cost of these drugs plays a role in decision-making (though often in indirect and complex ways). Rationing occurs with both human hearts and cancer drugs.

Rationing Chemotherapy

In their controversial book *The Painful Prescription* (subtitled *Rationing Hospital Care*), Aaron and Schwarz contrast the use of cancer drugs for various classes of cancer patients in the United States and England. They note that England spends about 70 percent less per capita on cancer-fighting drugs than the United States does (Aaron and Schwarz 1984, p. 47), and that the most dramatic difference lies in the tendency of American physicians to treat, and British physicians *not* to treat, patients who have metastatic solid tumors and who have few symptoms that might be relieved by chemotherapy and for whom chemotherapy rarely produces an extension of life and even less frequently a cure. Aaron and Schwarz report that the rate at which American physicians treat such patients is five to six times greater than that for British physicians (Aaron and Schwarz 1984, p. 48).

British physicians interviewed in the study justified their practice on the grounds that, for this group of patients, the disability and discomfort that are often side effects of chemotherapy are not worth the small chance or benefit. American physicians, in contrast, seemed more frequently to be committed to treating such cancer aggressively, even though they admitted that the prospects for success were very small.

The responses of some British physicians support the hypothesis that financial considerations are playing a role in this pronounced difference in patterns of practice (Aaron and Schwarz 1984, p. 50). British physicians know that they are custodians of a scarce public resource—that the British National Health Service must operate within a limited budget. American physicians operate under no such overall budget constraint and, as Aaron and Schwarz point out, American cancer specialists under the third-party, fee-for-service system have a strong financial incentive to treat patients aggressively.

However, Aaron and Schwarz neglect to mention that American physicians in some cases are already beginning to find themselves subject to budget constraints that give them incentives to take a harder look at *how much* benefit can reasonably be expected from chemotherapy. The director of an oncology department at a hospital owned by a large Health Maintenance Organization (HMO) in the United States reported that he only ordered extremely expensive new cancer drugs if their expected benefit exceeded a certain threshold—say, a .2 probability of "significant" improvement in terms of life extension with "reasonable" quality of life.[1] Unless some such rationing device were employed, he stated, his oncology unit, by using every new cancer drug that promised some net benefit, would bankrupt the entire HMO in a month's time. Although this case comes from an HMO, it could have occurred in any hospital in which close attention is paid to how resources are allocated among different services.

The differences in prescribing patterns for chemotherapy illustrate two important points. First, the question of what level of expected benefits to the patient is high enough in relation to costs to the patient (in terms of side effects) to justify the treatment is *not* a medical question. For persons who value the extension of their life very highly, gaining a rather small chance of longer survival may be worth considerable disability and discomfort; others may have a more demanding standard for what counts as an acceptable quality of life. Even when all the medical facts are in, a decision about whether, strictly from the patient's standpoint, chemotherapy is appropriate, depends on personal values. Second, the greater the extent to which physicians come to regard themselves as operating under budget constraints—imposed by society or by their own hospital administration—the more likely it is that the cost–benefit threshold they use to determine whether to prescribe expensive drugs will be influenced by broader cost considerations, not by what is best for this particular patient.

As cost-containment pressures mount, one of the most vexing questions concerning the allocation of health-care resources is: How can the physician play an effective role in efforts to ration scarce resources responsibly without undermining his or her traditional and valued role as advocate for the individual patient? Once the fact that rationing decisions are not only morally permissible but morally required for the fair and efficient use of scarce social resources, it will become harder to sustain the illusion that different practices concerning the use of cancer drugs or other expensive therapies simply reflect differences in medical judgment.

Allocating Hearts

The system—or rather the inconsistent patchwork of processes—by which human hearts for transplantation are allocated in the United States is neither efficient nor fair according to any reasonable standard (Mathieu 1988). There are several sources of inefficiency. A study by the national Task Force on Organ Transplantation (a committee appointed by the U.S. Department of Health and Human Services) found that regionalization of heart transplant centers, rather than the current proliferation of centers as individual physicians and medical centers compete for dollars and prestige, would save resources and increase the quality of care (Department of Health, Education, and Welfare 1986). Perhaps just as important, a coordinated, regionalized system of transplant centers would provide better prospects for developing and monitoring more ethical and more efficient procedures for allocating hearts. At present, hearts are sometimes allocated to patients who will almost certainly die even though they receive a heart, despite the fact that there are other potential recipients who have a much better chance of living if they were to receive the heart.

This inefficient—and morally irresponsible—use of the public resources used in the development and deployment of transplant technology can occur because of the defective way in which the human heart allocation "hotline" works. A registered transplant surgeon who wants a heart for his patient may call the hotline and request a heart. The most abusable feature of this system is that the physician who makes the request unilaterally classifies his patient according to a priority classification. In one recent case, a transplant surgeon designated his patient a "priority 1" on the grounds that the patient would die almost immediately if he did not receive a heart. Although this was true, it was in fact not a sufficient reason for bestowing the heart on this patient instead of another. The patient's condition had already so deteriorated that competent medical opinion agreed it was virtually certain that he would die even if he received the heart (Mathieu 1988). An allocation system that allows "urgency"—without consideration of relative expected benefit—to determine priority and that relies on interested parties to make priority classifications can only be expected to waste precious social resources.

Quite aside from the problems of inefficiency, the current processes by which human hearts are allocated also can be criticized as unfair. The chief criticism is that morally arbitrary factors often play a decisive role in determining who lives and who dies. The most obvious of these is ability to pay: most transplant centers require as much as $60,000 "cash up front." Further, some centers give first priority to in-state residents; thus, where one happens to live may mean that one will not get a heart, even if the medical need and potential benefit are greater than that of a person fortunate enough to be living in the right state. Geographical discrimination is especially suspect because millions of federal tax dollars (not state funds) were spent to develop the technology. Some transplant centers are, in effect, selling hearts to the highest bidders—in many cases foreign nationals (chiefly Saudis and Greeks, according to one study; Mathieu 1988).

Ethicists who recognize the need for a more satisfactory method of dealing with the problem of allocating scarce organs for transplantation have recognized two polar approaches. On the one hand, an exclusive concern with efficiency or with producing the most benefit possible requires that allocations be made according to what would maximize quality-adjusted life-years. Such an approach simply assumes the correctness of utilitarianism as a moral theory and is subject to the charge that it disregards all issues of fairness. Perhaps most important, it can be argued that a strictly utilitarian system for allocating scarce organs fails to show proper regard for the equal worth of persons, a worth that cannot be equated with contribution to social utility.

Some who reject utilitarian allocation systems on the latter ground suggest that the only way to show proper regard for equal moral status or worth of persons is to give them equal chances to receive the scarce good, either by using a fair lottery method in which each has an equal probability of winning, or by using a first-come, first-serve system to approximate the randomness of a lottery. The latter proposal is clearly flawed: The poor would be disadvantaged by a first-come, first-serve system not only because they tend to be less educated and informed about medical matters but also because they are less likely to see a physician and be advised of the need to get in line for a transplant.

The lottery method (assuming the lottery is fair) would avoid this problem and could be seen as showing equal respect for persons, but it goes too far in eschewing entirely all considerations of how much benefit an allocation will produce. Unless some initial threshold of expected benefit to the patient is used as an eligibility requirement for participation in the lottery, use of a randomizing method will mean that lives of extremely poor quality will be prolonged, perhaps only briefly, at the expense of much longer lives of higher quality.

One ethicist has suggested that a three-tiered system for allocating hearts would better express the conviction that both efficiency (or maximizing benefit) and equal respect for persons are important values (Mathieu 1988). First, potential recipients would be selected according to a standard of *medical suitability* (i.e., the minimal expected benefit threshold). Only if their expected benefit (in terms of quality-adjusted life-years) exceeded a specified threshold would they be placed on the list of potential recipients. Second, those among the first group whose need was most urgent—those who would die soon unless they receive a heart—would be given top priority. Third, if the number of available hearts were greater than the number of people in the top priority group, the remainder of those who passed the medical suitability test would receive hearts on a first-come, first-serve basis.

This sketch of a system is not intended to solve all the problems of allocation for hearts—it does not address the issue of whether a person whose immune system rejects a first heart should receive another, for example, nor does it address the objection that a first-come, first-serve method may discriminate against the poor.

But it does illustrate how one system might incorporate both efficiency and fairness (or equity) considerations in a coherent way.

An alternative would be to rate each potential recipient according to expected benefit (number of quality-adjusted life-years), but allow expected benefit to be decisive only if there is a difference in expected benefit that exceeds some rather high threshold. In effect, such a system would show strong—not unlimited—regard for the equal worth of persons by allocating hearts randomly unless some nonrandom allocation would produce a very marked increase in benefit (Brock 1988). Although both the allocation models would be an improvement over the current arrangements inasmuch as each recognizes that both efficiency and fairness are relevant values, neither by itself avoids the perplexing issue of exactly what the trade-off should be when the two values are in conflict.

The Ubiquity and Inescapability of Rationing

Although politicians sensitive to public opinion and hospital administrators vulnerable to lawsuits are loathe to admit it, rationing of health-care resources is not limited to exotic therapies like transplants. *Rationing*—which means the withholding of care expected to be of net benefit—occurs throughout every health-care system and is unavoidable. Rationing is a necessity because resources are finite and because there are other goods worth pursuing besides health care. To use the language of economics, the opportunity costs of attempting to provide everyone with all the health care that is expected to be of any net benefit are unacceptable.

It is important to understand that rationing is not confined to government health-care systems. In a purely private insurance system, health care is rationed according to ability to pay, with the result that those who are at greatest risk for illness may not be able to afford any health care. Regardless of the type of system, rationing takes a number of forms, some overt and dramatic, as in the allocation of scarce organs for transplantation, others subtle and even hidden. For example, an HMO administrator, recognizing that the elderly use more care on average and are less able to travel considerable distances to receive care, may decide to build a new clinic in an area with fewer elderly people. Thus, the choice of location has the effect of rationing care by limiting utilization. Or, a managed care organization may require patients to clear a number of hurdles (e.g., seeing a nurse practitioner first, then a primary care physician, before gaining access to a specialist) and work their way through a waiting list as a way of limiting utilization.

One of the most perplexing and urgent issues we now face in health care is the question of *who* should make rationing decisions. Different forms of delivery assign responsibility for rationing to different agents at different locations within the institutional structure. In the British National Health Service, a consensus on rationing policies develops among medical specialty groups through interaction with regional health authorities, but the public appears to have little opportunity for input and may not even know that rationing is occurring. In sharp contrast, Oregon recently instituted an explicit rationing program for Medicaid services, utilizing rationing criteria that were developed through a political process with a rather high degree of public participation. At this point, it is not clear whether the trend will be toward broader democratic participation in rationing decisions or toward a complex array of highly localized, largely hidden, and for the most part unaccountable rationing processes. The question of whether, or to what extent, rationing policies should be developed through democratic processes, whether directly participatory or representative, raises profound issues of political ethics.

There are two general ethical issues concerning rationing in health-care delivery systems. The first is the fairness of the system of rationing as it affects patients. A system that arbitrarily concentrates the burdens of rationing on certain classes of individuals (e.g., the elderly, as in the example stated earlier) or the poor (as some critics of the Oregon Medicaid rationing plan have complained) is ethically defective.

The second issue is the fairness of the rationing system toward the providers of care who must comply with the system. Increasingly, physicians in the United States complain that the rationing policies they are required to implement create unacceptable conflicts of interest and compromise their role as patient advocates.

Depending on who the agents of rationing are and the location of rationing decisions within the system, different health-care delivery systems will exacerbate or ameliorate the problem of conflict of interest for providers. For example, in a highly competitive health-care environment, administrators, through the use of various penalties and rewards, will exert pressure on physicians to limit utilization of care. Thus, a physician who orders more tests than the average physician of the same specialty working in the organization may be told that his or her contract will not be renewed, but one who is especially successful in limiting utilization may receive a year-end bonus. Obviously, in such a situation conflicts can occur between the physician's interest in remuneration, professional advancement, and job security, on the one hand, and the commitment to providing the best care available to each patient, on the other. A system that minimizes the strains of commitment on physicians and reduces the incentives for behavior that puts patients at risk is ethically preferable.

The "Access Problem" and the Ethical Evaluation of Large-Scale Allocation Patterns

Ethical theorizing about large-scale allocation patterns has arisen in part from the recognition that "macro" decisions shape "micro" problems and that piecemeal approaches (such as those sketched in the discussion of the preceding two examples) are inadequate. In addition, two powerful social factors motivate the search for coherent ethical criteria for evaluating large-scale allocation patterns. First, there is the growing perception that the rapid rise in health-care expenditures constitutes a "crisis"—and that serious cost-containment measures are a necessity. Second, there is the sobering recognition that from 30 to 37 million Americans lack any health-care coverage, either through private insurance or public programs such as Medicare and Medicaid, and that as many as 22 million more have coverage that is inadequate by virtually any reasonable standard (President's Commission 1983). Systematic theorizing is needed: (1) to determine when differences in access to health care for various individuals or groups constitute ethically objectionable inequalities, and (2) to determine which cost-containment measures are ethically acceptable.

RIGHTS TO HEALTH CARE

Until very recently, the prevailing view has been that to resolve the important large-scale allocation issues in health care, it is necessary to determine whether there is a moral right to health care, and if so, what its content is. However, this assumption is now being challenged by persons who maintain that it is unduly restrictive to limit the discussion to matters of justice and, more specifically, of individual rights. Their point is that allocations may be criticized for being uncharitable or ungenerous even if they are not unjust and violate no one's right. Just as respecting others' rights is not the whole of moral virtue for an individual, so justice, even if it is the first virtue of social institutions, is not the sole virtue.

Positions on the right to health care range from the denial that there is a moral right to health care to the claim that there is a strong egalitarian right, a right of each to an equal share of health resources. Another view holds that the right to health care is derivative and is based exclusively on considerations of utility maximization. The opposing thesis is that the right to health care is independent of and overrides all appeals to utility maximization. To appreciate these disagreements over the existence or scope of a right to health care it is first necessary to clarify the general import of the assertion that a person has a right to something. The distinctive features of such "right" are typically said to be as follows (Feinberg 1979, p. 87; Buchanan 1984b, p. 63):

1. If Jones has a right to X, he has a valid claim or entitlement to it. This is not captured by saying that Jones would benefit from X or that Jones's having it is desirable (to him or others). Because to have a right is to have a basis for making a claim to the thing in question, the appropriate posture

for the right-holder is not that of the supplicant pleading for a favor, but rather that of someone demanding what is due to him or her.

2. Consequently, if Jones' right is violated, it is not merely that an unfortunate or less than morally optimal situation has occurred; in addition, Jones has been wronged by those who failed to fulfill their obligations and is therefore the appropriate recipient of compensation or restitution.
3. If Jones has a right to X, someone or some collectivity (society, the government as the agent of society) has an obligation to make X available to Jones.
4. The existence of Jones's right provides a strong prima facie justification for enforcing these obligations if necessary.

Many discussions of rights assume a fifth feature:

5. A valid right-claim overrides appeals to utility maximization; in other words, the mere fact that failing to respect the right would maximize utility is not itself a sufficient reason for doing so (Dworkin 1977, pp. 184–205).

Writers who focus on the fifth feature sometimes fail to point out that it is quite compatible with viewing rights as being derivative from and ultimately justified by appeals to utility maximization.

A Utilitarian (Derivative) Right to Health Care

Utilitarianism purports to be a comprehensive moral theory, of which a utilitarian theory of justice, including an account of justice in health care, would be only one part (Buchanan 1981, pp. 4–5). There are two main types of comprehensive utilitarian theory: act and rule utilitarianism. Act utilitarianism defines rightness with respect to particular acts—an act is right if and only if it maximizes net utility. Rule utilitarianism defines rightness with respect to rules of action and makes the rightness of particular acts depend on the rules under which those acts fall. A rule is right if general compliance with that rule (or with a set of rules of which it is an element) maximizes net utility, and a particular action is right if it falls under such a rule.

The most prevalent form of the theory, sometimes called *classic utilitarianism,* (Buchanan 1981)[2] defines the rightness of acts or rules as maximization of aggregate utility. The aggregate utility produced by an act or by general compliance with a rule is the sum of the utility produced for each individual affected. *Utility* is defined as pleasure, satisfaction, happiness, or as the realization of preferences, as the latter are revealed through individuals' choices.

The distinction between act and rule utilitarianism is important for a utilitarian theory of justice because rule utilitarianism must include an account of when institutions are just. Thus, institutional rules may maximize utility even though the rules do not direct individuals as individuals or as occupants of institutional positions to maximize utility in a case-by-case fashion. For example, it may be that a judicial system that maximizes utility will do so by including rules that prohibit judges from deciding a case according to their estimates of what would maximize utility in that particular case. Thus the utilitarian justification of a particular action or decision may not be that it maximizes utility, but rather that it falls under some rule of an institution or set of institutions that maximizes utility.

Some utilitarians hold that principles of justice are the most basic moral principles because the utility of adherence to them is especially great. According to this view, utilitarian principles of justice are those utilitarian moral principles that are of such importance that they may be enforced, if necessary. Some utilitarians also hold that among the utilitarian principles of justice are principles specifying individual rights, in which the latter are thought of as enforceable claims that take precedence over appeals to what would maximize utility in the particular case.

A utilitarian moral theory, then, can include principles of rights that themselves prohibit or trump appeals to utility maximization, as long as the justification of the principles is that they are part of an institutional system that maximizes utility. In cases in which two or more rights principles conflict, considerations of utility may be invoked to determine which rights principles are to be given priority. Utilitarianism is incompatible with rights only if rights exclude appeals to utility maximization at all levels of justification, including the most basic institutional level. Rights founded ultimately on considerations of utility are called *derivative* rights, to distinguish them from rights in the strict, fundamental sense.

Whether an overarching total institutional system that maximizes net utility will include a right to health care will depend on a wealth of empirical facts not deducible from the principle of utility itself. A utilitarian system of derivative rights will designate certain goods as being the goods that make an especially large contribution to the maximization of net utility. It is reasonable to assume, on the basis of scientific empirical data as well as commonsense experience, that health care, or at least certain forms of health care, would be among them. Consider, for example, perinatal care, broadly conceived as including genetic screening and counseling (at least for special risk groups), prenatal nutritional care and medical examinations for expectant mothers, medical care during delivery, and basic pediatric services in the crucial months after birth. If empirical research indicates (1) that a system of institutional arrangements that maximizes net utility would include such services and (2) that such services can best be ensured if they are accorded the status of a right, with all that this implies, including the use of coercive sanctions where necessary, according to utilitarianism, there is such a derivative right. The strength and content of this right relative to other derivative rights is determined by the utility of various forms of health care relative to one another as compared with other kinds of goods.

It has been argued that utilitarianism is not capable of providing a secure foundation for a universal right to health care—a right to at least some minimal core of health-care services for everyone (Buchanan 1984a, p. 60). Certain classes of individuals might be excluded from virtually all health-care services. The class of newborns with Down syndrome (formerly called Mongolism), for example, might well be excluded from the "decent minimum" of health care (and other goods and services), which others should receive as a matter of derivative right on utilitarian grounds. These retarded individuals, who often also suffer from serious physical disabilities, tend to require a rather large outlay of social resources over the course of their lives. Relative to the costs of caring for them, the contribution these individuals make to social utility may not be large, at least so far as we are limited to a concept of contribution that permits quantification. If this is the case, utilitarianism will permit—indeed will require—that these individuals be excluded from the right to health care.

To understand why this is taken to be a serious criticism of utilitarianism, two points require emphasis. The first is that these infants are generally capable of enjoyment, purposeful activity, and meaningful interpersonal relationships, and can often attain something approximating a normal life span. In these respects, they are unlike more severely disabled individuals, such as those who become permanently comatose due to disease or trauma, anencephalics (babies born with no brain above the brain stem or with no cerebral cortex), or even profoundly demented patients with Alzheimer's disease. If utilitarianism only rendered problematic the claim that the latter sorts of individuals have a right to health care, it would be significantly less ethically problematic because the moral status of such individuals, our obligations to them, and even their capacity to benefit from our aid are more dubious.

Second, utilitarian calculations may require that the Down syndrome babies (or other groups of moderately disabled people) be excluded, not just from extremely expensive, exotic medical technology, but also from the most basic care. In sum, utilitarianism may mandate that even for basic and relatively inexpensive goods and services, what is guaranteed for most should not be provided for some, even though their needs are as great and they would benefit very much.

Criticism of the utilitarian account of the right to health care is simply an application of the more general objection that utilitarianism fails to provide a secure foundation for any of the most important moral rights as rights of all, not just some, persons. Rawls has argued that the case for equal, basic, civil and political rights for all should not depend, as it does according to utilitarianism, on contingent assumptions about what will in fact maximize overall utility. He also contends that this deficiency, as well as utilitarianism's inability to accord proper recognition to the values of fairness and desert, stems, ultimately, from its failure to take seriously the "separateness of persons" (Rawls 1971). According to utilitarianism, the ultimate objects of moral concern in the universe are desires or preferences, not the persons (or even sentient organisms) whose desires or preferences they are. For the utilitarian, persons are mere receptacles or loci for utility.

The fundamental ethical objections to utilitarianism as a general theory count heavily not only against the attempt to base a right to health care on strictly utilitarian grounds, but also against exclusive reliance on the principle of utility as a guide to more limited allocation decisions both within and outside health care. None of this, however, supports the more extreme conclusion that utilitarian considerations should have no weight whatsoever in allocating health-care resources. In virtually every ethical theory other than libertarianism (in its more extreme forms), and in commonsense moral thinking, maximizing overall utility is often a weighty consideration, even when it is not the sole or even the preponderant factor. This is hardly surprising, assuming that ethics is concerned in some fundamental way with human welfare.

Libertarianism: The Challenge to All Welfare Rights, Including the Right to Health Care

There are a number of different types of theories that are sometimes called libertarian, but Robert Nozick's is often taken to be paradigmatic.[3] Nozick begins by assuming, not arguing for, a very strong right to private property, a right to exclusive control over whatever one can attain through voluntary exchanges in the market (assuming that both parties in fact own what they exchange), through gifts voluntarily bestowed by others, and by appropriating previously unowned things by "mixing one's labor" with them, so long as (1) one's appropriation does not worsen the condition of others by creating a situation in which they are "no longer... able to use freely [without exclusively appropriating] what [they]... previously could" or (2) one properly compensates those whose condition is worsened in the way specified in (1) (Nozick 1974).

Apart from the special case of rectifying past injustices, Nozick's view strictly prohibits any coercive efforts to redistribute wealth, even for the purpose of providing the most minimal welfare rights, including all forms of a right to health care. The legitimate role of the state, according to this view, is restricted to the protection of so-called negative rights. The state may wield its coercive power only to protect citizens from assault, theft, and fraud, and for national defense.

According to Nozick, the competitive market with private property is the only social structure compatible with respect for these individual rights. Consequently, for Nozick, there is no need for a theory of the just allocation of resources in general, including health-care resources. Resources will be allocated by market processes; insofar as people exchange or give what they have rightfully acquired, whatever allocation of resources that results is just.

Nozick's libertarianism has been effectively criticized on a number of grounds, but two major objections are especially potent. First, it has been noted that Nozick fails in his attempt to show that every principle of justice that requires redistribution either (1) is intuitively unjust or (2) would require unacceptable disruptions of people's expectations by frequently appropriating their holdings for the sake of preserving the overarching pattern of distribution specified by the principle.

To support the first prong of his attack on redistributive principles of justice Nozick tries to persuade us that it is counterintuitive to think that injustice could arise merely from voluntary exchanges among people, each of whom owns what he exchanges, and that, consequently, any principle of justice that requires allocations arising from such exchanges to be overturned must be unjust.

As several critics have pointed out, however, Nozick's intuitions will not be shared by anyone who takes seriously the problem of cumulative harms. Once the cumulative negative effects on both welfare and liberty are appreciated, the need to avoid or minimize the negative externalities can provide strong ethical grounds for limiting the individual's right to acquire and exchange goods—and thus for challenging the virtually unlimited private property right Nozick merely assumes without argument. For example, strictly voluntary exchanges of property may lead to such extreme concentrations of wealth that the rich are able, even through largely legal means, to undermine the civil and political liberties of the poor (Cohen 1978).

The second prong of Nozick's attack is weak as well. It is true that a very demanding principle of justice that required, for example, strict equality in resources, might necessitate frequent redistributions that would be intolerably coercive and disruptive. It is much less plausible to argue, however, that *all* redistributive principles suffer from this defect. Implementing a principle requiring only that everyone is to have a decent minimum of certain basic goods, including food, shelter, and a core set of important health-care services, need not result in frequent or severe disruptions. Long-standing, publicized laws specifying predictable tax obligations can be and are used to fund such a core of welfare goods.

Another major objection to Nozick's libertarianism turns against him his own provocative suggestion that the ultimate foundation for his strong right to private property (and hence for the denial of welfare rights it entails) is an appreciation of the central role of autonomy in the leading of a meaningful life. This vague suggestion seems to backfire on Nozick. An autonomous person who wishes to lead a meaningful life—which for most of us would not be a life in which poverty limits our aspirations to securing the next meal, finding shelter for the night, and coping with suffering and disability due to health problems that could have been avoided—will require at least a modicum of material resources, including access to health care. An autonomous person values opportunity, and our opportunities can be limited not only by deliberate interferences by others but also by lack of resources, by illness, and by disability.

Libertarians such as Nozick have a reply to the charge that justice as they see it shows too little concern with the human welfare and with the material resources for meaningful, autonomous living. They emphasize that justice is not the whole of morality and that the harsh effects of the libertarian ban on enforced redistribution can be moderated by voluntary adherence to principles of beneficence. However, an examination of approaches to health-care allocation that rely chiefly on principles of beneficence (or "humanity," or "charity"), rather than on principles of justice, shows serious obstacles exist to efficient, coordinated voluntary redistribution, which libertarians tend to overlook.

Rawls's Theory and the Right to Health Care

In his widely acclaimed book, *A Theory of Justice*, John Rawls offers a new and highly sophisticated version of the traditional theory of the social contract, as developed by Hobbes, Locke, Rousseau, and Kant. Although Rawls supplies several distinct lines of justification for the principles of justice he advances, the hypothetical contract argument is the most distinctive:

> The principles of justice for the basic structure of society are the principles that free and rational persons concerned to further their own interests would accept in an initial position of equality as defining the fundamental terms of their association. These principles are to regulate all further agreements; they specify the kinds of social cooperation that can be entered into and the forms of government that can be established. This way of regarding the principles of justice I shall call justice as fairness. (Rawls 1971, p. 11)

One of the chief functions of this hypothetical choice situation, which Rawls calls the *original position*, is to capture a particular conception of impartiality or fairness. Thus, the parties in the original position must choose principles of justice from behind a "veil of ignorance" that deprives them of information about their own socioeconomic class, race, or gender—facts that might bias their choice by enabling them to tailor the principles to their own particular advantage. The basic idea is that fair principles of social cooperation are those that would emerge from a choice situation that is fair to all individuals as autonomous persons who have a highest-order interest in being free to choose and revise their ends and to pursue them effectively.

Rawls produces a number of arguments to show that the parties would agree on the following principles of justice:

First Principle

Each person is to have an equal right to the most extensive total system of equal basic liberties compatible with a similar system of liberty for all.

Second Principle

Social and economic inequalities are to be arranged so that they are both:

(a) to the greatest benefit of the least advantaged, and
(b) attached to offices and positions open to all under conditions of fair equality of opportunity.

Rawls calls the first principle *The Principle of Greatest Equal Liberty*. The second principle includes two parts. Part (a) is the *difference principle*, which states that social and economic inequalities are to be arranged so that they are to the greatest benefit of those who are least advantaged. Part (b) is the *principle of fair equality of opportunity*, which states that social and economic inequalities are to be attached to offices and positions that are open to all under conditions of fair equality of opportunity.

A vast literature on Rawls's theory and a number of serious criticisms of his view have emerged. It has often been noted, for example, that the difference principle would be chosen in the original position only if, as Rawls assumes, the choosers have such an extreme aversion to risk that all they care about is avoiding a situation in which, should they turn out to be among the worst-off, they have a lesser share of primary goods than they would have if they were the worst-off in some other arrangement. In other words, they care only about minimizing losses should they turn out to be among the worst-off; they do not care about reaping the higher gains they might make if they were among the better off under a less egalitarian principle. Once this implausibly strong assumption about the attitude toward risk is dropped, it can be argued that a principle requiring only that everyone be guaranteed a "safety net" or decent minimum of welfare goods, rather than the difference principle, would be chosen.

Even if this and other major objections to Rawls's general theory can be met, however, it is far from clear that Rawls's theory as he himself presents it, contains the conceptual resources for justifying a right to health care that is specific enough to provide a useful goal for policy. To understand the limitation on Rawls's theory, let us suppose that health care is either itself a primary good covered by the difference principle or that health care may be purchased with income or some other form of wealth that is included under the difference principle. In the former case, depending on various empirical conditions, the best way to satisfy the difference principle might be to establish a state-enforced right to health care. But whether maximizing the prospects of the worst-off will require such a right and what the content of the right would be depends on what weight is assigned to health care relative to other primary goods included under the difference principle. Similarly, a weighting must also be assigned if we are to determine whether the share of wealth one receives under the difference principle would be sufficient for both health-care needs and for other ends. Until we have some solution to the weighting problem, Rawls's theory can shed only limited light on the question of priority relations between health care and other goods and among various forms of health care.

It is important to see that the informational constraints imposed by Rawls's veil of ignorance preclude a solution to the problem of weighting health care against other primary goods because the solution depends on facts about the particular conditions of the society in which the notions in question would be applied. At best, Rawls's hypothetical contractors would choose a kind of "placeholder" for a principle establishing a right to health care, on the assumption that the content of the right can only be filled out at later stages of agreement in the light of specific information about their particular society.

However, nothing in Rawls's concept of rational decision suggests that once relevant, concrete information is available, rational persons will agree on a single assignment of weights to the primary goods. It follows that Rawls's theory does not itself supply any content for the notion of a right to health care. Instead, at best, it lays down a very abstract structure within which the content would be worked out through the democratic political processes specified by the list of equal basic liberties. Given this, Rawls's theory advances us very little beyond the idea that there is a universal right to health care (Buchanan 1984a, pp. 61–62).

Equality of Opportunity as the Basis for a Right to Health Care: Norman Daniels's Rawlsian Theory

In his book *Just Health Care*, Norman Daniels develops a substantive account of the right to health care by relying on Rawls's principle of fair equality of opportunity. Although Daniels offers no justification for that principle, he indicates that he believes that Rawls's contractarian derivation of it is plausible and also contends that there is a considerable consensus, at least within liberal democratic political philosophy, that equality of opportunity is a central element of justice (Daniels 1985).

According to Daniels, the right to health care is derived from the following principle of fair equality of opportunity:

> Basic institutions that affect the allocation of health care resources are to be arranged so that, as far as is possible, each person is to enjoy his or her fair share of the normal opportunity range for individuals in his or her society.

The normal opportunity range for a society is the full set of individual life plans that it would be reasonable for individuals in that society to pursue, assuming that they enjoy "normal species functioning." Although Daniels makes it clear that normal species functioning as he understands it is a strictly objective, biological, nonnormative concept, he does little to say just what it encompasses. However, he does state that disease and disability are to be understood as departures from normal species functioning (Daniels 1985, p. 28).

For Daniels, an individual's fair share of the normal opportunity range is that set of life plans that it would be reasonable for that individual to pursue, given his or her particular "talents and skills," were the development of those talents and skills not impeded by departures from normal species functioning; that is, by disease or disability (Daniels 1985, p. 34), or by features of the social system (such as discriminatory hiring practices and inequalities in the social class into which one is born) that are arbitrary from a moral point of view. The allocation of health-care resources, then, is one important tool for ensuring that everyone has fair equality of opportunity, because health-care resources serve to prevent, minimize, or compensate for departures from normal species functioning and because departures from normal species functioning (i.e., disease and disability) constitute one important barrier to fair equality of opportunity understood as having one's fair share of the normal opportunity range.

Daniels's account is designed to help answer two important questions central to an ethical theory of health-care resource allocations: (1) What makes health care morally special? and (2) How should various kinds of health care be ranked relative to one another in terms of priority? The answer to the first question is that health care affects the attainment of normal species functioning and that lack of the latter is one important barrier to fair equality of opportunity. The answer to the second question is that those kinds of health care that have the greatest impact on preventing, minimizing, or compensating for departures from normal species functioning should have the highest priority, at least at the level of designing basic health-care institutions, including mechanisms for allocation.

There are, however, several serious problems with Daniels's approach quite apart from objections to the more general Rawlsian account of justice on which it builds. First, and perhaps most important, Daniels's fair equality of opportunity principle, especially if it is given lexical priority over all principles of distributive justice (other than a principle distributing basic liberties, like Rawls's first principle), seems to place too great a demand on overall social resources in the name of implementing a right to health care. What it requires is that we continue to pump social resources into health care as long as doing so continues to bring individuals closer to the ideal of normal species functioning—which is nothing less than a life free of disease and disability, because the latter are defined as departures from normal species functioning. The only constraint on the imperative to channel all available resources into health care is that doing so must not undermine other efforts needed to achieve fair equality of opportunity by eliminating impediments to one's fair share of the normal opportunity range other than disease and disability (and with satisfying a lexically prior principle of greatest equal liberty).

The objection is that the demand for fair equality of opportunity, understood according to Daniels's principle, makes the health-care sector a kind of "black hole" capable of sucking in almost unlimited quantities of social resources because, especially for persons with grave disabilities and diseases, there is virtually no limit to how much could be done, granted continuing technological advances, to bring such persons closer to the goal of normal species functioning. For example, being born blind, mentally retarded, and deaf is surely one of the most severe impediments to being able to pursue effectively that set of life plans that it would be reasonable for one to pursue in this society, given the talents and skills one would have, were the development of one's talents and skills not impeded by disease or disability. If this is so, efforts to remedy or compensate for these severe departures from normal species functioning should have high priority in overall efforts (inside and outside the health-care sector) to ensure that every individual enjoys equality of opportunity. The commitment to providing such resources might be so demanding that honoring it would amount to a virtually unlimited right to health care.

Second, Daniels's principle not only seems to create an excessive drain on resources, it also does not appear to provide guidance as to how we are to make priority decisions within efforts to achieve fair equality of opportunity through allocation of health-care resources. It is silent on the question of whether we should first try to improve the condition of the worst-off—persons whose disease or disability is so severe that they are the furthest from the ideal of normal species functioning—even if doing this means that the better off will get access to virtually no health-care resources, or whether everyone is to receive at least some of the basic health-care resources.

It is important to understand that Daniels's view that the normal opportunity range is society-relative does little to blunt the force of the black-holes objection. The normal opportunity range is society-relative, for Daniels, in the sense that whatever life plans are reasonable for various people in a society to pursue will be influenced by the resources, cultural attitudes, and so forth, of the society in question. But in response to a critic who pointed out that the distribution of health-care resources that exists in a particular society will also determine which life plans it is reasonable to pursue (Buchanan 1984a, p. 64), Daniels explicitly states that the normal opportunity range is that array of life plans it would be reasonable for people to pursue in the society if they enjoyed normal species functioning, that is, if they were free of disease and disability. And normal species functioning, Daniels emphasizes, is not society-relative (Daniels 1985, p. 28–29). Thus, even if everyone in a particular society suffered from a certain disease, say a kind of anemia, having that disease would still be a departure from normal species functioning and would be an impediment to everyone's attaining his or her fair share of the normal opportunity range because the normal opportunity range is that set of life plans that would be reasonable to pursue in that society in the absence of departures from normal species functioning. As Daniels puts it:

> The anemia in this case is a disease which keeps each individual from adequately carrying out *any* life plan that otherwise would be reasonable in his society. Remember, our reference point is normal species-functioning functional organization, not functioning in a certain society. (Daniels 1985, p. 55)

A third problem with Daniels's fair equality of opportunity principle is that it, like Rawls's narrower principle concerning access to offices and positions, is based on the fundamental belief that opportunity should not be limited by "morally arbitrary" factors. Yet again, like Rawls's principle, it arbitrarily takes an individual's talents and skills as a fixed baseline. In Daniels's case, the baseline is hypothetical—the talents and skills one would have were their development not impeded by disease or disability. The problem is that, as Rawls and Daniels both admit, there are factors other than disease and social position that influence the development of talents and skills, but that are equally arbitrary from a moral point of view. The most obvious of these is one's normal genetic endowment. Neither Rawls nor Daniels gives any reason why efforts to achieve fair equality of opportunity should not deal directly with this important, "morally arbitrary" determinant of opportunity. Moreover, new advances in genetic engineering may soon make such an extension of their notions of fair equality of opportunity technically feasible. Daniels believes it to be an advantage of his theory that it takes skills and talents (as they would be, absent the effects of disease and disability) as the baseline for determining fair share of the normal opportunity range and "...does not require us to 'level' all differences among persons" (Daniels 1985, p. 52). However, the same fundamental concern to eliminate the influences of morally arbitrary factors on opportunity that leads Daniels to require that resources be used to minimize departures from normal species functioning and the effects of socioeconomic class position also seems to require the use of resources for increasing the opportunity of those who are not genetically disabled or diseased but who are, nonetheless, at a genetic disadvantage relative to the more fortunate.

Less Systematic Accounts of the Right to Health Care

Some ethicists have attempted to approach the right to health-care issue in a somewhat less systematic fashion. Instead of undertaking the ambitious task of first developing a comprehensive theory of justice and then drawing its implications for the right to health care, they have operated mainly at the middle level of ethical theorizing and have offered one or more general principles concerning the distribution of health care and provided less formal arguments for them, arguments that do not rely on complex theoretical backdrops.

An Egalitarian Right to Health Care

Writers who advocate an egalitarian right to health care have generally taken the less formal approach (Gutman 1983). They contend that the right to health care is not to be understood simply as a guarantee of a certain safety net, decent minimum, or core set of basic health-care services. Instead, they advance a much stronger claim of rights—everyone having equal need for a health-care service or resource is to have equal access to it. In some cases, this alleged egalitarian right to health care is advanced as a corollary of a more general egalitarian welfare right—all resources are to be distributed so as to approximate, as nearly as possible, a condition in which everyone's net welfare over a lifetime is equal (Veatch 1981, pp. 264–68; Menzel 1983, p. 21).

Such a view can be criticized in two ways. On the one hand, those who provide a more systematic account of a less egalitarian right to health care can appeal to the strengths of the background theory from which that is derived and point to the lack of a well-articulated supporting theory for the egalitarian right. On the other hand, the egalitarian position on the right to health care can be criticized using two less formal sorts of arguments. The first attacks the more general egalitarian welfare rights principle by noting that it would be irrational for anyone—including the worst-off—to insist on equality if allowing certain inequalities would improve everyone's situation. Suppose that it is true, for example, that a system that gave higher salaries to physicians than to most other workers would stimulate more intelligent and able people to become physicians, with the result that a higher quality of medical care would be available to all. Without a convincing systematic theory to support egalitarianism, it is difficult to see why anyone would find such an arrangement objectionable, as long as the greater income of physicians did not have negative effects that outweighed the gain in quality of care to persons who have lesser salaries.

Of course, the egalitarian might object by saying that there will be a preponderance of negative effects in most real-world cases in which income differentials (or other inequalities) are allowed for the sake of increasing benefits for the worst-off—those with higher incomes will wield undue political influence, the self-esteem of the lower-paid will suffer, and so forth. This defense of the general egalitarian principle is in a sense, however, a retreat from it. What it amounts to is the claim that, even though inequality is acceptable and perhaps even preferable to equality in principle, striving for the goal of equality is a more appropriate practical goal in an imperfect world.

The second objection is directed against those who do not hold that there is an egalitarian right to welfare goods in general but only an egalitarian right to health care. The egalitarian right to health care requires that no one is to have access to any health care that is not also available to everyone else in similar need. The objection takes the form of a dilemma (President's Commission 1983, pp. 18–19). Either the level of health care to which everyone is entitled—and more than which no one is allowed to have—is set as high as is technically possible or it is set lower. If the former, then the commitment to providing everyone with the very best care technically possible for every condition will place an unacceptable strain on overall social resources and the loss of opportunities to secure important non-health-care needs would be too great.

If, on the other hand, the equal level of health care is set sufficiently below the technically possible optimum to avoid irrational allocation of overall resources, so long as there are inequalities in income and differences in preferences for health care, some people will be prohibited from purchasing higher levels of or better quality health care, even though they wish to do so with their own resources. Such a situation would be inefficient because lifting the stricture that levels of health care must be equal would allow a pareto improvement—those who are better-off and have a preference for more or better care would gain by being allowed to satisfy it, and the worse off would not lose so long as they received an adequate share of the non-health-care benefits that could be reaped by keeping the level of health care guaranteed to all lower than the technically possible optimum. Quite apart from the objection on grounds of inefficiency, an egalitarian right to health care that sets the level lower than the technically possible optimum would require unacceptable interferences with individuals' liberty to use their after-taxes income to purchase the health care they desire, but would permit them to use their money for luxury goods such as fine wines or antique cars, perhaps much more questionable choices.

The Right to a Decent Minimum or Adequate Level of Health Care

The force of the objections to the claim that there is an egalitarian right to health care helps to explain the popularity of the view that, although there is a right to health care, it is a limited right, a right to a decent minimum or adequate level of care. Such a position has several attractions (President's Commission 1983, p. 20). First, the notion that people have a right to a decent minimum or adequate level, rather than to *all* health care that produces any net benefit, clearly acknowledges that, because not all health care is of equal importance, allocational priorities must be set within health care and that resources must also be allocated to goods other than health care.

Second, this position is also consonant with the intuitively plausible conviction that our obligations to the less fortunate, although fundamental enough to be expressed in the language of rights, are nonetheless *not unlimited.* Third, the decent minimum is a floor beneath which no one should be allowed to fall, not a ceiling above which the better off are prohibited from purchasing services if they wish. Thus, this position avoids the troublesome interferences with individual liberty, which an egalitarian right requires (President's Commission 1983, p. 20).

The chief objection to this way of understanding the right to health care is that it is virtually devoid of content. The chief import of the claim—that the right to health care is the right to a decent minimum or adequate level of care—is negative. It indicates only that neither a right to all care that is of any net benefit nor to only all technically possible care is appropriate. Beyond this cautionary function, little is conveyed, unless a reasonable way of filling out the content is supplied.

Although it acknowledges the inadequacies of various ad hoc proposals for specifying the adequate level of care, the President's Commission offers little by way of a concrete alternative. At one point, the report offers the apparently plausible suggestion that the fundamental idea behind the notion of an adequate level is the belief that everyone is to have access to "...enough care to achieve sufficient welfare, opportunity, information, and evidence of interpersonal concern to facilitate a reasonably full and satisfying life" (President's Commission 1983, p. 20). Unfortunately, this statement, in effect, takes back much of what was said about the obligation being a limited one because some individuals are so badly off that enormous amounts of resources could be spent in attempting to ensure them of "...a reasonably full and satisfying life." Further, there may be considerable disagreement over what counts as a "reasonably full and satisfying life." This is simply the notion of quality of life that crops up elsewhere in medical ethics—a mask for sharply conflicting values.

In an attempt to provide practical content to the notion of a decent minimum of care while avoiding an unlimited obligation that would raise the specter of the black holes problem, Alan Gibbard has proposed a seemingly simple but ingenious hypothetical choice procedure or thought experiment (Gibbard 1983, pp. 153–78). To determine which health-care services should be included in the decent minimum, Gibbard asks us to think of a person as choosing among different lifetime health-care insurance policies, each of which represents a different mix of preventive and curative services, medical and nonmedical services, and so forth. Because different persons would choose different policies tailored to their own particular health-care needs if they could predict them, it is necessary to impose a veil of ignorance—a set of informational constraints—upon the choosers. Gibbard suggests that it would be necessary to think of a person as choosing among policies before his or her own conception because, from conception on, our health-care prospects diverge. Granted this restriction, the rational choice of an insurance policy would be based on general statistical information about overall morbidity and mortality rates for one's society.

Before a determinate choice could be made, however, another parameter of the choice situation must be specified—the chooser must know his or her budget, what his or her total disposable wealth is. The choice of a particular health-care insurance policy will then depend not only on one's estimate of the comparative health-care benefits of the different policies, but also on how much one values the health-care benefits in question relative to benefits that could be obtained by using one's resources on goods and services other than health care.

The fundamental limitation on this strategy for specifying the ethically required decent minimum, of course, is not simply that it yields a determinate outcome if a fixed budget for the individual is assumed, but also what that budget should be is itself an ethical question. Gibbard frankly acknowledges this when he describes his thought experiment as a way of giving content to the guaranteed decent minimum of health care once we know what the appropriate guaranteed income share is. In other words, until we know what individuals have a right to, by way of the allocation of income, we cannot determine how health-care resources ought to be allocated. So it seems that we have merely substituted the problem of specifying one kind of decent minimum for another. Further, there is also a problem of circularity—whether something is a fair income share (or an adequate level of income) depends on whether it would be sufficient for providing adequate levels of various important goods, including health care. Both these objections point to the conclusion that the rational health-care insurance chooser approach cannot settle the most fundamental ethical issues concerning the allocation of health-care resources and fails to provide a fully satisfying response to the objection that the notion of a right to a decent minimum or adequate level of care is too vague to be of much practical value (Baily 1986).[4]

Indeed, once the problem of vagueness is appreciated, it may even become difficult to distinguish between the decent minimum view and the egalitarian view that its proponents reject. Those who believe that there is an egalitarian right to health care but who are not committed to across-the-board egalitarianism presumably hold that there is something special about health care that requires it to be distributed equally even if (some) other goods need not be. But if health care means all forms of health care, then this is a most implausible position, because, at best, only some of the most important forms of health care could have this special status. Consequently, the claim that there is an egalitarian right to health care should be understood as meaning that everyone is to have equal access to some especially important subset of health-care services and resources. Until these are specified, and until it is determined whether they exceed those included in a decent minimum, it will not be possible to distinguish between the egalitarian view and the decent minimum view. After all, the right to a decent minimum is an egalitarian right—everyone is to have equal access to whatever it is that constitutes the decent minimum. Without a clearer specification of what the decent minimum includes, it is possible to distinguish between it and the claim that there is an egalitarian right to health care only if the latter is taken in an unrestricted sense, as meaning that everyone is to have equal access to all beneficial forms of health care that anyone else is getting (assuming equal need).

Fair Financing as an Element of Distributive Justice in Health Care

Remarkably enough, theorists of the right to health care have usually proceeded as if distributive justice concerned only the question: Who is to get what? and have neglected the question Who is to pay how much, for whom? In other words, discussions have focused on only one aspect of distributive justice, the nature and justification of the right to health care, and they have neglected the issue of fair financing, the just distribution of the costs of providing that health care to which individuals are supposed to have a right.

Different systems for ensuring a right to health care for all distribute costs differently. For example, a single-payer system, such as the Canadian national health insurance system, finances the right to health care from taxes. If the taxation arrangements are progressive, the financing of the right to health care is just, at least if it is assumed that a just distribution of costs requires those with greater resources to bear a larger portion of the costs. On the other hand, if, as in some health-care reform plans now under consideration in the United States (including President Clinton's plan), everyone is required to pay the same dollar amount in premiums for the standard benefit package to which all are supposed to be entitled, the distribution of costs is regressive. (A janitor making $15,000 a year will pay the same premium as the chief officer of a major corporation, even though the latter earns 20 times as much money.) Similarly, a system that has uniform rates for deductibles or co-payments (regardless of ability to pay) will be to that extent regressive in its distribution of costs. A co-payment of $20 will have a much greater impact on a poor person than it will have on a rich person. Clearly, the comprehensive ethical evaluation of a health-care delivery system must consider the distribution of costs as well as the distribution of benefits.

When theorists of the right to health care have mentioned the distribution of costs, they have tended to assume that the question of the content of the right to health care can be answered independently of and before the question of who pays how much for whom. Yet if, for reasons noted earlier, the right to health care should not be understood as an unlimited right to *all* care that is expected to be of any net benefit, but rather a right to an adequate level or decent minimum of care, the assumption proves false. Part of what should go into determining how generous the adequate level or decent minimum of care should be is how burdensome ensuring the amount of care will be on those who must pay for it. An extremely generous package of benefits to be ensured for all might impose excessive burdens on the better off, even if the financing arrangements were strictly progressive. Thus, the question of what the right to health care includes cannot be answered without considering how the cost of providing care is to be distributed.

It is worth noting that, even if a systematic discussion of just cost distribution has been lacking in theories about distributive justice in health care, the topic has not been ignored in the area of health-care policy, albeit it has not been dealt with systematically in that area. For example, the primary justification given for instituting the Medicare program (1965) was that, without subsidized insurance, the elderly were forced to bear an excessive cost in securing health care. The argument was not that the elderly absolutely could not afford to obtain care, but that the cost they would have to bear to obtain it was unacceptable. Because it is financed from general tax revenues, the Medicare program represents a political judgment that others should pay a share of the costs of providing health care for the elderly.

BENEFICENCE RATHER THAN JUSTICE: OBLIGATIONS WITHOUT RIGHTS

Partly because of dissatisfaction with the forgoing attempts to settle major allocation questions by an appeal to principles specifying a right to health care, and partly because of a growing perception that justice is not the only ethical value bearing on allocation, some recent works have begun to focus instead on principles of beneficence or charity. The President's Commission argues for a societal obligation to provide an adequate level (or decent minimum) of care for all and that the ultimate responsibility and authority for seeing that this is achieved lies with the federal government (President's Commission 1983, pp. 3–6). The Commission approach, like that advocated in an earlier article by Buchanan, rejects a premise that has guided much of the ethical literature on allocation—the assumption that any policy for allocating health-care resources that involves nonvoluntary transfers of wealth from the better off to the worse off is justifiable only if it can be shown to be based on a moral right to health care. Uncritical subscription to this assumption has led, quite naturally, to the belief that very little can be said about the ethical evaluation of the current pattern of health-care resource allocation in the absence of a convincing defense of the claim that there is such a moral right. This in turn would require clear adjudication between rival theories of justice.

There may be an even more fundamental—and even less thoroughly examined—assumption that underlies the exclusively rights-based approach to allocation issues. This is the view that the government is morally justified in using coercion (in this case to enforce transfers of wealth) only for purposes of guaranteeing moral rights. The latter view is a very strong and usually inadequately defended assumption about the sole condition under which the use of state power is morally legitimate.

Implicit in the Commission's approach is the thesis that, even if it is true that the need to guarantee rights is the strongest and most obvious moral justification for enforcing allocation policies, it is not the only justification. The Commission argues that, because of the special moral significance of health care (or, rather, of some forms of it), because health-care needs are often to a significant extent underserved, and because health-care needs are typically so unpredictable, costly, and unevenly distributed among people that it is implausible to expect everyone to be able to meet them using only their own resources, society has a moral obligation to provide an adequate level of care or set of health-care services to those who cannot provide them for themselves. In effect, the Commission contends that this obligation is of such fundamental moral importance that it may be enforced, if necessary, regardless of whether there is a corresponding individual right to an adequate level of care.

The general line of argument can be fleshed out in a more systematic and convincing way (Buchanan 1984a, 1985, 1987).[5] The basic premises employed are the following:

1. The provision of at least some of the more important forms of health care to the needy can be viewed as a collective good, and strictly voluntary schemes for securing them may succumb to familiar obstacles to successful collective action—in particular, the free-rider problem and the assurance problem.
2. In some cases, enforcement of obligations to contribute is both necessary and sufficient for the successful provisions of collective goods, including important forms of health care for the needy.
3. The fact that enforcement is necessary and sufficient for achieving such a morally fundamental collective good as the provision of the most important forms of health care to the needy is a strong prima facie justification for enforcement, independently of whether the individuals who will receive the good have an antecedent moral right to it.

Whether this strong prima facie justification is a decisive justification, all things considered, depends on a number of factors. Is use of enforcement compatible with avoiding unacceptably dangerous concentrations of power in the government? Can a system of enforced contributions be achieved—one that fairly distributes the burden of providing for the needy among the better off and that avoids unpredictable, arbitrary, and excessively burdensome appropriations of individuals' wealth? Only if these questions can be answered affirmatively can the prima facie justification become a decisive justification.

The attractiveness of this line of argument becomes clearer once premises 1 and 2 are explicated. Without an effective enforcement mechanism, strictly voluntary compliance with duties to aid the needy may founder due to the fact that a system of aid is a collective good. Even if rational individuals agree to a system of duties to contribute to the good, they may find it rational to defect from it, to be free riders, as long as compliance is voluntary. The situation has an incentive structure similar to that of a many-person prisoners' dilemma. Each individual may reason as follows: Either enough others will contribute to the good in question, regardless of whether I contribute, or they will not. Because my contribution is a cost to me, the rational thing for me to do is not to contribute, so long as I will be able to partake of the good regardless of whether I contributed.

It might be replied that, in fact, individuals will not behave thusly because their desire to maximize their own utility will be constrained by altruism. The extent to which individuals observe moral constraints on their individual utility-maximizing behavior is an empirical issue. But this much seems clear: Because altruism is generally limited, the scope of duties to aid that we can expect people to fulfill voluntarily is probably considerably narrower than that of duties they would discharge if those duties were enforced.

The free-rider problem arises on the assumption that the good at which each individual aims is accurately described as the provision of aid to the needy. If this is the goal, the individual may withhold his contribution if he believes that the needy will be provided for by others or that they will not, regardless of whether he contributes. And there are several different ways in which one may benefit from the attainment of this good without having contributed to it. Some may derive satisfaction or avoid discomfort simply by knowing that the needy are provided for. Others may view the provision of aid to the needy as instrumentally good—it makes for a more stable social structure, in which those who have wealth and power may enjoy them in greater security, and it increases overall productivity by enabling more people to work. Indeed, it is often said that the major social welfare programs initiated in western Europe in the late nineteenth century were motivated chiefly by the latter sorts of considerations rather than by a sense of justice or a direct concern for the well-being of the needy.

On the other hand, the free-rider problem will not block successful collective action if a sufficient number of people desire to provide for the needy, rather than simply desiring that the needy be provided for. If I regard the good to be attained as "a system of aid to the needy to which I contribute," then, of course, I cannot partake of that good without contributing to it.

Whether a sufficient number of people will be effectively motivated by the desire to be charitable to achieve a particular goal of collective charity (rather than simply by the desire that charity be done) is an empirical question whose answer will vary from case to case, depending on the psychology of the individual involved.

But even if an individual does not himself wish to take a free ride on the contributions of others to a system of aid to the needy, he still may be unwilling to render aid to the needy unless he has assurance that others (with resources as great as or greater than his) will also render aid to those in need. He may be unwilling to contribute without assurance that others will do so for either or both of two distinct reasons: (1) He may conclude that it is better to expend his "beneficence budget" on an act of independent charity toward some particular person in need, rather than risk contributing to a collective charity in which the threshold of contributions needed for success is not reached; (2) his commitment to being charitable may be limited by a requirement of fairness or reciprocity. That persons who are strict individual utility maximizers may fail to achieve systems of aid that are public goods is hardly surprising. What is striking is the more general conclusion that collective action to create and maintain systems of aid may falter even if some individuals are significantly altruistic.

Whether enforcement will be necessary to achieve goals of collective charity does not appear to admit of a general answer. Under certain rather strong conditions, strictly voluntary contributions may suffice. However, in the case of systems of aid that are collective goods, as with collective goods generally, there seem to be no strictly voluntary strategies that will work in all circumstances. If this is so, and if enforcement is justified in any such cases, it is not the case that enforcement of a duty to contribute is justified only where there is an antecedent moral right to a share of the good in question, whether it be national defense or a system of health care for the needy.

The non-rights-based or enforced beneficence approach has four important advantages. First, it represents, in effect, a kind of end run around the conceptual impasse created by the deadlock of rival theories of distributive justice in health care because it provides an ethical basis for evaluating current allocations and for designing new allocation policies without having to adjudicate decisively among such theories. Indeed, the enforced beneficence arguments can be seen as providing moral support for establishing a legal right to health care in the absence of a clear justification for a moral right on which to found the legal right.

Second, obligations of beneficence are traditionally understood to be limited by the proviso that rendering aid to the needy is not to be unduly burdensome to the benefactor. Consequently, the enforced beneficence approach avoids objections to which more demanding egalitarian concepts of the right to health care are vulnerable.

Third, the notion of enforced beneficence gains some plausibility from the widespread acceptance of the legitimacy of arguments for enforcement to secure more familiar collective goods, such as national defense. It is well known that free-rider problems, assurance problems, or both can block voluntary contribution to such goods and there is a rather broad agreement that enforced contribution is at least sometimes justifiable.

Fourth, the enforced beneficence approach can be seen as a step toward rectifying two unfortunate biases of much of contemporary ethical thinking, both within and outside medical ethics—a tendency to proceed as if morality were limited to justice and a propensity to concentrate exclusively on matters of individual, rather than collective, responsibility and action, which thereby glosses over problems of social coordination.

On the other side of the ledger, there are two main difficulties with the enforced beneficence view. Perhaps the most important is that the obligation of beneficence in health care may be so vague that it, like the alleged right to a decent minimum, may not provide sufficient guidance for substantive policy decisions. In addition, a systematic, society-wide effort to specify and coordinate obligations to contribute may seem to run contrary to what many take to be a distinctive feature of those obligations of beneficence that do not have correlative rights. Such obligations, often called *duties of charity*, are traditionally thought to allow a broad sphere of discretion for the benefactor, who may choose either the form his aid will take or to whom it will be given, or both. If a coordinated, enforced system of contributions to the needy is to avoid this objection, the system must be designed in such a way as to allow a significant exercise of autonomy for benefactors, either within the system or outside it.

CONCLUSION

The foregoing critical survey has exposed a number of serious difficulties with each of the main strategies for making ethical evaluations of health-care resource allocation. None of the strategies has emerged as fully adequate or uniquely attractive. Such a result should prompt neither surprise nor pessimism. Systemic thinking about these difficult issues has barely begun. Only in the past few years have economists, other policy analysts, and those who actually make policy begun to recognize that ethical issues are unavoidable and that they are not merely matters of taste, but that they can be reasoned about. Similarly, systematic ethical theorizing about matters of distributive justice is also a relatively recent phenomenon, and the hard work of teasing out the concrete implications of such general theories for real-world allocation problems is in its infancy.

DISCUSSION QUESTIONS

1. What resources (time, energy, money, etc.) should be put into health care and into other social goods such as education, defense, eliminating poverty and homelessness, and improving the environment? Are

health-care professionals appropriate persons for making these allocational decisions?

2. Within the area of health care (once we have determined its budget), how much time, energy, money, and the like should we allocate for prevention and how much for rescue and crisis medicine? Are health-care professionals appropriate persons for making these decisions?
3. Within either preventive care or rescue medicine, who (if anyone) should receive resources such as vaccines or artificial hearts when we cannot meet everyone's needs?
4. Often, because of their conditions, the sickest and most needy patients are not the ones who would benefit the most from health-care interventions. For example, the worst-off heart patients may not benefit from a heart transplant as much as patients who are in somewhat better physical condition. Under ethical principles of utility and justice, who should receive the scarce resource?
5. If health care is to be allocated at least in part on the basis of need, do people who have great need because of voluntary lifestyle choices have high-priority claims on scarce resources or, because of their lifestyle choices, have they waived their claim on these resources?

3

PUBLIC AND PRIVATE RESPONSIBILITIES IN THE U.S. HEALTH-CARE SYSTEM

Allen Buchanan

THE EXPERIENCE OF ETHICAL CONFLICT IN THE PRIVATE SECTOR

Some private health-care insurers report that they are experiencing conflicts between what they take to be their ethical obligations and the pressures of escalating competition and cost-containment strategies. Following are the questions they are asking among themselves:

1. Is it ethically permissible to charge higher premiums or to deny coverage to individuals who presently have or have had a specific disease or who test positive for a high probability of some disease (e.g., those who are HIV positive or those whom genetic testing or screening indicates are at high risk for certain diseases)?
2. Is it ethically permissible for the insurer to limit payment to care received from providers selected by the insurer in order to reduce the insurer's costs?

Some provider–insurers are asking similar questions about the scope and limits of their ethical responsibilities. Should health maintenance organizations (HMOs) continue their traditional commitment to "comprehensive coverage" for all subscribers even if this means that fewer potential subscribers will be able to afford to join the plan? Should the organization depart from its traditional "first-dollar coverage" philosophy and introduce substantial co-payments or deductibles to reduce costs?

Similarly, administrators of private health-care provider organizations also report that they are increasingly grappling with ethical dilemmas that arise because of competition and cost-containment pressures.[1] Now that the use of diagnosis-related groups (DRGs) has reduced the surplus revenues from Medicare hospital payments and private insurers are much more careful about which services and procedures they will reimburse, hospitals find it much more difficult to "cross-subsidize" uninsured patients. Is it, therefore, ethically permissible for a hospital to target its marketing strategies only to insured patients or simply to adopt a policy of not admitting the uninsured (except where law requires emergency treatment regardless of ability to pay)?[2]

It is tempting to plunge immediately into these ethical issues, but before doing so there is a prior puzzle to be solved: Why are these private organizations—these business concerns—exercising themselves over these issues in the first place? What assumptions about the ethical obligations or responsibilities of their organizations must they be making for it even to be possible for them to experience these ethical conflicts?

OBLIGATIONS CONCERNING ACCESS

It is important to understand that the ethical problems listed are not the familiar ones that virtually any large corporation faces and which are grist for the mill of the emerging discipline of business ethics—the standard dilemmas concerning truth-telling, exploiting the misfortune or ignorance of competitors (or customers), whistle-blowing, and all the rest.[3] Instead, the chief ethical issue common to these concerns of private insurers and providers is something quite different. It is the question of the scope and limits of the ethical responsibilities these organizations have to help solve or at least not to worsen the problem of access to health care in the United States.

Even to pose this question is to assume or at least strongly to suggest that such private organizations do have some ethical obligations concerning access. Indeed, unless members of these organizations made this assumption, they would not experience the ethical conflicts in question. It is this assumption that we should first probe. There are two distinct ways in which an obligation to help people secure access might be understood, but neither of them by itself implies that private health-care insurers or providers have any special obligations concerning access.

The first focuses upon the potential recipient of care and assumes that all citizens have a moral right to health care, the sort of right which has as its correlative an obligation on the part of someone to provide health care to those who have the right. The most plausible arguments for such a right, however, imply that the correlative obligation falls upon society as a whole, not upon some particular organizations within society.[4] If any institution or agency can be said to be ultimately responsible for seeing that this societal obligation is met it would have to be the state, not any particular organization. And in American society it is both customary and reasonable to assume that the federal government has the ultimate responsibility for seeing that societal obligations are met. The federal government alone, because of its taxation powers, is equipped to provide adequate resources for securing all citizens' rights to health care and to do so in such a way that the burden of providing these resources is distributed fairly in society, with no segment of society bearing a disproportionate share of the costs of fulfilling what is a societal obligation.[5]

The second way of understanding the assumption that there is an obligation (on someone's part) to provide access to health care focuses not primarily upon the individual who is the recipient of care but upon various benefits to society at large of having a healthy citizenry—a more productive work force, a sturdy army to preserve national security, and so on. It is generally thought that this way of conceiving of the obligation to provide access to health care rather than any assumption that access to health care is a fundamental individual moral right, provided the ideological underpinnings of the first modern health and social welfare programs in Western Europe. The obligation to provide access to health care, then, is based upon the need for the social goods derived from a healthy populace, and the ultimate responsibility for seeing that the obligation is met rests again with the state as the entity that is authorized to ensure that important social goods are achieved. Whether or not any private organizations have obligations to provide access to health care cannot be inferred from the assumption that an individual has a moral right to health care or that public health is an important social good. Much more must be said about what the division of responsibility is (or ought to be) before any determinate claims about obligations can be warranted.

What is common to both approaches is the assumption that the obligation to provide access to health care is primarily a *societal* obligation rather than an individual obligation or one that falls primarily on particular private organizations or entities within society. The President's Commission on medical ethics summarized the chief reasons for regarding this obligation as societal. "Securing equitable access is a societal rather than a merely private or individual responsibility for several reasons. First, while health is of special importance for human beings, health care—especially scientific health care—is a social product requiring the skills and efforts of many individuals; it is not something that individuals can provide for themselves solely through their own efforts."[6]

Second, because the need for health care is both unevenly distributed among persons and highly unpredictable and because the cost of securing care may be great, few individuals could secure adequate care without relying on some social mechanism for sharing costs. Third, if persons generally deserved their health conditions or if the need for health care were fully within the individual's control, the fact that some lack adequate care would not be viewed as an inequity. But differences in health status, and hence differences in health-care needs, are largely undeserved because they are, for the most part, not within the individual's control.[7]

Still, even if the primary obligation to provide adequate access to care falls on society as a whole, this does not mean that particular social entities and individuals have no obligations regarding access. Although a distinction must be made between society and government as one institution within society, in a system such as that of the United States the central, or federal, government has a special responsibility for ensuring that basic societal obligations are met, for reasons already noted. In particular, the federal government alone has the authority and the resources to devise and enforce an effective and coordinated societal effort to ensure access. Moreover, whereas modern pluralistic societies are composed of many communities, each with its own collective obligations, the federal government alone can serve as the ultimate agent for meeting collective obligations that transcend the boundaries of various communities within society.

The nature and extent of governmental activity required to ensure that the societal obligation is met will vary depending on the particular circumstances, resources, and ethical and political traditions of the society in question. Thus "the recognition of a collective or societal obligation does not [itself] imply that government should be the only or even the primary institution involved in the complex enterprise of making health care available."[8]

ALTERNATIVE SCHEMES FOR SECURING ACCESS

There are four different ways in which the federal government might discharge its responsibility for seeing that the societal obligation to provide access to health care is met. Each constitutes a different division of responsibilities among organizations and institutions within society.

1. Government provision of an adequate level of health care for all: a national health service, with health-care professionals serving as direct employees of the government.
2. Government funding of care with private provision: national health insurance—that is, a single insurer, the federal government—which allows individuals to choose among private providers; or insurance vouchers supplied by the federal government, which individuals can use to purchase insurance from whichever private insurer they choose.
3. Mixed system: some government provision of care and/or funding of privately provided care, along with private insurance and private provision

(the current U.S. system, which includes the VA CHAMPUS [the government health-care program for families of active military personnel], Medicaid, Medicare, a large number of private insurers and private providers, as well as some private charitable institutions).

In the fourth system the government would have to do nothing positive to discharge its responsibility to see that the societal obligation is met:

4. Purely private system: adequate access to care achieved for all through a combination of private insurance markets and private provisions, supplemented by private charity.

Current policy debates about access to health care as well as the ethical conflicts experienced by private insurers and providers assume that this fourth approach would not be adequate and I will proceed in this discussion upon that assumption as well. (It is worth pausing for a moment to reflect, however, upon whether the assumption that a purely private system will not suffice reflects skepticism about the extent of the charitable impulse, appreciation of the difficulties of coordinating charitable efforts in an efficient way so as to fill the gaps left by market provision, or an uneasy suspicion that there really is no social consensus that individuals do have a moral right to health care).[9] The present U.S. health-care system is, of course, of the third type, but in almost any interpretation of what an adequate level of care is, this system is not providing it for everyone. Estimates vary, but there is a broad consensus among health-care researchers that at least thirty-five million Americans have no private health-care insurance and are not eligible for any government programs, including Medicare, Medicaid, VA, and CHAMPUS. Perhaps another fifteen million or more have private insurance whose benefits fall below what would count as an "adequate level of care" in any reasonable interpretation of that rather vague concept.[10]

TWO CONTRASTING MODELS OF THE ROLE OF PRIVATE ORGANIZATIONS IN A MIXED SYSTEM

There are two quite different ways in which ethical responsibilities for access could be distributed in a mixed system. First, the federal government could itself assume full responsibility for filling in any gaps left by the combined operations of the private insurance market and private charity. In other words, the scope of government provision and/or funding of care or of private insurance would be determined by the size of the gap between an adequate level of care for all and the care provided through private insurance and charity. According to this arrangement, neither private insurers nor private providers (nor private insurers/providers such as HMOs) have any obligations to help ensure access to an adequate level of care for all. They will, presumably, have obligations to pay taxes, and some portion of their taxes will be used by the federal government to see that the gap between the level of care provided by the private sector and an adequate level of care for all is closed, but in this respect they will be indistinguishable from other taxpayers. Private insurers and providers, in this model, are simply businesses like any other. They have no more of an obligation to provide access to care to those who cannot purchase insurance coverage or pay directly than automobile dealers are obligated to give cars to the poor or grocers are obligated to hand out free food.[11]

If such private organizations could be said to have obligations concerning access at all, they are obligations only in a very loose sense, what moral philosophers call imperfect duties or duties of charity. These are not specific obligations to provide some determinate level of aid to any particular needy persons, but rather simply a duty to do something to benefit some of the less fortunate.[12] The standard form of an imperfect duty or charitable obligation is as follows: one ought to help (some) persons in need (in some way or other), so long as one can do so without "excessive cost" to oneself. The looseness of their obligations strongly affects the possibility of ethical appraisal of the organizations' practices. They cannot be judged deficient if they fail to provide any particular kind or level of aid to any particular potential recipient, and it is not appropriate for society to hold them accountable, by public censure or through legal penalties or regulative actions.

The second way of conceiving of the obligations in a mixed system has quite different implications for the ethical status of private insurers and providers. The idea is that private insurers and providers have special obligations, just as the government has its own obligations. The extent of the government's obligations is limited by the extent of the obligations of private organizations. In the first model, any gap in access signals a failure on the part of the government, since its obligation is simply to fill whatever gap is left by the operation of the competitive market plus charity. In the second model, a gap in access need not signal a failure on the government's part. Instead, the fault may lie with private insurers or providers who have not fulfilled the special obligations that are assigned to them in the overall social division of responsibility. There are various ways in which such special obligations might be assigned. As in the case of the Hill-Burton Act, private organizations might receive public resources (in outright grants or subsidized loans) in exchange for discharging certain obligations to improve access. Alternatively, tax exemptions or other tax incentives may be granted in exchange for organizational policies that improve access. Finally, the government (federal or state) may unilaterally impose obligations on certain institutions or types of organizations, as in all-payers schemes that require all licensed insurers in a particular jurisdiction to share the burden of insuring some of those who could not afford insurance on terms the market offers or as in taxes on hospital revenues to create a fund for the medically indigent. For case of reference let us call the first conception of a mixed system the "governmental responsibility conception" and the second the "shared responsibility conception." The difference between these two ways of conceiving of how the job of providing equitable access gets done in a mixed system is crucial. Once the difference is clearly articulated it becomes evident how ambiguous appeal to cooperative private sector/public sector solutions to the access problem is, and what a handy tool of obfuscation this ambiguity supplies to the federal government for rationalizing its failure to discharge its fundamental responsibility for ensuring that the societal obligation to provide equitable access to all is actually met. It is all too easy for the federal government to divert attention from its failure to fulfill its distinctive responsibility to ensure that the societal obligation is met by suggesting that private entities should do more. The common slogan that health care in the United States is provided by the combined efforts of the public and private sectors, then, is descriptively true but tends to obscure the ethical issues. Unless the division of responsibility is more clearly specified, it is simply not possible to evaluate the ethical behavior of actors within the system.

Under the governmental responsibility system it will not be possible to say that a particular private organization is not fulfilling any particular obligation—at most it will be possible to say that this or that organization is ungenerous or uncharitable or "ought to do more," just as we might say this of an individual who did little or nothing to help the needy. But nothing of substance can be said about how much more should be done or precisely what should be done by this or that actor, since all of the "duties" that they have will be imperfect or indeterminate, duties of charity. Nor will it be possible to say that this or that organization is not doing its fair share, since there will be no basis for ascertaining what a fair share is. The very notion of a fair share, at least as far as it can serve as the basis for determinate ethical appraisals, has sense only where there is an integrated, systematic assignment of specific responsibilities. And where no determinate sense can be given to the notion of a fair share, no organization can rightly be publicly censured or penalized for failing to do its fair share. In a mixed system of the governmental responsibility type, then, the "ethical obligations" of private insurers or providers are a matter of private morality, the corporate analog of the question of conscience which an individual may pose herself when she asks whether her charitable contributions are adequate.

This last statement admits, however, of one important qualification. Some private organizations have imposed upon themselves and their members certain specific obligations, or, perhaps more precisely, have voluntarily taken on certain special commitments through their collective choices. The "constitution" of a particular HMO or of a private insurer such as the Blue Cross/Blue Shield system could be understood as including a self-imposed special obligation of a very general and somewhat abstract sort—a self-chosen mission of providing "affordable, comprehensive coverage," for example.[13] By such an organization's "constitution" I mean, not necessarily a written, explicit document, but rather something that is to be constructed from certain documents and from authoritative interpretations and elaborations of them as well as the long-standing patterns of official behavior of the organization in question. In the process of its development, such an organization may translate these rather abstract mission statements or ideals into more concrete, self-imposed obligations. To the extent that these obligations are self-imposed and flow from the organization's own interpretation of its self-chosen mission, they may be modified or even repudiated through appropriate processes within the organization. This places a severe limitation on the appropriateness of public ethical appraisal of the organization's behavior, in effect removing the possibility of society holding the organization accountable for failing to live up to these obligations (unless, of course, their doing so happens to violate contractual obligations or involves illegalities).[14]

COST-CONTAINMENT AND COMPETITION IN MIXED SYSTEMS

In an effort to curb rising health-care expenditures, the federal government, as well as a number of health policy analysts, has advocated increasing competition.[15] But when the governmental-responsibility type of mixed system is subjected to serious competitive pressures, altruism becomes more costly for any particular organization and the scope of its imperfect duties shrinks. Unless a particular organization has assurance that its competitors are making commensurate transfers of resources to the needy, it risks putting itself at a competitive disadvantage by shaping its policies so as to improve access. But its imperfect duty—the only "duty" concerning access it has in a governmental-responsibility mixed system (unless it happens to choose to impose on itself some special, determinate obligation)—is only a duty to render aid *if this does not involve excessive costs* to the organization itself. And as competition increases, the cost of being charitable rises.

Even if every private organization in such a system sincerely desires to do something substantial to ameliorate the access problem, each may find it not only rational but ethically permissible to reduce its contributions to coping with the access problem. Purely voluntary agreements among organizations in the private sector are not likely to solve this problem for two reasons. First, it may be very difficult to achieve a consensus among all potential competitors as to the level of contribution for each that would put none at a competitive disadvantage. For one thing, they may lack the institutional mechanisms and authority structures for creating such a consensus. But second, and more important, as long as the agreement is purely voluntary there will be an incentive to defect either because one hopes thereby to gain a competitive advantage or because one fears that someone else will do so and that this will damage one's own competitive position. Let us call this the "shrinking imperfect duty phenomenon." In sum, as competition raises the costs of altruism, the threshold at which a private organization's efforts to improve access begin to involve "excessive costs" lowers, and the scope of its imperfect duty shrinks. Purely voluntary efforts to avoid the shrinking imperfect duty phenomenon are likely to be of limited value.

At present the U.S. government not only permits but also encourages increasing competition in health care (as a means of reducing costs), while at the same time abdicating more and more of its responsibility for ensuring access and attempting to justify this policy by emphasizing the role of the private sector in achieving adequate access. The result is likely to continue to be a widening access gap, as the government's contribution and the level of charity that it is reasonable to expect from private organizations both shrink. In general, the strategy of containing costs by increasing competition in the private sector makes sense only if one or the other of three circumstances obtain. (1) A governmental-responsibility type mixed system is utilized and the government is willing and able to fill the widening access gap that will result from the shrinking scope of private imperfect duties (as ever smaller contributions tend toward "excessive costs"). (2) A shared-responsibility type mixed system is successfully implemented so that each organization's specific obligations are fairly assigned and in such a way that no organization is thereby put at a competitive disadvantage, and these obligations are adequately enforced by the government. (3) A governmental-responsibility type system is utilized but private organizations develop arrangements for binding agreements among themselves so as to ensure that all will do their part and so as to eliminate the incentive to be a free rider, thus avoiding the shrinking imperfect duty phenomenon. For example, private (i.e., nongovernmental) providers or insurers might make a multilateral contract with each other to divide among themselves the burden of ensuring access for some or all of those individuals who are not covered by government programs and who cannot afford private insurance at market rates. If such contracts were deemed legally valid, then the ordinary mechanisms of contract law would provide enforcement to overcome the problems of purely voluntary agreements mentioned earlier. There would be no need for the government to specify and assign special obligations to private-sector organizations and to enforce them.

As a way of coping with the access problem, the third approach suffers from serious limitations. I have already noted that private organizations may lack collective decision-making and authority structures. Yet these may be indispensable for creating a consensus as to what a fair division of responsibility for access among private organizations would consist of. Unless such a consensus can be gained, no multilateral contract will be made and the shrinking imperfect duty problem will not be averted. The larger the number of parties to the attempt to work out such contracts and the more diverse and conflicting their interests, the slimmer the prospects will be for achieving the needed consensus. Further, while smaller-scale, local arrangements are more likely to succeed in gaining sufficient consensus to create multilateral contracts that will assign specific special obligations to private organizations, merely local efforts are of limited efficacy as a response to the access problem for two reasons. First, the result is likely to be an uncoordinated patchwork of local arrangements with redundancies here and gaps there. Second, small-scale arrangements are prone to instability. A new provider or insurer that comes on the scene will not be a party to the multilateral contract, and its presence will give those who are an incentive to defect from the agreement or let it lapse. Indeed the inability to control entrance into local markets will be a barrier to achieving an agreement in the first place, since local organizations will not wish to make themselves vulnerable to newcomers who will not be under the constraints of an agreement and who will consequently enjoy a competitive advantage. Finally, and perhaps most important, if, as I have suggested, the obligation to provide adequate access is a societal obligation, then a fair division of responsibility for achieving adequate access must be all-inclusive, society-wide, not merely local. Merely local efforts have in fact been rightly criticized on grounds of fairness. For example, in some states "all-payer schemes" have been instituted requiring all health-care insurers to contribute to a fund for the medically indigent. Critics of all-payer schemes point out that these arrangements improve access for the poor by, in effect, placing a special tax on one segment of the population, the insured sick. The general problem is that merely local efforts are unlikely to be coordinated in such a way that a fair overall division of responsibility across institutions and organizations is achieved. Instead, local arrangements are likely to shift the burden of securing adequate access onto others in ad hoc ways. The implementation of the second way of conceiving of obligations concerning access in a mixed system, the shared responsibility model, then, encounters serious difficulties. An appreciation of these difficulties might well lead private organizations to opt for a governmental-responsibility type of system, if they had the choice.

THE OBLIGATIONS OF PRIVATE INSURERS AND PROVIDERS UNDER EXISTING CONDITIONS

The current U.S. health-care system is much closer to a governmental-responsibility type of mixed system than a shared-responsibility type. Neither social consensus nor federal law provides a clear and systematic, much less fair, distribution of determinate obligations for securing access among private-sector institutions and organizations. Tax laws provide exemptions or other advantages to health-care providers or insurers that are legally classified as not-for-profit, and the justification of these privileges is that of a pro quid pro: these organizations are thought of as earning the advantages in question in virtue of providing a public benefit, a contribution to the fulfillment of the societal obligation to provide adequate access for all. There are, however, two serious defects in these arrangements. First, the nature of the pro quid pro ensures that we have no reason to believe that what the private organization contributes and what it receives are even roughly equivalent, much less that this is the most efficient way of eliciting private contributions to fulfilling the societal obligation. Second, these are isolated instances, developed in an ad hoc way, not integral elements of a systematic, fair division of responsibilities.

Given the assumption that providing access to health care is a societal obligation and that the responsibility for seeing that this obligation is met rests ultimately with the federal government, the federal government can be faulted for failing *either* to specify, assign, and enforce a fair division of responsibilities among private organizations *or* to do an adequate job of filling in the gaps in access left by the private sector. But what, then, are the obligations of private insurers and private providers under these imperfect conditions?

Apart from any special pro quid pro arrangements and special, self-imposed commitments (which they may revise if they wish), private insurers and private providers have no determinate obligations to help provide access to an adequate level of health care to all. They are at most obligated only in the loose and indeterminate way in which individuals are said to have imperfect duties of charity. In neither case is the obligation sufficiently determinate to justify society or the state holding these private organizations accountable.

It can be argued, however, that at least the larger and more powerful private provider and insurer organizations do have an important higher order obligation: an obligation to take a leadership role in exerting pressure upon the federal government to fulfill its basic responsibility in one of two ways, either by implementing an effective governmental responsibility system and discharging the responsibility of filling gaps in access left by the private sector or by creating an effective shared-responsibility system in which the obligations of private organizations will be sufficiently determinate so as to justify holding them accountable. If, as may well be the case at present, the prospects for succeeding in getting the federal government to fulfill its basic responsibility are dim, then major private insurers have an obligation to work together to develop arrangements to share among themselves some of the burdens of providing access that the federal government has failed to bear, just as private citizens are obligated to try to coordinate their efforts to aid the needy in the absence of adequate state-directed welfare programs. Because of the special problems created by increasing competition and cost-containment pressures in health care, there may be a greater need for larger scale coordination and cooperation and for developing private enforcement mechanisms (such as reliance on multilateral contracts) in the case of private health-care organizations than is generally the case with individuals who seek to fulfill imperfect duties of charity. Although, as I have already indicated, such private-sector efforts to create a determinate structure of obligations and to overcome free-rider and assurance problems are fraught with difficulties, they may for the forseeable future be the best alternative available. This obligation to help create a system that more effectively addresses the access problem is not, of course, absolute or unconditional. But it seems clear that at least many of the more powerful private insurers and providers could afford to expend significant efforts toward this end without incurring such costs as to undermine their competitive positions. My suggestion is that the effort currently wasted on trying to ascertain the scope and content of specific obligations which do not in fact exist or in attempts to point the finger of blame at other organizations for not doing "their fair share" when no real sense can be given to this notion, should be directed toward developing a system in which obligations are determinate and substantive moral appraisal and social accountability are possible.

4

PRIVATIZATION AND JUST HEALTH CARE

Allen Buchanan

INTRODUCTION

When advocates of insurance privatization consider whether private-insurance-dominated systems achieve justice at all, they tend to rely on an incomplete set of criteria for a just health-care system. They also mistakenly assume that it is enough to show that justice is in principle achievable within a private-insurance-dominated system. This essay offers a more complete set of criteria for a just health-care system. It then argues that the motivational assumptions needed to make insurance privatization at all plausible (on grounds of choice, efficiency, and quality of care) are inconsistent with the motivational assumptions needed to show that in practice a private insurance-dominated system will achieve justice. A private-insurance-dominated system can be expected to satisfy the criteria for just health care only if (a) there is extensive and effective regulation to constrain the normal competitive behavior of private insurers or if (b) generous public funds are provided to fill the gaps in access left by the private insurance market. Yet the assumptions about the motivations and abilities of the public, regulators, and public officials needed to satisfy conditions (a) or (b) contradict the privatization advocate's explanations of how privatization will maximize efficiency, choice, and quality of care.

Originally published in *Bioethics* ISSN 0269-9702, Volume 9, Number 3/4, 1995.

THE PROBLEM OF EVALUATING PRIVATIZATION

Critics of privatization in health care usually attack on one or both of two fronts. They try to show that privatization does not achieve the benefits invoked to justify it—increased efficiency, greater consumer and provider choice, and higher quality of services.[1] Or they argue that privatization destroys the physician–patient relationship by converting altruistic caregivers into profit-seeking business people.[2] Both lines of attack raise serious doubts about privatization. Nevertheless, there is the danger that they will divert attention from what should be the primary question: Is privatization likely to move us closer to a just health-care system? It is on this question that I shall focus.

To make any progress in answering it, we must first distinguish among the many disparate phenomena that are promiscuously lumped together under the term "privatization." Privatization can mean:

1. selling public health-care facilities and delivery organizations to private enterprises;
2. contracting out publicly provided services to private enterprises through competitive bidding;
3. government policies to encourage the growth of for-profit health-care entities (hospitals, nursing homes, outpatient facilities);
4. government policies to encourage greater reliance on private health-care insurance (insurance provider–insurer entities, i.e., HMOs);
5. de-insurance practices—introduction or escalation of out-of-pocket payment for health-care services (co-payments, deductibles, charges for prescription drugs).

I shall concentrate primarily on 4., privatization as the effort to achieve greater reliance on private health insurance—call it *insurance privatization.*

One advantage of doing so is that this form of privatization is probably the most widespread at present and for the foreseeable future—occurring in a wide range of systems from those in developed countries such as the United States, Germany, and the Netherlands, to those in less-developed countries such as South Africa, and countries of intermediate developmental status such as Chile. Another advantage is that the system in which reliance on private health-care insurance is greatest—the U.S. health-care system—is one in which data relevant to assessing the relationship between this form of privatization and the achievement of the goal of just health care is most abundant.

Although my concern is with justice, I should note that privatization as reliance on private health insurance is very far from being a clear winner even if we meet the proponents of privatization on their own chosen ground. The system that has the greatest reliance on private insurance also has the highest cost of health care in the world (without compensating advantages in terms of better health outcomes according to any recognized criteria). Moreover, the administrative costs of this system are estimated to be several times higher than those of the single (government) payer system of its neighbor to the North.[3] In addition, there is growing evidence that as the private insurance market in the United State continues to develop, the result is less rather than more choice, for both consumers and providers, as insurers exclude more conditions from coverage, sharply curtail coverage for some conditions that for which they do insure, and exert ever greater pressures on providers to reduce utilization of care.[4] And this is so quite apart from that one further very significant limitation on choice which is the most shameful feature of the U.S. system: the fact that nearly 40 million people lack insurance at all, while perhaps another 20 million are underinsured according to any reasonable standard of adequacy.[5]

Finally, it is also worth noting that there is no good evidence that privately insured individuals in the United States receive higher quality care on the whole either than U.S. citizens covered by Medicare or by citizens in comparably developed countries which depend largely on government subsidized health insurance.[6]

It is true that in some countries, especially some of those in Africa and Latin America, those with private insurance receive higher quality care than those who depend on government-provided care, but this only counts as a forceful argument for private insurance if one regards justice as irrelevant. For it is in precisely those countries in which the discrepancy between the quality of care provided publicly and that gotten through private insurance is greatest that it is least likely that private insurance will become affordable to the majority of the people. To summarize: Even from the standpoint of efficiency, choice, and quality of care, the burden of argument has not been borne by proponents of privatization as greater reliance on private health-care insurance. Indeed, where reliance on private insurance is greatest, the application of these three criteria do not yield a powerful argument for it.

It is crucial to keep this point in mind, for one simple reason. If, as I shall argue, a preponderant reliance on private insurance is likely to produce a system that scores poorly on criteria of justice, then the fact that the case for such a system is not strong on grounds of efficiency, choice, and quality, makes criticisms on grounds of justice all the more telling.[7]

THE ELEMENTS OF JUST HEALTH CARE

There is a growing and increasingly sophisticated literature on just health care.[8] Without providing a review of this literature here, I shall simply take the core of a just health-care system to include the following:

1. universal access
2. to an "adequate level" of care
3. without excessive burdens.

This analysis, which is based on that offered by the U.S. President's Commission on Medical Ethics report, *Securing Access To Health Care* (1983), can be further explicated in this way. Every citizen is to have access, as a matter of effective legal entitlement, to a socially defined "decent minimum" or "standard benefit package" of preventive, palliative, and curative services.[9] The phrase "without excessive burdens" is designed to emphasize that mere legal entitlement to services is not sufficient, if the individual faces serious obstacles in actually utilizing services in the form of debilitating financial costs, excessive waiting periods, informal barriers of class, gender, racial, or ethnic prejudice, or geographical remoteness from the point at which services are delivered.

A word of caution is in order. I am simply assuming that a just health-care system is one that ensures all citizens access to a minimal package of services. Here I offer no arguments against those who maintain the extreme libertarian view that there is not even such a minimal right to health care (nor to any other welfare goods). My interest, rather, is in addressing those who acknowledge at least this minimal commitment to universal access, but also advocate insurance-privatization.[10]

The most obviously unsatisfying feature of this sketch of the elements of a just health-care system is its vagueness. What is to count as an "adequate level" or "decent minimum" of care? How and by whom is it to be decided what goes into the standard benefit package to which all citizens are to have legally guaranteed access without encountering undue burdens in actually utilizing care?

I will make no attempt to answer this question here. However, I will provide three considerations that suggest that it can be answered. First, what the "adequate level" of care will be for a given society, will be less than the best, technically available care that would be of any net benefit, and there is no assumption that the health care available to all individuals, from any source, will be strictly equal for those in equal need or who could equally benefit from a given service. In other words, just health care, according to what I have referred to as the core account, does *not* require either that every individual have access to the same level or kind or services that any other individual with the same health condition has, nor that anyone has access to all care that would be of any net benefit to him or her. Thus a just health-care system, on the core account, will be one in which (a) the better off are free to purchase services that exceed the adequate level if they so choose, and (b) the adequate level, whatever it turns out to be, will be a constrained benefit package—it will lack some services which would be of some net benefit to some.

There are two reasons for the second condition (b). First, given that resources are scarce, society's commitment to ensuring access to health care should be limited by an appreciation that there are other socially valuable goods (education, scientific and cultural pursuits, etc.). Second, there are moral limits as to what we owe our fellow citizens, limits that are ultimately based in a recognition that we are separate persons, with our own goals and projects, to which we may rightly give a certain priority. Ideals of generosity or charity may exhort us to more, but *justice* does not require more.

Once it is acknowledged that justice requires only a limited entitlement to health care, it becomes clear why individuals should be allowed to purchase services that exceed the adequate level if they have the resources and inclination to do so. Given that such discretionary purchases do not interfere with the achievement of universal access to the adequate level, and given that we think it permissible for individuals to spend discretionary income on other goods (finer clothing, bigger houses, etc.) there seems to be no reason for preventing them from spending more on health care.

Rather than dwelling on the problem of how to flesh out the notion of an adequate level of care, I will simply take it for granted that any sound account of just health care will include the three elements mentioned previously. However, I wish to add three more elements to our list of criteria that a just health-care system must satisfy, but which are often overlooked.

4. the financial costs of ensuring access to an adequate level for all are fairly distributed;
5. the burdens of rationing care are fairly distributed;
6. the system has the capacity for reform and improvement toward a closer approximation of a perfectly just system.

Each of these additional criteria is at least as plausible as the first three. A system that achieved universal access at the price of imposing unfair financial burdens on some individuals or groups would not be a just health-care system. For the reasons noted earlier in support of the idea that the entitlement to health care must be a limited right, rationing health care is unavoidable. But a system that arbitrarily concentrates the burdens of rationing on some individuals or groups would not be a just health-care system.

The last criterion (6) may be somewhat less intuitive than the others, but in the real world, as opposed to the world of abstract theory (especially the neoclassical theory of economics), it is of singular importance. For after all, it is highly unlikely that a perfectly just health-care system (or a perfectly just state, or a perfectly just legal system) will ever be achieved. Nevertheless, it is more than desirable that the imperfect systems we do have include the capacity for improvement. Even more importantly, a proposed system should not, when implemented, unleash economic and political forces that will tend to make it *less just* over time.

Once these three additional criteria are acknowledged, the assessment of privatization in general and of increased reliance on private health-care insurance will appear in a different—and far less favorable—light.

Before proceeding to an examination of how insurance-privatization stacks up against the criteria for a just health-care system, I wish to mention three more criteria that should figure in any evaluation of privatization proposals, even though these criteria do not pick out elements of justice per se. Privatization proposals, if implemented, should not hinder the pursuit of the following three goals:

7. the education and training of appropriate numbers and types of health care providers,
8. the effective pursuit of high-quality biomedical research,
9. the cost-effective utilization of the fruits of biomedical research for the improvement of human health.

All nine criteria are relevant for assessing privatization policies. Once the multiplicity of dimensions of assessment is seen, it becomes clear how incomplete—if not to say, self-serving—most attempts to justify privatization initiatives are. Even if it were clear (which it is not) that privatization (or certain varieties of privatization) increase efficiency, expand consumer and provider choice, and improve quality of care, this would not be sufficient to make the case for privatization. Since my objective is to concentrate on the criteria for a just health-care system (1–6), I will only illustrate very briefly the serious questions that the last three criteria (7–9) raise about privatization, before proceeding to concentrate on the justice criteria.

First, there is a serious risk, especially in developing countries where facilities for training providers are meager or nonexistent, that capital, as well as talented personnel, will flow into the private health-care sector and away from educational and research facilities. And even in more developed countries, there is a serious question about whether teaching hospitals will be able to maintain their commitment to educating a broad complement of specialists and primary care providers and conducting a wide range of research activities if they sell their facilities or practice plans to for-profit hospital chains. For even if each for-profit health-care organization recognizes that comprehensive medical education and a diversity of research efforts is in everyone's interest, each will have an incentive to attempt to take a free ride on collective efforts to achieve these goods. However, if the flow of capital and human resources from the public to the private sector becomes great enough, there will be no free ride to be taken.

Second, there is growing evidence that where private insurance is dominant, there are perverse incentives that result in a suboptimal utilization of the fruits of biomedical research. One concrete example will graphically illustrate the very general problem. A simple blood test for serum feratin, confirmed either by a liver biopsy or an HLA match with a relative already diagnosed as having the disease, provides an accurate diagnosis of a genetic disorder called hemochromatosis. If untreated, this disease is invariably fatal, as a result of iron deposits accumulating in and destroying the heart, liver, and pancreas. Among the most serious genetic disorders, hemochromatosis is relatively common: in the general population of the United States as well as in Northern Europe, 3–5 persons per 1000, according to some estimates. If diagnosed early enough, all damage can be avoided through a simple process of regular phlebotomies (periodic removal of quantities of blood).

Yet in any system in which there is reliance on a competitive private health insurance market, insurers will have an incentive not to insure persons known to have this disease, if they utilize existing actuarial data on the morbidity and mortality of persons with hemochromatosis. (In spite of the fact that the disease can be treated successfully if detected early enough, average life expectancy from the time of diagnosis is only two and one-half years.) This prediction is supported by growing evidence of uninsurability of persons with genetic disorders generally and with hemochromatosis in particular.[11] In addition, individuals will have an incentive not to be tested for this disease, even if they suspect that, for reasons of family history, they are at risk for it. For once there is a record of a diagnosis of hemochromatosis the individual may not be insurable (or may have to perpetrate insurance fraud by not reporting his illness when applying for insurance).

A system that discourages detection and treatment of a disease that is far from rare, invariably fatal if not treated, inexpensively and accurately diagnosable, and easily, cheaply, and completely treatable is surely one we should think long and hard about endorsing, to say the least. Moreover, as the Human Genome Project yields more and more information about genetically-based diseases, the ability of insurance companies to exclude individuals from coverage can only increase—unless individuals avoid being tested, or unless insurers are effectively denied access to information about genetic risk. Yet if they are denied such information, they will be vulnerable to adverse selection: Individuals who know themselves to be at risk will purchase more insurance, and the cumulative effects of many instances of adverse selection can in principle lead to the collapse of the private insurance market.[12]

So quite apart from whether privatization does in fact produce greater efficiency, expand choice, and improve quality, there are serious questions about its compatibility with the goals of achieving balanced medical training and education, furthering a comprehensive biomedical research agenda, and optimally utilizing the fruits of biomedical research. If, as I shall now argue, insurance privatization also fares poorly when judged by the central criteria of justice, then the case for it is shaky indeed.

JUST HEALTH CARE AS A COOPERATIVE VENTURE BETWEEN THE PUBLIC AND PRIVATE SECTORS: THE CRUCIAL COORDINATING ROLE OF THE STATE

If, as I am assuming, justice matters in the evaluation of health policy initiatives, then any proposal for privatization, including insurance-privatization, must be understood to rest upon the following, usually unstated premise:

Justice in healthcare is to be achieved through a division of labor between the private and public spheres.

The reason for this premise is simple: No serious party to the health-care systems debate is under the illusion that a *fully privatized health-care system*—one in which all access to care is through private insurance—will achieve justice. The reason is straightforward: Where the only access to health care is through competitive health-care insurance markets, some of those most in need of health care will be unable to afford it.[13] Accordingly, all proposals for privatization, of whatever variety, must be seen (if they are to be taken seriously) as prescriptions for shifting the boundary in the social division of labor toward a greater role for the private sector, rather than for eliminating public sector involvement entirely. It is for this reason that I have phrased the question as whether *greater* reliance on private insurance is likely to secure justice in health care.

Before developing several criticisms of insurance privatization from the standpoint of justice, it is necessary to understand precisely how the social division of labor between the private and public sectors is supposed to achieve just health care. The idea is that the normal, competitive behavior of private insurance markets (plus, perhaps, some private charitable provision of care) will provide access to an adequate level of care for many or even most people, and that government action will (1) see that *whatever gaps in access remain will be filled*, while at the same time (2) ensuring that *inequities in the distribution of the costs of ensuring access* that would otherwise occur are eliminated or at least reduced. Though it is rarely mentioned, a third role of government in a mixed system, if the system is to be just, is (3) ensuring that there is a *fair distribution of the burdens of rationing*. In other words, the ultimate responsibility for seeing that rationing is not achieved through discriminatory or otherwise unfair policies in the private or public sector also lies with the government.

Unless some agency or institution takes ultimate responsibility for coordinating the division of labor between the private and public sectors in the provision of just health care, there is no reason to think that gaps in access left by the private insurance market and charity will be filled, and financial costs, as well as the burdens of rationing will be fairly distributed, automatically. (No theory of the "spontaneous order" of the market is capable of predicting such felicitous, unplanned coordination in the division of labor between the private and public sectors.) Furthermore, the reasonable assumption is that only the highest level of government—the state—has the authority and resources to play the coordinating role required by functions (1), (2), and (3).[14]

THE STATE AS THE ULTIMATE GUARANTOR OF ACCESS TO CARE IN A MIXED SYSTEM

Consider the first of the state's two essential roles in achieving just health care in a mixed (private–public) system, that is, of ensuring that gaps in access are filled. There are two ways in which government can play this coordinating role, and they may be undertaken in combination. First, government can simply let the private health-care sector operate without hindrance and commit itself to providing whatever is necessary to fill the access gap. In principle this is the role of government subsidized insurance (chiefly Medicaid and Medicare) in the United States, along with some direct government provision of health care (in Veterans Administration hospitals and military base hospitals).

Second, the state can attempt to regulate the behavior of private-sector insurers and providers in such a way as to cause them to provide wider access than they would if they responded purely to market incentives. In other words, government can attempt to regulate private sector actors in such a way as to restrain their normal competitive behavior. For example, the Clinton Healthcare Plan would have prevented insurers from charging higher premiums for the standard benefit package to those at greater risk of illness. If such regulations were successful, their effect would be to make insurance available to some who otherwise could not afford it, because they would result in those at lower risk subsidizing those at higher risk.

It is important to emphasize that this second approach to fulfilling the government's role responsibility in a mixed system for ensuring access requires private insurers to behave in ways that are diametrically opposed to the behavior which competition naturally stimulates. Accordingly, the second approach requires effective regulation; and regulation is costly even when it fails to be effective.

There are two situations in which regulation designed to ensure that private insurers do not succeed in doing what they do naturally (as competitors in the marketplace) is likely to be exceptionally ineffective. The first is where the private insurance market is highly developed and includes a number of extremely wealthy corporations. In the United States the larger corporations have management personnel and legal counsel who have an impressive record of "gaming" the regulator rules (finding loopholes one step ahead of government efforts to close them) and of "capturing the regulators".[15] As a broad generalization, it is fair to say that where private insurance markets have flourished the most, the attempt to fill part of the access gap by restraining the competitive behavior of market entities has been far from successful. Insurance company interests have simply proved too powerful, either by successfully lobbying to draw the teeth of legislative proposals for powerful regulation or by avoiding effective compliance with those regulations that do make it through their lobbying gauntlet.

One concrete example among many will illustrate how regulations can be circumvented. Even in areas where state regulations restrict the freedom of insurer–provider organizations (such as HMOs) from explicitly rejecting high-risk individuals or charging them higher premiums, competition has stimulated the development of ingenious strategies for avoiding high-risk patients and enrolling low-risk ones. To avoid high-risk (and hence costly) patients, organizations engage in a variety of "de-marketing" strategies—policies to deter high-risk individuals from purchasing or utilizing services. Perhaps the most common is to locate their facilities in more affluent areas where poor public transportation prevents high-risk patients from utilizing them. To garner a higher proportion of low-risk patients (without formally departing from regulations requiring community-rating), organizations also target their advertising to healthier groups (by direct mailings to members of health clubs, etc.).[16]

The second situation in which regulation to constrain the normal competitive behavior of private insurers is likely to fail is that in which the state simply lacks the financial resources and administrative know-how to achieve effective regulation. A number of studies support the unsurprising hypothesis that this is usually the case in the poorer, less-developed countries in which insurance-privatization is now being actively promoted.[17] Even the World Bank, generally an enthusiast (if not a zealot) for privatization, acknowledges this as a serious problem in its 1993 *World Health Report*.[18] Instead of drawing the obvious conclusion that where an adequate regulatory infrastructure is lacking, insurance-privatization cannot be expected to achieve broadened access to health care, the World Bank report lamely suggests that in countries where this is the problem the solution is reliance on the professional ethics of health-care providers.

The naivete of this proposal will be most apparent to those who are well acquainted with the repeated failures of the medical profession to play a constructive role in efforts to widen access to care in the United States.[19] However, even if the medical profession showed a much stronger commitment to ensuring universal access than it historically has, it is not clear that this would be effective in the face of the pressure that private insurers can and do bring to bear on the behavior of physicians. After all, it is one of the chief complaints of physicians in the United States that competitive pressures from insurers are eroding their professional autonomy and forcing them to behave more and more like "mere businessmen" purveying "just another commodity in the marketplace."[20]

The World Bank report offers not so much as a hint of evidence to support its faith that professional ethics can render just an otherwise unjust system by filling the regulatory void. Moreover, I know of no data to support the view that the professional ethics of physicians in poorer, less-developed countries will be better able or more willing to resist competitive pressures than their colleagues in developed countries.

Nor does historical experience in the United States warrant much confidence in the other strategy by which government can in principle see that the access gap is filled—by largely leaving the private insurance market alone and supplementing its workings through government funded insurance and/or direct provision of care. For as was noted earlier, government programs, especially those targeted at the poor, have been chronically underfunded and have fallen far short of filling the access gap. This has also been the case in many other countries which employ mixed systems in which government is supposed to fill the access gap by providing care or providing payment for it.[21]

THE STATE AS THE ULTIMATE GUARANTOR OF THE FAIR DISTRIBUTION OF COSTS IN A MIXED SYSTEM

Since a just health-care system not only ensures universal access, but also achieves (or at least approximates) a fair distribution of the costs of providing universal access, government at the highest level must also exercise ultimate responsibility for ensuring that taxation and other policies result in a fair distribution of costs. Yet it is not hard to see why the same political and economic factors that tend to thwart the achievement of universal access to adequate care in mixed systems in which private insurance dominates also make it unlikely that there will be a fair distribution of costs. The burden of argument is on the advocates of insurance-privatization to explain why we should expect anything resembling a fair distribution of costs to occur in a mixed system in which there is a large role for private insurance.

There are two reasons for placing the burden of argument on the shoulders of the proponent of insurance-privatization. First, the distribution of costs *within* the private-insurance sector of a mixed system will *necessarily* be unfair, if, as seems plausible, it is assumed that fairness requires that there be a significant degree of subsidization by those who are healthy and well-off of those who are unhealthy and poor. This is because competitive health insurance companies by definition engage in risk-rating: Unless prevented from doing so, they either do not offer insurance to those at greatest risk of ill-health or only do so at exorbitant rates. But since in every society of which we have any knowledge poor health and poverty are positively correlated, this means that those who are most in need of insurance and least able to afford it will not get it unless others subsidize them. It follows, therefore, that if a fair distribution of costs is to be achieved in a system that relies heavily on private insurance, it must be achieved through political institutions, not through the normal competitive workings of the private insurance market. So the advocate of insurance privatization owes us an account of how a just distribution of costs can be achieved through political institutions in a society in which there is a large and successful private insurance market for health care.

The second reason for demanding an account of how the fair distribution of costs is to be accomplished in a system that relies heavily on private insurance is that existing systems in which there is significant reliance on private insurance tend to include *politically created* features that ensure that the distribution of costs is *not* fair. I have in mind here primarily the fact that in many systems in which there is a major or growing reliance on private insurance, including those of the United States, Germany, and Chile, private insurance is largely employment-based, with the employer's contribution to insurance premiums being tax-deductible. The effect of this arrangement is to give better-off individuals—those who are fortunate and healthy enough not only to be employed, but to be employed in businesses big enough to offer insurance—a tax subsidy that is inherently regressive. The regressivity of the employer-contribution tax exemption guarantees that the distribution of the costs of ensuring access will be unfair, unless government compensates for this inequity by some other effective mechanism. However, there is no evidence that in any of the systems in which this regressive cost-distribution is present, such a mechanism is in place. Moreover, the popularity of this subsidy among the most politically powerful segment of society—namely, those in the middle and upper classes who receive it—has understandably made it extremely unlikely that it will be abolished.

Although my main focus in this paper is on universal access as one element of just health care, I hope to have shown that the fair distribution of costs in an important though usually neglected criterion for evaluating insurance-privatization proposals and that it would be a grave mistake to assume that a fair distribution of costs will be achieved in a system that relies heavily on private insurance. Similar points, I believe, can be made regarding the fair distribution of the costs of rationing, though I will not attempt to argue for them here.[22]

INSURANCE-PRIVATIZATION AND THE PROSPECTS FOR REFORM TOWARD A MORE JUST SYSTEM

A system in which private insurance is predominant is not only unlikely to achieve a successful division of labor for the achievement of justice; it is likely to generate economic and political forces that will make movement toward justice more difficult. The very phenomena that explain the failures or private-insurance dominated systems to ensure universal access and to achieve a fair distribution of costs also explain why reforming such systems is so difficult. This becomes clear once one unpacks the premises that would have to be substantiated for a successful division of labor to occur in a system in which private insurance was the predominant way of financing health care.

In a system in which insurance privatization is successfully implemented, either the majority of citizens or at the very least the majority of the more affluent citizens (call them the elite) will be covered by private insurance. To the extent that the private insurance system is delivering the goods that are supposed to justify it, the most powerful people in society will have no direct interest in the adequacy of the public system, unless they are exceptionally altruistic. Yet the whole point—the whole motivational underpinning—of privatization proposals generally is that the most reliable and powerful (if not the only) human motivation is self-interest.

In other words, the virtue of privatization (like all market-based approaches to social life) is supposed to lie in the fact that it is a form of interaction that *economizes on altruism*. And it is only necessary to economize on altruism, of course, if altruism is in short supply. Why is it then, that the advocate of insurance privatization assumes that altruism will be in short supply in all areas of life except politics? What *theoretical* reason or *empirical evidence* available to the proponent of privatization is there for assuming that the more powerful (who by hypothesis are being well served by the predominant reliance on private insurance when reliance on private insurance performs as its advocates say it will) will be willing to incur additional costs in order to ensure that those who cannot afford private insurance will have access to an adequate level of care without undue burdens in actually utilizing it?

Again, the case of the United States is instructive and a propos because it is there that insurance-privatization is most developed. As noted earlier, the patchwork called the U.S. health-care system, considered as a joint venture to achieve just health care between the private and public sectors has failed. Millions lack secure access to anything other than care for dire emergencies. Moreover, the most recent effort to improve access—and hence to move a bit closer to a just system—the Clinton Plan, failed utterly, in part because its advocates were unable to convince the middle and upper classes that they could no longer rely upon private insurance for secure access to adequate care for themselves. The lesson is clear: When a large private insurance sector performs the way it should (competitively, efficiently, with a reasonable degree of consumer satisfaction) it tends to reinforce existing class divisions and thus make it more difficult to mobilize support for access reforms across class divisions.

This unsurprising result is not confined to the United States or even to more developed countries generally. There is mounting evidence that in South Africa and other sub-Saharan countries, as well as in Latin America, elites seeking better care for themselves through private insurance arrangements are less likely to be vigorous advocates for improving access to care for the majority and especially for the rural poor.[23]

The point is this. It is not enough to argue that insurance privatization (or other varieties of privatization) are *in principle* compatible with a social division of labor between the private and public sectors that achieves a reasonable approximation of justice in health care. The economic theory that predicts gains in efficiency, choice, and quality from privatization must be in harmony with an accurate account of the *political* motivation and behavior of those consumers of health care who also happen to be concerned with the shape of public policy. But not only are the privatizers' predictions about gains in efficiency, choice, and quality undersupported; even worse, the motivational assumptions on which they base them must be studiously denied in order to have any confidence that there will be sufficient political support for the public sector to do its part in the division of labor.

I have already suggested that the stronger the private insurance sector becomes, the less likely influential citizens are to give their wholehearted support to public programs designed to fill the access gap and to achieve a fair distribution of costs—at least if the motivational assumptions required for privatization to be at all plausible are correct. I now want to make a similar suggestion concerning the motivational assumptions that proponents of privatization must attribute to *political leaders* and *regulators* if they are to supply the claim that insurance-privatization will be compatible with just health care.

Consider, first, the case of political leadership. If, as the motivational assumptions of privatizers imply, the more influential citizens will do well in the private insurance market and have no direct interest in extending access to those who cannot achieve it through private insurance, then what motivations must the proponent of privatization attribute to political leaders if justice is to be secured?

The answer is straightforward: Political leaders will be likely to exhibit the firmness of will required to achieve justice in such a system only if they are willing and able to mount a heroic resistance to pressures from their most powerful constituents, namely, large private insurance companies and the more affluent voters who are satisfied with reliance on private insurance and who benefit from the unfair distribution of costs. It follows that political leaders can be expected to exhibit the political resolve to make the division of labor between the private and public sectors in achieving just health-care work only if their motivation also is strikingly different from that upon which privatization strategies are premised.

The same point can be made about the privatization advocate's assumptions about the motivations of government regulators. Why is it that we are to assume (contrary to much historical evidence in the system most dependent on private insurance) that those government officials who regulate private insurers will be diligent, savvy, and efficient, while those who administer single-payer government insurance schemes or public health-care facilities will be slothful, ignorant, and inefficient?

What has been largely overlooked or ignored is that privatization that has a chance of achieving just health care requires a good deal of regulation or a good deal of government financing or provision of care, and that for this reason privatization does not necessarily mean less government. Instead, it is likely to mean more of a change in the character of government involvement in health care rather than a net reduction in it. And so far, there is to my knowledge no theory of bureaucratic behavior—and least of all a theory compatible with the motivational assumptions upon which privatization advocates rely—capable of distinguishing so dramatically between the behavior of bureaucrats who are regulators of private insurers (or providers) and bureaucrats who are administrators of single-payer systems or of government health-care programs. More specifically, there is nothing in the theory of public choice as it now exists that can convincingly explain why the bureaucratic behavior needed to achieve justice in a mixed system with a preponderance of private insurance will be forthcoming but that the bureaucratic behavior required for the reasonably efficient functioning of a mixed system in which there is a larger role for government financing or provision of health care and a lesser role for private insurance will not be available.[24]

Advocates of insurance privatization radically underestimate what is necessary to make their case. It is not enough to show that insurance privatization produces gains in efficiency, choice, and quality. Nor is it enough to do that and to show that *in principle* the state can intervene so as to render the overall system just by filling access gaps, distributing costs fairly, and preventing an unfair distribution of the burdens of rationing. In addition, what is needed is an empirically supported theory of political and bureaucratic behavior capable of showing that at least in relevant, real-world circumstances the state can be expected to do these jobs in a system in which insurance-privatization is present. However, not only have the advocates of insurance-privatization failed to even acknowledge the magnitude of this task, much less accomplish it; they have also rendered it virtually impossible for themselves because of the motivational assumptions upon which they have attempted to build their limited and incomplete case for privatization.

What could explain such deeply flawed reasoning? My suspicion is that proponents of insurance privatization have failed to see the discordance between their general motivational assumptions and what they would have to assume about the motivations of citizens, political leaders, and regulators if privatization were to be compatible with justice for one of two reasons. Perhaps they simply don't take the problem of justice (as opposed to that of efficiency or cost-reduction) seriously. Or perhaps they do, but grievously underestimate how much regulation—and how much political commitment to public programs for filling gaps in access and achieving a fair distribution of costs—is needed to achieve justice in a system in which private insurance plays a dominant role. Privatizers adopt an extremely critical and pessimistic view of politics and bureaucracy when arguing for privatization, but either ignore the very demanding role for politics and government if privatization is to function in a system that achieves justice or uncritically and optimistically assume that this role will be successfully discharged.

CONCLUSION

We have at last arrived at a conclusion sufficiently ironic to serve as a fitting end to our investigation. While the predictions that advocates of privatization make about the benefits of privatization (in efficiency, choice, and quality) are not well supported by the available data, the motivational assumptions that privatization advocates rely on to make those predictions do help to explain why it is naive to think that private health insurance will play a major role in a system that achieves just health care. However, to change their motivational assumptions in such a way as to make it more plausible to predict that justice will be achieved in a system that relies heavily on private insurance, the proponents of privatization would have to abandon the very assumptions about motivation that are needed to make a case for insurance-privatization on grounds of considerations other than those of justice.

5

ETHICAL ISSUES IN FOR-PROFIT HEALTH CARE

Dan W. Brock and Allen Buchanan

The American health-care system is undergoing a rapid socioeconomic revolution. Within a general environment of heightening competition, the number of investor-owned for-profit hospitals has more than doubled in the past 10 years, while the number of independent proprietary for-profit hospitals has declined by half.[1] Investor-owned for-profit corporations are controlled ultimately by stockholders who appropriate surplus revenues either in the form of stock dividends or increased stock values. Independent proprietary institutions are for-profit entities owned by an individual, a partnership, or a corporation, but which are not controlled by stockholders. Nonprofit corporations are tax-exempt and are controlled ultimately by boards of trustees who are prohibited by law from appropriating surplus revenues after expenses (including salaries) are paid. Although the increase in investor-owned hospitals has been most dramatic and publicized, a rise in investor-owned health-care facilities of other types, from dialysis clinics to outpatient surgery and "urgent care" centers has also occurred.

The aforementioned definitions treat "for-profit" rather narrowly as a legal status term referring to investor-owned and independent proprietary institutions. However, much of the current concern over "for-profit health care" has a wider, though much less clear focus. It is often said, for instance, that health care in the United States is being transformed from a profession into a business like any other because of the growing dominance of those types of motivation, decision-making techniques, and organizational structures that are characteristic of large-scale commercial enterprises.

A recent book published by the Institute of Medicine bears the title *The New Health Care for Profit*, with the subtitle *Doctors and Hospitals in a Competitive Environment*. The difference in scope between the title and subtitle is but one example of a widespread tendency of discussions of "for-profit health care" to run together concerns about the effects of increasing competition in health care, which affects both "for-profit" and "nonprofit" institutions in the legal sense, and special concerns about the growth of those health-care institutions which have the distinctive "for-profit" legal status.

This essay will focus primarily on the ethical implications of the growth of for-profit health-care institutions in the legal sense. However, although the ethical problems we shall explore have been brought to public attention by the rapid rise of for-profit institutions (in the legal sense), it would be a mistake to assume that they are all peculiar to institutions that have this legal form.

In what follows, "for-profit" will be used only to denote a distinctive legal status and not as a vague reference to "commercial" motivation or decision-making and organizational structure, or as a synonym for the equally nebulous concept of "competitive health care." We shall explore, however, some moral concerns about the rise of for-profit institutions in the legal sense that focus on the profit motivation, decision-making forms, and organizational structures common to those institutions.

Serious moral criticisms of for-profit health care have been voiced, both within and outside of the medical profession. Before they can be evaluated, these criticisms must be more carefully articulated than has usually been done. In each case, after clarifying the nature of the criticism, we shall try to answer two questions: (1) Is the criticism valid as a criticism of for-profit health care? (2) If the criticism is valid, is its validity restricted to for-profit health care?

The most serious ethical criticisms of for-profit health care can be grouped under six headings. For-profit health care institutions are said to (1) exacerbate the problem of access to health care, (2) constitute unfair competition against nonprofit institutions, (3) treat health care as a commodity rather than a right, (4) include incentives and organizational controls that adversely affect the physician–patient relationship, creating conflicts of interest that can diminish the quality of care and erode the patient's trust in his physician and the public's trust in the medical profession, (5) undermine medical education, and (6) constitute a "medical–industrial complex" that threatens to use its great economic power to exert undue influence on public policy concerning health care. Each of these criticisms will be examined in turn.

FOR-PROFITS EXACERBATE THE PROBLEM OF ACCESS TO HEALTH CARE

Twenty-two to twenty-five million Americans have no health-care coverage, either through private insurance or through government programs including Medicare, Medicaid, and the Veterans Administration. Another 20 million have coverage that is inadequate by any reasonable standards.[2] The charge that for-profits are exacerbating this already serious problem takes at least two forms. First, it is said that for-profits contribute directly to the problem by not providing care for nonpaying patients. This is an empirical question to which the accompanying Institute of Medicine (IOM) report devotes a chapter. The data are not fully consistent on whether for-profit hospitals provide less or as much uncompensated care as do nonprofit hospitals; data from several states show that they provide less, but national data show minimal differences between for-profits and nonprofits, both of which do much less than publicly owned hospitals. In any event, our concern here is to analyze the arguments that have been advanced regarding the issue of uncompensated care.

Second, it is also alleged that for-profits worsen the problem of access to care in an indirect way because the competition they provide makes it more difficult for nonprofits to continue their long-standing practices of "cross-subsidization." Cross-subsidization is of two distinct types: Nonprofits have traditionally financed some indigent care by inflating the prices they charge for paying patients, and they have subsidized more costly types of services by revenues from those that are less costly relative to the revenues they generate.

It is sometimes assumed that, in general, for-profits are more efficient in the sense of producing the same services at lower costs and that these production efficiencies will be reflected in lower prices. At present, however, there is insufficient empirical evidence to show that for-profits on the whole are providing significant price competition by offering the same services at lower prices, though this may change in the future. In fact, what little data there are at present indicate that costs, especially of ancillary services, tend to be higher, not lower, in the for-profits.[3]

However, the argument that for-profits are making it more difficult for nonprofits to continue the practice of cross-subsidization does not depend upon the assumption that for-profits are successful price competitors in that sense. Instead, it is argued that for-profits "skim the cream" in two distinct ways. First, they capture the most attractive segment of the patient population, as noted earlier, by locating in more affluent areas, leaving nonprofits with a correspondingly smaller proportion of paying patients from which to subsidize care for nonpaying patients. Second, by concentrating on those services that generate higher revenues relative to the costs of supplying them, for-profits can achieve greater revenue surpluses, which provide opportunities either for lower prices or for investment in higher quality or more attractive facilities, both of which may worsen the competitive position of nonprofits, making it more difficult for them to cross-subsidize.

Critics of for-profits predict that access to care will suffer in two ways: Fewer nonpaying patients will be able to get care and some paying patients, that is, some who are covered by public or private insurance, will be unable to find providers who will treat them for certain "unprofitable" conditions.

Although these predictions have a certain a priori plausibility, they should be tempered by several important considerations. First, as already indicated, there is at present a dearth of supporting data concerning differences in the behavior of for-profits and nonprofits, and this is hardly surprising since the expansion of the for-profit sector has been so recent and rapid. However, preliminary data do support two hypotheses which tend to weaken the force of the criticism that for-profits are exeracerbating the problem of access to care by making it more difficult for nonprofits to continue cross-subsidization. One is that at present there seems to be no significant difference in the proportion of nonpaying care rendered by for-profits and nonprofits.[4] The other is that at present the proportion of nonpaying care rendered by nonprofits is on average only about 3 percent of their total patient care expenditures.[5] Here again, however, it may be important to separate from the overall data for nonprofits, the public hospitals in which the proportion of nonpaying care is both higher than in the for-profits and substantially in excess of 3 percent of overall total patient care expenditures.[6] If the public hospitals experience a decrease in their paying patients, their ability to carry out their mission of serving the indigent could be seriously jeopardized.

A third reason for viewing predictions about the effects of for-profits on access to care with caution is that there are other variables at work that may be having a much more serious impact. In particular, the advent of a prospective reimbursement system for Medicare hospital services and other efforts for cost-containment by state and federal regulatory bodies and businesses, as well as the general increase in competition throughout the health-care sector, are making it more difficult for any institution to cross-subsidize.

In addition, as defenders of for-profits have been quick to point out, in some cases for-profits have actually improved access to care not only by locating facilities in previously underserved areas thus making it more convenient for patients to use them, but also by making certain services more affordable to more people by removing them from the more expensive hospital setting. The growth of outpatient surgical facilities in suburban areas, for example, has improved access to care in both respects. Indeed, there is some reason to believe that by making decisions on the basis of the preferences of their boards of trustees (which may be shaped more by their own particular preferences or considerations of prestige than by demands of sound medical practice or response to accurate perceptions of consumer demand), nonprofits have in some cases duplicated each other's services and passed up opportunities for improving access by failing to expand into underserved areas.

This latter point drives home the complexity of the access issue and the need for careful distinctions. For-profits may improve access to care in the sense of better meeting some previously unmet demand for services by paying patients, while at the same time exacerbating the problem of access to care for nonpaying patients. However, there is clearly a sense in which the latter effect on access is of greater moral concern. We assumed that the members of a society as affluent as ours have a collective moral obligation to ensure that everyone has access to some "decent minimum" or "adequate level" of care, even if they are not able to pay for it themselves. Surely providing basic care for those who lack any coverage whatsoever then should take priority over efforts to make access to care more convenient for those who already enjoy coverage and over efforts to reduce further the financial burdens of those who already have coverage, by providing services for which they are already insured in less costly nonhospital settings.

So far we have examined the statement that "cream-skimming" by for-profits exacerbates the problem of access to care. Ultimately, this is largely an empirical question about which current data are inconclusive. There is another way in which the "cream-skimming" charge can be understood. Sometimes it is suggested that for-profits are acting irresponsibly or are not fulfilling their social obligations by failing to provide their "fair share" of indigent care and unprofitable care, as well as making it more difficult for nonprofits to bear their fair share through cross-subsidization. To this allegation of unfairness, defenders of for-profits have a ready reply: "No one is *entitled* to the cream; so for-profits do no wrong when they skim it. Further, for-profits discharge *their* social obligations by paying taxes. Finally, since the surplus revenues that nonprofits use to subsidize nonpaying or unprofitable care are themselves the result of overcharging—charging higher prices than would have existed in a genuinely competitive market—then it is all the more implausible to say that they are entitled to them."

While this reply is not a debate-stopper, it should give the critic of for-profits pause since it draws attention to the unstated—and controversial—premises underlying the contention that cream-skimming by for-profits is unfair because it constitutes a failure to bear a fair share of the costs of nonpaying or unprofitable patients. The most obvious of these is the assumption that, in general, nonprofits are (or have been) bearing their fair share.

To determine whether for-profits or nonprofits are discharging their obligations we must distinguish between two different types of obligations—general and special. For-profit corporations, like individual citizens, can argue that they are discharging their *general* obligation to subsidize health care for the poor by paying taxes. To see this, assume that the fairness of the overall tax system is not in question, and in particular its taxation of corporate profits. For-profits can then reasonably claim that they are doing their fair share to support *overall* government expenditures by paying taxes. If the government is subsidizing health care for the poor as part of overall government expenditures, then for-profits would appear to be doing their fair share toward supporting subsidized health care for the poor. If the government is providing inadequate subsidization of health care for the poor, then the fair share funded by the for-profits' taxes will in turn be inadequate, but proportionately no more so than every other taxpayer's share is inadequate, and *not unfair* relative to the subsidization by other taxpayers. The responsibility for this inadequacy, in any case, would be the government's or society's, not the for-profit health-care corporation's.

A for-profit hospital chain cannot say that if it is paying, for example, $30 million in taxes, it is providing $30 million toward funding health care for the poor. Its taxes, whether at the federal, state, or local level, should be understood as a contribution to the overall array of tax-supported programs at those levels. But it can claim to be subsidizing health care for the poor with the portion of its taxes proportionate to the portion of overall government expenditures devoted to subsidizing health care for the poor.

On the other hand, those who raise the issue of fairness have apparently assumed that health-care institutions have *special* obligations to help care for indigents. Even if this assumption is accepted, however, it is not obvious that in general nonprofits have been discharging the alleged special obligation successfully for the reasons already indicated. First, even if cross-subsidization is widespread among nonprofits, the proportion of nonpaying and nonprofitable care that is actually provided by many nonprofits appears not to be large. Second, some of the revenues from "overcharging" paying patients apparently are not channeled into care for nonpaying patients or patients with unprofitable conditions.

It was noted earlier that while many *publicly owned* nonprofit hospitals provide a substantial proportion of care for nonpaying patients, nonpublicly owned nonprofits ("voluntaries") as a group do not provide significantly more uncompensated care than for-profits. One rationale for granting tax-exempt status is that this benefit is bestowed in exchange for the public service of providing care for the indigent. If it turns out that many nonprofit health-care institutions are in fact not providing this public service at a level commensurate with the benefit they receive from being tax-exempt, then this justification for granting them tax-exempt status is undermined.

It is also crucial to question the assumption that for-profit health-care institutions have special obligations to help subsidize care for the needy over and above their general obligation as taxpayers. As the for-profits are quick to point out, supermarkets are not expected to provide free food to the hungry poor, real estate developers are not expected to let the poor live rent-free in their housing, and so forth. Yet food and housing, like health care, are basic necessities for even a minimal subsistence existence. If there are basic human rights or welfare rights to some adequate level of health care, it is reasonable to think there are such rights to food and shelter as well as health care.

Whose obligation is it then to secure some basic health care for those unable to secure it for themselves? Assuming that private markets and charity leave some without access to whatever amount of health care that justice requires be available to all, there are several reasons to believe that the obligation ultimately rests with the federal government. First, the obligation to secure a just or fair overall distribution of benefits and burdens across society is usually understood to be a general societal obligation. Second, the federal government is the institution society commonly employs to meet society-wide distributive requirements. The federal government has two sorts of powers generally lacking in other institutions, including state and local governments, that are necessary to meet this obligation fairly. With its taxing power, it has the revenue-raising capacities to finance what would be a massively expensive program on any reasonable account for an adequate level of health care to be guaranteed to all. This taxing power also allows the burden of financing health care for the poor to be spread fairly across all members of society and not to depend on the vagaries of how wealthy or poor a state or local area happens to be. With its nationwide scope, it also has the power to coordinate programs guaranteeing access to health care for the poor across local and state boundaries. This is necessary both for reducing inefficiencies that allow substantial numbers of the poor to fall between the cracks of the patchwork of local and state programs, and for ensuring that there are not great differences in the minimum of health care guaranteed to all in different locales within our country.

If we are one society, a *United* States, then the level of health care required by justice for all citizens should not vary greatly in different locales because of political and economic contingencies of a particular locale. It is worth noting that food stamp programs and housing subsidies, also aimed at basic necessities, similarly are largely a federal, not state or local, responsibility. These are reasons for the federal government having the obligation to guarantee access to health care for those unable to secure it for themselves. It might do this by directly providing the care itself, or by providing vouchers to be used by the poor in the health-care marketplace. *How* access should be guaranteed and secured—and in particular, to what extent market mechanisms ought to be utilized—is a separate question.

Granted that the obligation to provide access to health care for the poor rests ultimately with the federal government, is there any reason to hold that for-profit health-care institutions such as hospitals have any special obligations to provide such care? The usual reason offered is that health-care institutions, whether nonprofit or for-profit, are heavily subsidized directly or indirectly by public expenditures for medical education and research and by Medicare and Medicaid reimbursement which have created the enormous predictable demand for health-care services that has enabled health-care institutions to flourish and expand so dramatically since the advent of these programs in 1965. However, we believe it is less clear than is commonly supposed that these subsidies redound to the benefit of the for-profit institution in such a way as to ground a special institutional obligation to subsidize health care for the poor.

The legal obligation of nonprofit hospitals to provide free care to the poor is principally derived from their receipt of Hill–Burton federal funds for hospital construction. However, the for-profit hospital chains secure capital for construction costs in private capital markets and do not rely on special federal subsidies. Even when they purchase hospitals that have in the past received Hill–Burton monies, they presumably now pay full market value for the hospitals. If there is a subsidy that has not been worked off in free care, that redounds to the nonprofit seller, not the for-profit purchaser. What of other subsidies?

There is heavy governmental subsidy of medical education; it is widely agreed that physicians do not pay the full costs of their medical education. Perhaps then they have a reciprocal duty later to pay back that subsidy, though it would need to be shown why the form that duty should take is to provide free care to the poor as opposed, for example, to reimbursing the government directly. However that may be—it is physicians and not the for-profit hospitals who are the beneficiaries of medical education subsidies. Physicians are the owners of these publicly subsidized capital investments in their skills and training, and are able to sell their subsidized skills at their full market value. Physicians, and not the owners of for-profit health-care institutions in which they practice or are employed, are the beneficiaries of education subsidies and so are the ones who have any obligation there may be to return those subsidies by in turn subsidizing free care for the poor.

Another important area of public subsidy in the health-care field is medical research. Much medical research has many of the features of a public good, providing good reason for it to be publicly supported and funded. (Where these reasons do not apply, as for example in drug research, the research is largely privately funded by the drug companies.) Medical research makes possible new forms of medical technology, knowledge, and treatment. Because it is publicly funded, and once developed is generally freely available for use by the medical profession, for-profit health-care institutions are able to make use of the benefits of that research in their delivery of health care without sharing in its cost.

But who ultimately are the principal beneficiaries of this public subsidy of research? Not, we believe, the for-profits, but rather the patients who are the consumers of the new or improved treatments generated by medical research. It may or may not be true that for-profits will not bear the research costs of these treatments as part of their delivery costs. But if, as is increasingly the case, the for-profits operate in a competitive environment concerning health-care costs or charges, they will be forced to pass on these subsidies to consumers or patients. (And if they operate in a largely noncompetitive environment, there will be a strong case for some form of regulation of their rates.) The price that patients pay for health-care treatments whose research costs were subsidized by the government will not include those research costs and so will not reflect true costs. It is then consumers of health care, not the for-profits, who principally benefit from research subsidies, and any obligation arising from this subsidy presumably lies on them.

Finally, consider the large public subsidy represented by Medicare and Medicaid. These programs created a vast expansion in the market for health care which many for-profits serve and from which they benefit. This is new health-care business which heretofore did not exist and on which they make a profit. Perhaps this benefit grounds a special obligation of for-profit institutions to provide subsidized care for the poor. The most obvious difficulty with such a view is that the subsidized health-care consumers, not the deliverers of the health care, are by far the principal beneficiaries of Medicare and Medicaid. Any profit that the for-profits receive from serving Medicare and Medicaid patients is only a small proportion of the overall cost of their care.

It must be granted, nevertheless, that the for-profits do earn profits from these subsidized patients. But it is difficult to see how this fact by itself is sufficient to ground a special obligation of the for-profits to subsidize free care for the poor. In the first place, for-profits can again respond that they pay taxes on these profits, like other profit-making enterprises. Moreover, they can point out that in no other cases of government-generated business of for-profit enterprises is it held that merely earning a profit from such business grounds a special obligation similar to that claimed for for-profit health-care enterprises. Virtually no one holds that defense contractors, supermarkets who sell to food stamp recipients, highway builders, and so forth have any analogous special obligation based on the fact that their business is created by government funds. Nor is it ever made clear why this fact should itself ground any special obligation of for-profits in health care to provide access to health care for the poor. Thus, we conclude that none of the current forms of public subsidy of health care will establish any significant *special* obligation of for-profits to provide free care, and so the claim cannot be sustained that for-profits do not do their fair share in providing access to health care for the poor. We emphasize that we believe there *is* an obligation to guarantee some adequate level of health care for all, but the obligation is society's and ultimately the federal government's and not a special obligation of for-profit health-care institutions.

Even if there are insufficient grounds for the assumption that for-profit health-care institutions, or health-care institutions as such, have special obligations to provide a "fair share" of uncompensated care, it can be argued that a nation or a community, operating through a democratic process, can impose such a special obligation on the institutions in question as a condition of their being allowed to operate. According to this line of thinking, a community may, through its elected representatives, require that any hospital doing business in that community provide some specified amount of indigent care, either directly or by contributing to an indigent care fund through a special tax on health-care institutions (so far as they are not legally exempt from taxes) or through a licensing fee.

Whether or not such an arrangement would be constitutional or compatible with statutory law in various jurisdictions is not our concern here. One basic ethical issue is whether the imposition of such special obligations would unduly infringe on the individual's occupational and economic freedoms. Although no attempt to examine this question will be made here, this much can be said: A community's authority to impose a special obligation to contribute a portion of revenues (as opposed to an obligation to contribute services) for indigent care seems no more (or less) ethically problematic than its authority to levy taxes in general.

A second basic ethical issue is then whether such taxes, or requirements to provide uncompensated care as conditions of doing business for health-care institutions, fairly distribute the costs of providing care to the indigent. That will depend on the details of the particular tax or requirement to provide uncompensated care, but since any are likely to be ultimately a tax on the sick, it is doubtful that such provisions will be fairer than financing care, for the indigent through general tax revenues.

There is, moreover, an additional difficulty with any claim that by skimming the cream for-profits fail to fulfill an existing special obligation to bear a fair share of the burden of providing at least some minimum level of care for all who need it but cannot afford it. This is the assumption that in the current U.S. health-care system any determinate sense can be given to the notion of a "fair share" of the burden of ensuring access to care (in the absence of specific legislation such as the Hill–Burton Act). Unless a rather specific content can be supplied for the notion of a fair share, the nature and extent of an institution's alleged special obligation will be correspondingly indeterminate. In particular, it will be difficult if not impossible to determine whether for-profits have met such a special obligation. But it will also be problematic to assert what some defenders of nonprofits imply, namely that nonprofits have in the past done their fair share through cross-subsidization.

The current U.S. health-care system is a patchwork—or, less charitably, a crazy quilt—of private insurance and public program entitlements. There is no generally accepted standard for a "decent minimum" or "adequate level" of care to be ensured for all, no system-wide plan for coordinating local, state, and federal programs, charity, and private insurance so as to achieve it, and no overall plan for distributing the costs of providing care for those who are unable to afford it from their own resources. Absent all of this, no determinate sense can be given to the notion of an institution's special obligation to provide a "fair share" of the burden of ensuring an "adequate level" or "decent minimum" of care for everyone.

Furthermore, even if it were possible at present to determine, if only in some rough and ready way, what an institution's "fair share" is, this would still not be enough. Whether an institution has an *obligation*—a duty whose fulfillment society can require—will depend upon whether it can do so without unreasonable risks to its own financial well-being. But in a competitive environment, determining whether one institution is contributing its "fair share" will be unreasonably risky for it will depend upon whether other institutions are doing *their* "fair share."

The establishment of a coordinated system-wide scheme in which institutions share the costs of providing some minimum level of care for all is a "public good" in the economist's sense. Even if every governing board of every institution agrees that it is desirable or even imperative to ensure some level of care for all, so long as contribution to this good is strictly voluntary, each potential institutional contributor may attempt to take a free ride on the contribution of others with the result that the good will not be achieved.

It is important to understand that failure to produce the public good of a fair system for distributing the costs of care by voluntary efforts does *not* depend upon the assumption that potential contributors are crass egoists. Even if the potential contributor has no intention of taking a free ride on the contributions of others, he may nonetheless be unwilling to contribute his fair share unless he has *assurance* that others will do their fair share. For unless he has this assurance, to expect him to contribute his fair share is to expect him to bear an unreasonable risk—a cost which might put him at a serious competitive disadvantage. In the absence of an *enforced* scheme for fairly distributing the costs of care for the needy, the current vogue for containing costs by increasing competition in health care will only exacerbate this free rider and assurance problem. And unless an institution can shoulder its fair share without unreasonable risk to itself, it cannot be said that it has an *obligation* that it has failed to fulfill. Granted that this is so, what is needed is an effective mechanism for enforcing a coordinated scheme for distributing the costs of providing some minimal level of care for all without imposing unreasonable competitive disadvantages on particular institutions.

It is important not to overstate this point. Although the notion of unreasonable risk is not sharply defined, it is almost certainly true that many for-profit (and nonprofit) institutions could be spending more than they currently are for nonpaying or unprofitable patients without compromising their financial viability. So it is incorrect to conclude simply from this that in the current state of affairs institutions have no special obligations whatsoever. The point, rather, is that debates over which institutions are or are not fulfilling their obligations are of limited value and that the energy they consume could be more productively used to develop a system in which institutional obligations could be more concretely specified and in which society would be morally justified in holding those who control the institutions, whether government or private, accountable for the fulfillment of those obligations.

Moreover, there is at least one obligation which *now* can be justifiably imputed to for-profit (and nonprofit) health-care institutions and that is the obligation to cooperate in developing a system in which determinate obligations (whether general or special) can be fairly assigned and enforced. It is much less plausible to argue that the initial efforts needed *to develop* a coordinated, enforced system would undermine an institution's competitive position, even if it is true that in the absence of such a system an institution's acting on a strictly voluntary basis to help fund indigent care would subject it to unreasonable risks.

Assuming that as members of this society we all share a collective obligation to ensure an "adequate level" or "decent minimum" of health care for the needy, those who control health care institutions, as individuals, have the same obligations the rest of us have. However, because of their special knowledge of the health-care system and the disproportionate influence they can wield in health policy debates and decisions, health-care professionals may indeed have an additional *special* obligation beyond the general obligations of ordinary citizens to help ensure that a just system of access to health care is established.

It can still be argued that whether or not they fail to fulfill their obligations, for-profits have at least contributed to the decline of cross-subsidization and that the cross-subsidization system has made some contribution toward coping with the problem of access to care. Whether this provides a good reason for social policy designed to restrain or modify the behavior of for-profits will depend upon the answer to two further questions: (1) Are cross-subsidization arrangements the best way of coping with the access problem, and, just as important, (2) is it now feasible in an increasingly competitive environment to preserve cross-subsidization even if we wish to do so?

Objections to cross-subsidization are not hard to find. On the one hand, cross-subsidization can be viewed as an inefficient, uncoordinated welfare system hidden from public view and unaccountable to the public or to its representatives in government. Further, it can be argued that widespread cross-subsidization is incompatible with effective efforts to curb costs. Surely an effective solution to both the access and cost containment problems requires a more integrated, comprehensive, and publicly accountable approach. Consequently, the demise of cross-subsidization should be welcomed, not lamented.

This last conclusion, however, is simplistic. It assumes that an explicit public policy designed to improve access for those not covered by private or public insurance is presently or in the foreseeable future politically feasible. Perhaps the strongest argument for cross-subsidization is the claim that it does—though admittedly in a haphazard and inefficient way—what is not likely to be done through more explicit social policies.

It might be tempting to protest that even if this is so, cross-subsidization ought to be rejected as an unauthorized welfare system since it did not come about through the democratic political process as a conscious social policy. However, if providing some minimum of care for the needy is a matter of right or enforceable societal obligation and not a matter of discretion, then the lack of a democratic pedigree may not be fatal, since rights and obligations place limitations on the scope of the democratic process.

Controversy over the ethical status of cross-subsidization may soon become moot if a point is reached where it is no longer feasible to shore up or rebuild an environment in which cross-subsidization is economically viable for health-care institutions. So even if cross-subsidization has been the best feasible way of coping with the problem of access it does not follow that it will continue to be a viable option. Perhaps too much energy has already been wasted in policy debates defending or attacking cross-subsidization when the real issue is: How can we now best achieve the purpose that cross-subsidization was supposed to serve?

FOR-PROFITS ARE UNFAIR COMPETITION FOR NONPROFITS

This criticism of for-profits can be interpreted in either of two different ways: The first understands it as a charge we have already examined in detail, that for-profits skim the cream and gain a competitive advantage over nonprofits by failing to discharge their institutional obligations to bear their fair share of the costs of providing care for indigents and those with unprofitable diseases. But the metaphor of cream-skimming suggests another possible aspect of the charge of unfair competition that it is worth saying a little more about. This is that besides not taking a fair share of the "bad" (unprofitable) patients, the for-profits also take more than their share of the "good" (profitable) patients.

As we noted earlier, if no one is *entitled* to the profitable patients, it is unclear why seeking to get as many as possible of them is unfair. Nor is it clear that the nonprofits do not also seek as many as possible of the profitable patients. If the for-profits get a disproportionate share of the profitable patients, which may be true at some places but not others, why would that be? Since paying patients have a choice about where and from whom they receive care, their choice of for-profits must in significant part reflect their view that for-profits offer a more attractive product: for example, more convenient location, more modern and higher quality facilities, additional amenities, cost-saving efficiencies, and so forth. It is difficult to see why getting a disproportionate share of the profitable patients simply because one offered a better product is unfair. Of course, when for-profits get more of the profitable patients because of factors such as tie-in arrangements with physicians, this may constitute unfair competition, but non-profits may engage in such anticompetitive practices as well.

According to the second interpretation of the unfair competition charge, non-profit health-care institutions make a distinctive and valuable social contribution—one that is so important that they ought to be protected from the threat of extinction through competition with for-profits. Three main arguments can be given in favor of perpetuating the nonprofit legal status for health-care institutions and, hence, for social policies that are designed to protect them from destructive competition from for-profits. First, nonprofit health-care institutions are properly described as charitable institutions. As such they help nurture and perpetuate the virtue of charity among members of our otherwise highly self-interested society, and this virtue is of great value. The nonprofit legal form stimulates charity by exempting charitable institutions from taxes. Because it also ensures that those who administer charitable funds do not appropriate revenue surpluses, the non-profit legal form encourages charity by providing potential donors with the assurance that they will not be taken advantage of and that their donations will be used for the purposes for which they were given. This assurance is especially vital in the case of donations for health care because donors usually lack the knowledge and expertise to determine whether the providers they support are using their resources properly.

Second, nonprofit health-care institutions both function as and are perceived to be an important community resource, serving the entire community, rather than a commercial enterprise ultimately serving its shareholders and restricted to "paying customers." Like the virtue of charity, the sense of community is an important though fragile value in modern American society, and institutions that contribute significantly to it should not be lightly discarded.

Third, nonprofit health-care institutions nurture a professional ethos that is more likely to keep the patient's interest at center stage than do for-profit institutions, in which the commercial spirit is given freer rein. Hence nonprofits are valuable because they protect quality of care. The quality-of-care argument will be examined in detail later.

The first argument dealt with earlier assumes that most nonprofit health-care institutions are properly described as charitable institutions in the sense that a substantial portion of their financial resources comes from donations. At present, however, most nonprofit hospitals are not charitable institutions in this sense; they are "commercial" rather than "donative" institutions insofar as the major portion of their resources comes from selling services rather than from donations.[7] The more closely nonprofit health-care institutions approximate the purely "commercial" nondonative type, which is becoming the dominant form among nonprofit hospitals, the weaker the value of charity appears as a justification for perpetuating the nonprofit legal status. Nevertheless, even if only a small portion of most nonprofits' revenues comes from charitable donations and is in turn used for unpaid care, nonprofits may still be properly regarded as "charitable" *if* they do in fact serve as the provider of last resort for those who are unable to pay for their care and who are not covered by any insurance or government program to fund their care. Even if such care represents only a small portion of a hospital's overall revenues, it may still be perceived as an important charitable activity and thereby reinforce altruistic and charitable motivations.

It should be clear that the charity and community arguments are not unrelated. It is partly because nonprofits stand ready to provide unpaid health care to the poor (if they do) that they are seen to be a community resource available to the entire community. They can serve to symbolize a shared community commitment that no member of the community should be denied access to an adequate level of health care. This commitment is especially important in the mission of public hospitals. Moreover, control of nonprofits will commonly rest with a board of trustees composed of members of the local community, rather than with a board of directors of a large national or multinational chain. This effect of nonprofits on the sense of community as shared by members of the community is somewhat intangible and difficult to measure. It is also certainly true that nonprofit hospitals are not the only institutions supporting this sense of community, or even the only means of supporting it within health care, and that for-profit hospitals can often contribute to it as well. Nevertheless, we believe the nonprofits are in general more likely than the for-profits to promote this significant value of community.

FOR-PROFITS TREAT HEALTH CARE AS A COMMODITY TO BE BOUGHT AND SOLD IN THE MARKETPLACE RATHER THAN AS A RIGHT OF EVERY CITIZEN

This next collection of ethical concerns about the growth of for-profit health care is steeped in stirring rhetoric. We are told that "health care is not a commodity," that "health care ought not be left to the market," that "access to health care ought not depend on ability to pay," and that "everyone ought to have access to a single level of health care." And it is often said that the ethical acceptability of for-profit health care delivery systems depends on whether health care is properly viewed as a right or as a commodity.[8] In this section we attempt to sort out just what the implications of claims like these are for for-profit health care.

The slogan that health care is not a commodity is best understood as a normative, rather than a purely descriptive claim. As a descriptive claim, it is quite false: If a commodity is defined as something which has a market price or relative exchange value, then health care is a commodity since various treatments, tests, and services are assigned a market price in our society. (Until recently, of course, codes of professional ethics for physicians, backed up by the coercive power of legislation, have made it difficult for most consumers to learn the market price of most forms of health care; but this is a fact about the profession's success in restricting consumer information about health care, not a fact about the nature of health care.)

As a normative claim, the slogan that health care is not, that is, should not be treated as, a commodity implicitly depends on two sorts of assumptions: (1) empirical assumptions about what health care will be distributed to which persons if production and distribution of health care are carried out by for-profit institutions in a marketplace and (2) moral assumptions about what is a just distribution of health care, and what moral right, if any, there is to health care. With regard to the moral assumptions, we believe it is crucial to distinguish the claim that justice requires some level of access to health care for all from the claim that it requires equal access for all persons. We shall argue here that only the view that justice requires *equality* in access to health care, not merely that it implies a right to health care, is incompatible with for-profit provision of health care in a free marketplace.

If the goal is only to ensure that everyone is guaranteed access to some minimally adequate level of health care, why not leave its distribution to the market and so to for-profit institutions? The difficulties with doing so are well known and need not be rehearsed in detail here. Generally, a market system for the distribution of health care, like a market distribution of all other goods and services, will be influenced by the initial natural endowments and wealth that people bring to the market, rather than simply by their need for health care. The market distribution of health care, as with other goods, will only be just if the distribution of initial assets, including income and wealth, is just.

However, there are specific characteristics of health care, and of health-care markets, which further ensure that a market distribution of health care will fail to satisfy the demands of any theory of justice requiring that some minimally adequate level of access to health care be guaranteed to all. Health care needs are highly unpredictable for any particular individual, vary greatly between different individuals (unlike other basic needs for food or shelter), and in the context of modern health care are very expensive relative to most other goods and services. As a result, it is difficult if not impossible for any but the very richest to budget their health-care expenditures.

The market solution to this situation, of course, is the development of a market in insurance, a device for *risk-sharing* that enables individuals to protect themselves from substantial unforeseen financial losses and to secure very expensive professional help in coping with disease or disability when it occurs. However, competition in the market for health-care insurance will lead to differentiation of risk pools. Different insurance packages, with different premiums, will be developed for different groups of individuals with similar risks of sickness and disability with the result that those individuals who have the greatest risk of ill health—that is, those who need insurance the most—will find it prohibitively costly. Regulatory measures requiring community rating of insurance risks and unlimited access to insurance pools can be used to counter risk-pool differentiation, although a market proponent will view these as inefficient interferences in the operation of health care markets.

With either different risk pools or community rating, however, health-care insurance will remain extremely expensive, and beyond the financial reach of substantial numbers of the poor in this country. This would be true even if access to health insurance were less closely tied to employment than it is in the United States today. Thus, even with health insurance the market will make access to even some minimally adequate level of health care depend upon ability to pay, an ability that many millions of Americans today lack (and would lack even under a system of perfectly competitive markets for the distribution of income).

On virtually any general theory of distributive justice, and in particular any theory of justice in health care other than a rather austere libertarian view, no one in a country as wealthy as ours ought to have to go without access to at least a minimally adequate level of health care. There is a general moral obligation of society to ensure that level of access for all, and we have argued that the obligation falls ultimately on the federal government. While general theories of rights are not well developed, nevertheless, we believe this obligation supports the claim that there is a moral right of all Americans to that level of health care. Market distribution systems employing for-profit health-care delivery systems will fail to meet this obligation, or to secure the correlative right, and so will distribute health care in an unjust way.

To this extent, then, the rhetoric with which we began this section is correct: The distribution of health care ought not be left to the market and ought not depend on ability to pay. But this fact provides no reason for preferring for-profit health care to nonprofit health care, or for attempting to protect nonprofits or to stem the growth of for-profits. As noted earlier, until quite recently nonprofit institutions have dominated the health-care system, but they did not solve the problem of access to care. The greatest extension of access to care to those who previously had virtually no access came from Medicare and Medicaid, not from the private insurance market working within a largely nonprofit system. Whether or not a predominantly nonprofit system, a predominantly for-profit system, or a more evenly mixed system will remedy the ethical deficiencies of a purely market distribution of health care will depend upon the specific arrangements for modifying the market distribution by subsidizing care for the worse off.

In a system in which virtually all health care institutions were of the for-profit form, the distributional inequities of the market might be avoided by the use of health insurance vouchers for the poor, financed by taxes, including taxes of health care institutions. Of course, if some health care markets are sufficiently noncompetitive so that supply problems still remain, for example in poor rural or innercity ghetto areas, then supplementary, nonmarket direct provision programs such as the National Health Service Corps may be needed. The fundamental point, however, is that unjust gaps in access left by a market system of health care distribution require redistributive measures (probably by the government), whether the overall health care system is predominantly nonprofit or for-profit, and that redistributive means are available for either a nonprofit or for-profit system. So here, as with the charge that for-profits exacerbate the access problem, analysis of a criticism which at first appears to be directed only at for-profit health care leads us back to more fundamental issues of distributive justice—issues that would perhaps be just as urgent if for-profit health care had never appeared on the scene.

If acknowledgment of a right to health care is compatible with either a nonprofit or for-profit delivery system, both of which require redistributive measures to fund access for the poor, why is it so often thought that for-profits and markets are incompatible with that right? A principal explanation, we believe, is the confusion of a right of all persons to an *adequate* level of health care (the right we have appealed to earlier) with a right of all persons to the *same* level of health care. A right to an adequate level requires some minimal floor of health-care access below which no one should be allowed to fall. That level does not, on the other hand, constitute a ceiling above which no one is permitted to rise, and so is compatible with individuals using their resources to purchase in the market more or better health care or health care insurance than the adequate level guarantees.

Without trying to specify what an "adequate level" would be, it also seems clear that it would be less than all medically beneficial care. A right to an adequate level of health care, then, is only minimally egalitarian in requiring an equal minimal level of access for all while permitting departures from equality in an upward direction from that minimum. A right of all persons to the same level of health care, on the other hand, is strongly egalitarian in not permitting departures from equality in either a downward or upward direction from the level specified by the right. If that level is something less than all medically beneficial health care, as we believe it inevitably would have to be, such a right would have the effect of prohibiting anyone from using his or her resources to purchase more or better health care than is guaranteed to all.

This strong egalitarian position regarding health-care distribution is incompatible with the unconstrained purchase and sale of health care in a market, *whether the seller is a for-profit or nonprofit institution*. Limited market price competition among providers offering only a single level of care to all would be possible, and so equality in health care does not foreclose all use of market competition, though it is likely that such competition would spread to quality and quantity of care, thereby undermining the single level of care for all. However, if markets for different amounts or quality of health care are allowed to exist alongside whatever system ensures the equal level to all, then any differences between persons in either income and wealth and/or preferences for health care as opposed to other goods and services will produce inequalities in the overall distribution of health care.

As several commentators have noted, the necessary prohibition of markets for health care to enforce this equality in health care, understood as requiring both a floor and ceiling, would have the effect of permitting persons to use their resources to purchase nonessential luxury goods like. Mercedes-Benz cars and Caribbean vacations while prohibiting their use for the basic and essential good of health care.[9] Without pursuing the matter further here, we believe this would require a stronger commitment to equality than is either plausible or widely accepted in American society, while at the same time conflicting with the freedom of individuals to decide for themselves how they will use their justly acquired resources.

There is another version of the concern that health care is a right whereas for-profits treat it as a commodity to be bought and sold in the marketplace. The important distinction here is between health care *needs* and market-expressed *wants* or preferences for health care. For-profits, it is argued, will respond to consumer wants for health care even if they are for frivolous amenities such as champagne breakfasts for obstetric patients and however unrelated they may be to the patient's true health care needs. The right to health care, on the other hand, is to some level of health care adequate to meet the patient's objectively determined, basic health care needs. There are two versions of this concern with a health-care system that responds to wants rather than needs that should be distinguished.

The first rejects the identification of patients' well-being or just claims to health care with the satisfaction of even their *fully informed* preferences or wants. This view depends implicitly on some objective account of human well-being that does not ultimately reduce to the satisfaction of fully informed wants, or on an account of individuals' just claims to health care that depends on some objective features or ranking of health care (e.g., its effects on a person's range of opportunity as in Norman Daniels' theory of justice in health care[10]). To evaluate this version of the concern would require us to evaluate the underlying objective theories of human well-being or the nonpreference-based theories of justice in health care. Most of these theories are not sufficiently well developed to permit their evaluation, and that task is in any case beyond the scope of this chapter.

The second version of the concern about a health care system that responds to wants rather than needs is the more common one. It is that the actual expressed wants for health care of real patients in real conditions often deviate sharply from both their objective health care needs and what their fully informed preferences for health care would be.

As we have noted earlier and will discuss further, health-care consumers are commonly in a poor position to evaluate for themselves their own need for health care. They lack information about the nature of their medical condition and of what alternative treatments might positively affect it in what ways. Moreover, in circumstances of serious illness, patients are often anxious, fearful, confused, and dependent in ways that further impair their capacities to assess for themselves their health-care needs in an informed and rational fashion. Thus, their actual health care wants will often be both ill-informed and unusually vulnerable to influence and manipulation by health-care professionals. It is these fundamental features of the setting in which decisions are made to utilize health care that support the importance both of the physician's commitment to act in the patient's best interests and of the patient's trust that the physician will do so.

One concern about the growth of for-profits is that they may contribute to strengthening physicians' motivations to act in their own economic interests and thereby weaken their commitment to their patients' well-being; we pursue this possible adverse impact on the physician–patient relationship later in this chapter. The other potential effect of health care coming increasingly to be viewed as a commodity to be aggressively marketed is that physicians will cater to ill-informed patient wants at the expense of their true health needs or take advantage of patients' vulnerable positions to manipulate their wants. In either case, the result will be the delivery of health care that fails best to meet patients' true health needs. We believe this is a reasonable worry that warrants careful future monitoring, although the data do not yet exist to show to what extent, if any, the phenomenon has begun to occur.

However, not all increased responsiveness to consumer wants constitutes a shift from serving patients' health needs to serving their mere wants. Increased responsiveness to consumer wants makes a genuine contribution to patient's well-being to the extent that which treatment, if any, best promotes a patient's well-being depends at least in part on the particular aims and values of that patient. If for-profits promote this form of responsiveness to patients they are to be commended, not condemned.

FOR-PROFITS DAMAGE THE PHYSICIAN–PATIENT RELATIONSHIP, ERODE TRUST, CREATE NEW CONFLICTS OF INTEREST, AND DIMINISH QUALITY OF CARE

It is undeniable that for-profit health care involves potential conflicts between the interests of providers (physicians, managers, administrators, and stockholders) and those of patients. In the most general terms, the conflict is simply this: An institution with a strong if not an overriding commitment to maximizing profit may sometimes find that the best way to do this is not to act in its patients' best interests.

This fundamental potential conflict of interest is said to be of special concern in health care, not only because health-care interests are so important, but also because the "consumer" of health care, unlike the consumer of most other goods and services provided by profit-seeking firms, is in an especially vulnerable position for two reasons. First, he will often lack the special knowledge and expertise needed for judging whether a particular health service is necessary or would be beneficial, whether it is being rendered in an appropriate way, and even in some cases whether it has been successful. Second, because illness or injury can result in anxiety and loss of self-confidence, the patient may find it difficult to engage in the sort of self-protective bargaining behavior expressed in the admonition "caveat emptor."

Whether this conflict of interest will damage the physician–patient relationship will depend on the extent that it also exists outside for-profit settings. And it is quite clear that this fundamental potential for conflict of interest is not peculiar to for-profit health care. A health-care institution may exhibit a strong commitment to maximizing profit, and this commitment may result in practices that are not in patients' best interests, even if the institution is of nonprofit form. When we ask whether an institution's or an individual's pursuit of profits is prejudicial to the patient's interests, the appropriate sense of the phrase "pursuit of profits" is quite broad, not the narrower legal sense in which nonprofit institutions do not by definition pursue profits. After all, the issue is whether the opportunities for attaining *benefits* for themselves provide incentives that influence behavior on the part of providers that is not in patients' best interest. Whatever form these incentives take and whatever kinds of benefits are pursued, they may all run counter to the patient's interests.

In any form of medical practice operating under a fee-for-service system, under any system of prepayment (as in health maintenance organizations [HMOs]), and under any system of capitation, where physicians are paid a salary determined by the number of patients they treat (as in independent practice associations [IPAs]), a basic conflict of interest will exist, regardless of whether the organization is for-profit or nonprofit. In a fee-for-service system, the conflict is obvious: Physicians have an incentive to overutilize services because their financial return will thereby be increased. The incentive for overutilization of services can conflict with the patient's interest in three distinct ways: it can lead physicians to (1) provide services whose *medical costs* to the patient outweigh their *medical benefits* (as in the case of surgery or X-rays that actually do more medical harm than good), (2) impose financial costs on the patient that exceed the medical benefits provided (greater out-of-pocket expenses for the patient), and (3) contribute to higher health-care costs (including higher insurance premiums) for everyone.

In prepayment or capitation systems, providers are subject to conflicts of interest because of incentives to underutilize care. In HMOs, providers have an incentive to limit care because the overall financial well-being of the organization requires it and because salary increases and year-end bonuses as well as new personnel, new equipment, and new services are all financed by these savings. In IPAs and other organizations that operate on a capitation system, conflicts of interest due to the incentive for underutilization are equally clear: Spending less time and using fewer scarce resources enable physicians to handle a larger number of patients, and this results in a larger salary. Whether, or to what extent, these incentives actually result in reduced quality of care is an extremely difficult question. But what is clear is that they create conflicts of interest, in both for-profit and nonprofit settings.

Some analysts have recognized that the preceding sorts of conflicts of interest are unavoidable because they result from two features that will be found in any form of health-care institution or organization: (1) the patient's special vulnerability and (2) the need to provide some form of incentive for providers that is related in some fashion to the amount and kind of services they provide. They have then gone on to argue that what makes conflicts of interest especially serious in for-profits is that for-profits provide physicians with opportunities for *secondary income*. This secondary income may come either from charges for services, which they themselves do not provide but which they recommend or which are provided by others under their supervision, or from being a shareholder in the for-profit health-care corporation.

Secondary income, however, and the conflict of interest it involves, is also neither a new phenomenon in health care nor peculiar to for-profits. Several forms of "fee splitting" are practiced by physicians working in nonprofit settings. One of the most common is an arrangement whereby a physician receives a percentage of the fee charged for X-rays, laboratory tests, other diagnostic procedures, physical therapy, or drug or alcohol counseling that he recommends but which are performed by people he employs or supervises. In some cases, licensing and certification laws and reimbursement eligibility requirements for Medicare, Medicaid, and private insurance require nonphysician health-care professionals to be supervised by a physician, thus creating a dependence which makes it possible for physicians to reap this secondary income. Physicians may also charge fees for interpreting diagnostic tests, such as electrocardiograms, that they recommend and which are performed by others even if they do not split the fee for the procedure itself.

It may still be the case that the opportunities for secondary income and other conflicts of interest tend to be *greater* in most for-profit institutions than in most nonprofit institutions. At present, however, neither the extent of these differences, nor, more importantly, the extent to which they are taken advantage of in ways that reduce quality of care, increase costs, or otherwise compromise patients' interests is documented. It may also be the case that even though serious conflicts of interest, from secondary income and other sources, already exist in nonprofit health care, the continued growth of for-profits, both in their own activities and the influence they have on the behavior of nonprofits, will result in a significant worsening of the problem. Our current lack of data, however, makes it premature to predict that this will happen or when it will happen.

There is another form of the charge that for-profit health care creates new conflicts of interest or exacerbates old ones. Some fear that even if the physician's behavior toward patients is not distorted by incentives for secondary income or by equity ownership, physicians in for-profits will be subject to greater control by management and that this control will make it more difficult for physicians to serve the patient's interests rather than the corporation's. There can be little doubt that American physicians are increasingly subject to control by others, especially by managers and administrators, many of whom are not physicians.

There are two major factors that have led to this loss of "professional dominance" which are quite independent of the growth of for-profits.[11] One is the institutionalization of medicine which itself arose from a variety of factors, including the proliferation of technologies and specializations which call for large-scale social cooperation and cannot be rendered efficiently, if they can be rendered at all, by independent practitioners. The other is the increased pressure for cost-containment in a more competitive environment, which has led to a greater reliance on professional management techniques within health-care institutions and more extensive regulatory controls by government. At most, the growth of for-profits may be accelerating the loss of professional dominance.

It should not simply be assumed, however, that diminished physician control will result in an overall lowering of the quality of care or a worsening of the problem of conflict of interests. Whether it will depends upon the answer to three difficult questions: To what extent will management or shareholders of for-profits exercise their control over physicians in the pursuit of profit and at the expense of patient interests or will their pursuit of profit be restrained by ethical considerations? To what extent will management and stockholders act on the belief that, in the long run, profits will be maximized by serving patients' interests? To what extent have physicians, in the physician-dominated system that has existed up until recently, actually acted in the best interests of their patients? The answers to the first two questions await data not yet available.

The third question is especially difficult to answer because of an ambiguity in the notion of the "patient's best interests." In a fee-for-service, third-party payment system in which physicians exercise a great deal of control in ordering treatments and procedures, a physician who makes decisions according to what is in the individual patient's best medical interests will tend to order any treatment or test whose expected net medical benefit is greater than zero, no matter how small the net benefit may be. Under such a system, the traditional ethical principles of the medical profession, which require the physician to do what is best for the patient (or to minimize harm to him), and the principle of self-interest speak with one voice, at least so long as the patient's interests are restricted to his medical interests. Indeed, even if the physician considers the patient's overall interests—financial as well as medical—so long as a third party is picking up the major portion of the bill, the physician may still conclude that acting in the patient's best interest requires doing anything that can be expected to yield a nonzero net medical benefit. Yet, as has often been noted, the cumulative result of large numbers of such decisions, each of which may be in the best interest of the particular patient, is that health care is overutilized and a cost crisis results.

"Overutilization" here does not mean the use of medically unnecessary care, i.e., care having no net medical benefit or which is positively harmful; instead what is meant is what one author has called "noncostworthy care"—care which yields less benefit than some alternative use to which the same resources could be put, either for other health care services or for nonhealth care goods.[12] Overutilization of health care in this sense, not just overutilization as nonbeneficial care, is clearly contrary to everyone's interest. If continued professional dominance means perpetuation of this problem of overutilization, then even if a continued loss of professional dominance will lead to medical decisions that are not, considered in isolation, in the individual patient's best interest, it may result in the elimination of one important conflict of interest and collective irrationality in the current system.

This does not rule out the possibility, of course, that greater control by nonphysicians will also lead to overutilization. If this occurs, then one system which works against everyone's best interest will merely have been replaced by another that does the same thing.

We have seen that in the fee-for-service, third-party payment system in nonprofit as well as for-profit settings, the cumulative result of many physicians acting on the desire to do what is best for the individual patient can result in overutilization that is contrary to all patients' best interest. Some critics of for-profits suggest that we must either pay the price of this overutilization or cope with it by methods that do not undermine physicians' commitments to doing what is best for their individual patients. They then conclude that even if it could be shown that the growth of for-profits would restrain overutilization by introducing greater price competition into health care, the price would be too high to pay because the physician's all-important commitment to do his best for each patient would eventually be eroded by the increasing "commercialization" of health care that is being accelerated if not caused by the growth of for-profits.

The force of this objection to for-profits depends, of course, not only upon the correctness of the prediction that the growth of for-profits will in fact contribute to a weakening of the physician's commitment to do the best he can for each patient, it also depends upon the assumption that under the current system that commitment has been a dominant force in physician behavior. This last point may be cast in a slightly different way. How concerned we should be about the tendency for the behavior of physicians to become more like that of businessmen depends upon how great the difference in behavior of the two groups is and has been. If one assumes that as a group physicians have been significantly more altruistic than businessmen and if one also assumes that altruism is the only effective safeguard against exploitation of the patient's special vulnerability, then one will oppose any development, including the growth of for-profit health care, which can be expected to make physicians more like businessmen.

Those who make the first assumption tend to overlook two points which call it into question. First, our society does in fact expect, and in some cases enforces by the power of the law, significant restrictions on the pursuit of profit by "mere businessmen." In fact, it can be argued that the moral obligations of businessmen to their customers are not significantly less demanding than those of physicians toward their patients *when equally important interests are at stake.* Robert Veatch has observed that if a physician becomes aware that another physician is acting on misinformation or performing a procedure incorrectly, then the first physician is under an obligation to bring this to the attention of the second and perhaps to help him remedy the defect.[13]

Veatch then goes on to say that a businessman who learns that a competitor is acting on misinformation or using sloppy production techniques is under no obligation to point this out to the competitor. Veatch's contrast between the moral obligations of physicians and businessmen, however, is overdrawn if not outright mistaken. It is not clear that a physician has a moral obligation to inform another physician that he is misinformed or even that his technique is deficient unless significant patient interests are at stake. It may be true, however, that important interests are more frequently potentially at stake in health care than in ordinary business transactions.

Yet surely a businessman has a moral obligation to inform a competitor that he is unwittingly endangering people's lives even if in giving his competitor this information he prevents his competitor from ruining himself and, thereby, foregoes a chance to eliminate the competition. Moreover, if a businessman lies to or defrauds a customer, we conclude not only that he has done something illegal but that he has acted immorally. And even if he breaks no law, we may nonetheless condemn him morally as a cheat and a scoundrel. All of this is simply to emphasize a simple point that critics of the "commercialization" of health care sometimes overlook, namely, that we customarily do apply not only legal but also moral standards to the behavior of businessmen. One would not want a physician who was motivated exclusively by financial reward, but then one would not want an electrician who was either. Nevertheless, even if there is a tendency to overstate the contrast between ethical and legal constraints on business transactions and the physician–patient relationship, we typically do expect a somewhat higher standard of conduct from physicians.

Many outside the medical profession and some within it greet the claim that physicians as a class are especially altruistic with some skepticism. This attitude is not groundless. One of the difficulties of determining the strength of altruistic motivation among physicians is that until very recently, the fee-for-service, third-party payment system has produced a situation in which altruism and self-interest converge: Doing what is best for the patient (pursuing all treatment that promises nonzero benefits) was often doing what was financially best for the physician. Nevertheless, critics of the thesis that physicians are especially altruistic can marshal a good deal of evidence to support their view, such as the profession's historical opposition to HMOs and to Medicare and Medicaid, each of which promised significant extensions of access to health care,[14] its failure to overcome the chronic geographical maldistribution of physicians in this country, and its support of strict entry controls to the profession through medical licensure together with relatively weak oversight of the continuing competence of those already licensed. We can make no attempt to evaluate such evidence here, but the self-interest of the profession seems a better prima facie explanation of it than does an altruistic concern for the health of the ill. It is important to emphasize that explanations of these phenomena need not assume that self-interest here is exclusively or even primarily *financial* self-interest. The profession's resistance to Medicare, for example, was probably more an attempt to preserve physician *autonomy.*

In assessing these questions of conflict of interest, we think it is helpful to distinguish the behavior of physicians acting as an organized profession addressing matters of health policy from the behavior of individual physicians toward individual patients. As we have noted above, much behavior of medicine as an organized profession (e.g., as reflected in the political role the American Medical Association [AMA] has played in seeking to maintain physician dominance in the health-care profession) to protect and enhance physician incomes, and so forth, has served the self-interest of physicians. Controversial is the extent to which the self-interested function of the motivation for supporting such practices as medical licensure is manifest or latent, explicit or implicit. In considering the conduct of professional trade associations such as the AMA, we believe that forwarding the economic and other interests of the members of the profession is often the explicit and conscious intent of the representatives of the profession. To the extent that the profession has been successful in forwarding its members' interests, we would expect to find an institutional, organizational, and legal structure shaping the practice of medicine that serves the economic and other interests of members of the profession. Moreover, it would be hard to look back over the evolution in this century of the position and structure of the medical profession without concluding that the profession has had considerable success in promoting its interests.

It would be completely implausible to attribute a high level of altruism to the medical profession if that was interpreted to mean a high level of economic self-sacrifice in favor of the public's health needs. The exceptionally high levels of physician incomes would belie that. Nor is it plausible to claim that the organized profession has led efforts to address some of the most serious moral deficiencies in our health-care system, such as the continued lack of access to health care of large numbers of the poor.

As we noted earlier, the history of the profession's opposition to national health insurance and to Medicare and Medicaid belies any such role of altruism or moral leadership. Nor finally have many members of the profession acting as individuals been remarkably self-sacrificing or acted as moral leaders in addressing these problems. Occasionally physicians have, of course, located in undesirable geographical areas to meet pressing health-care needs or have provided substantial unpaid care to the poor, but such behavior has not been sufficiently widespread to have a major impact on these problems.

Despite the extent that the profession has forwarded its members' interests and that individual members have not been self-sacrificing in addressing the most serious deficiencies in the health-care system, we believe it would be a serious mistake to conclude that the patient-centered ethic that has defined the traditional physician–patient relationship is mere sham and rhetoric, a thin guise overlaying the physician's self-interest.

An alternative, and we believe more plausible, perspective is that in part just because the medical profession has been exceptionally successful in promoting and protecting an institutional and organizational setting that well serves physicians' economic and other interests, individual physicians have thereby been freed to follow the traditional patient-centered ethic in their relations with their individual patients. Put oversimply, a physician whose overall practice structure assures him a high income need not weigh economic benefits to himself when considering treatment recommendations for his individual patients. As we have argued earlier, conflicts of interest between physicians and patients have long existed and are hardly a heretofore unknown consequence of for-profit health-care institutions. As one commentator has argued, much of medicine can be viewed as a conflict for the physician between self-interest and altruism, requiring a balancing of these sometimes conflicting motivations.[15]

What we are suggesting is that the self-interested organized professional behavior and institutional structure of medicine may have helped protect the possibility of altruistic behavior on the part of the physician when guiding treatment with his individual patients. (This hypothesis, of course, requires careful qualification. In some cases the self-interested behavior of organized medicine has clearly had a negative impact on patient interests. For example, licensure and other forms of self-regulation by the profession have often failed to protect patients from chemically dependent or otherwise incompetent physicians and have exacerbated the problem of access by inhibiting the development of less expensive forms of care utilizing nonphysician providers such as midwives and nurse practitioners.)

One virtue of this more complex perspective is that it allows us to accommodate the elements of truth that exist in each of two otherwise seemingly incompatible perspectives, each of which taken only by itself appears extreme and incomplete. One perspective views the physician simply as an economically self-interested businessman in his dealings with patients. Those who support this perspective can point to the various ways in which the actions of the medical profession and the institutional and financing structure in which medicine is practiced serve the interests of physicians, as we have done earlier, but they often end up denying any significant reality to the physician's commitment to promoting his patients' best interests. On the other hand, many defenders of physicians viewed as devoted professionals committed to the well-being of their patients seem also to feel it necessary to deny the extent to which medical practices and institutional structures serve physicians' interests.

Either perspective is by itself stubbornly one-sided in its view of physicians simply as self-interested economic accumulators or as devoted altruists. We favor a view which recognizes that these two perspectives are *not* incompatible and accepts the elements of truth in each of them.

One advantage of this more balanced perspective is that it permits the recognition of the reality and importance of the traditional patient-centered ethic, without denying the conflicts of interest between physician and patient that we have discussed earlier or the important historical role played by economic interests of physicians. A perspective that encompasses a balance between self-interested and altruistic motivations on the part of physicians can help articulate the concern of many observers that the rise of for-profit medicine while *not* representing an entirely new phenomenon nevertheless *does* pose a danger to the traditional physician–patient relationship by shifting the traditional *balance* between self-interested and altruistic motivations because it tends to bring motivations of economic self-interest more directly and substantially into the physician's relations with individual patients.

What, more specifically, is the worry about the erosion of the physician–patient relationship by the rise of for-profit health-care institutions? We think that worry can be most pointedly brought out by initially overstating the possible effect. The traditional account of the patient-centered ethic makes the physician the agent of the patient, whose "highest commitment is the patient."[16] The physician is to seek to determine together with the patient that course of treatment which will best promote the patient's well-being, setting aside effects on others, including effects on the physician, the patient's family, or society.

This commitment to the patient's well-being responds to the various respects discussed earlier in which patients are in a very poor position to determine for themselves what health care, if any, they need. Because the patient is unusually dependent on the physician, it is especially important to the success of their partnership in the service of the patient's well-being that the patient believe that the physician will be guided in his recommendations solely by the patient's best interests. Patients have compelling reasons to want the physician–patient relationship to be one in which this trust is warranted, quite apart from the putative therapeutic benefits of such trust.

Suppose the rise of for-profit health care so eroded this traditional relationship, and in its place substituted a commercial relationship, that patients came to view their physicians as they commonly now view used car salesmen. We emphasize that such a radical shift in view is not to be expected. We use this "worst-case" example of a caveat emptor commercial relationship only because it focuses most pointedly the worry about the effect on the physician–patient relationship of the commercialization of health care. Many factors will inhibit such a shift from actually taking place in patients' views of their physicians, including traditional codes of ethics in medicine, requirements of informed consent, fiduciary obligations of physicians, as well as powerful traditions of professionalism in medicine. Recognizing that the stereotype of the used car salesman substantially overstates what there is any reason to expect in medicine, nevertheless what would a shift in this direction do to the physician–patient relationship?

Most obviously and perhaps also most importantly, it would undermine the trust that many patients are prepared to place in their physicians' commitment to seek their (the patients) best interests. In general, there is no such trust of a used car salesman, but rather his claims and advice are commonly greeted with a cool skepticism. He is viewed as pursuing his own economic interests, with no commitment to the customer's welfare. It is the rare (and probably in the end sorry) consumer who places himself in the hands of the car salesman. Anything like the fiduciary relationship in which a patient trusts the physician's commitment first to the patient's interest is quite absent with the used car salesman.

This is not to say that some additional consumer skepticism of physician recommendations and increased attempts by patients to become knowledgeable health-care consumers would not be a good thing—they would. It is rather to say that many of the various inequalities in the physician–patient relationship are sufficiently deep and difficult to eradicate that some substantial trust of the physician's commitment to the patient is likely to remain necessary and valuable. The commercial model of arm's-length, caveat emptor bargaining is not promising for the physician–patient relation.

While there has been deception of patients by physicians, it seems to have markedly decreased in recent decades, and in the past this deception in medicine was justified as for the patient's own good (even if in fact it often was not). However, one does not expect the truth, the whole truth, and nothing but the truth from a used car salesman, nor that shadings of the truth are done for the customer's own good. We expect some concealment and distortion of information in order to make the sale, although this is not to say that some outright deception in commerce may not be fraudulent and immoral. It is also commonly believed that businessmen are in business to sell as much of their product as possible, however much the consumer may not "need" the expensive car being pushed by the salesman, whereas physicians are expected not to encourage needless consumption. Businessmen respond to consumer wants, not needs, and will do their best to manufacture such wants where they do not already exist.

A shift towards commercialization of health care could be expected to result in increasing emphasis on marketing strategies to secure an increasing segment of the market. Moreover, we expect no unprofitable products or services from a car salesman in response to consumer need. We have argued that the moral obligation to ensure access to health care for the poor is ultimately the government's, not an individual physician's or hospital's by way of cross-subsidization. Nevertheless, in the face of unmet need, physicians and health-care institutions often do, and are often expected to, respond to that need by furnishing the needed care. Other norms important to the practice of medicine have a weakened or nonexistent place in most commercial transactions, such as the requirement of confidentiality concerning information about the patient.

One must be careful not to overstate the contrast between medicine and commerce—we have already seen it is certainly not the case that commerce takes place in the absence of any ethical constraints (or legal constraints, reflecting ethical norms) or that the medical profession is never moved by self-interest. However, we believe there is a genuine and important difference in the ethos of the two enterprises that plays out in important differences in the physician–patient and businessman–consumer transaction. Oversimplifying, it is commonly believed that in business transactions individuals pursuing their own interests, though admittedly within some ethical and legal constraints, will best promote the overall social good. It is this view of the motivation of self-interest as ethically acceptable that quite reasonably worries many as medicine becomes increasingly commercialized. Since physicians are, of course, human like the rest of us and naturally concerned with their own interests, it is reasonable to view their primary commitment to the patient's well-being as inevitably fragile and always in danger of being undermined. In that light, it is unnecessary to view for-profit institutions as introducing a qualitatively new dimension of commercialization and new set of conflicts of interest into health care. As we have argued, such a view is indefensible. Nor need it be expected that physicians' concern with their patient's well-being will just disappear as soon as they go on the payroll of a for-profit hospital or, more likely, establish other types of contractual relations with it. That view too would be indefensible, indeed downright silly.

The realistic worry, concerning which the data are not yet in, is rather that over time the increased importance of investor-owned for-profit institutions may permit considerations of economic self-interest increasingly to invade the heretofore somewhat protected sphere of the physician–patient relationship, and thereby weaken the patient-centered ethic on which that relationship has traditionally depended. The difference would only be one of degree, but no less important for that. As we have noted earlier, there are other independent factors putting similar pressures on that relationship such as the expected oversupply of physicians. It would be a mistake to think that these possible adverse effects on the physician–patient relationship are uniquely due to the rise of for-profits. However, that is not a reason to be unconcerned with these effects of for-profits, but only a reason not to focus one's concerns solely on for-profits.

We emphasize that the traditional patient-centered ethic need not be incompatible with greater attention to costs in health-care utilization decisions and practices. Utilization of health care should reflect the financial costs as well as benefits of care, but that will not be appropriately achieved by, nor need it inevitably lead to, physicians making utilization decisions solely according to their own economic self-interest. Whatever the right mix of incentives for reasonably limiting health-care utilization and costs, simply making physicians fully subject to incentives of economic self-interest by breaking down the patient-centered ethic seems not the path to that mix. A physician weighing the true financial costs of care against its medical benefits *to the patient* is entirely different from one who simply weighs the economic consequences *to himself* of the patient utilizing care.

The most obvious worry, then, is that the increasing prominence of for-profits may contribute to a shift in physicians' patient-oriented behavior, which may in turn affect the patient trust important to a well-functioning physician–patient relationship. The test of that hypothesis would then be the extent to which physician behavior is actually different within for-profit settings. But it is important to realize that patient trust may be eroded, and so the physician–patient relationship adversely affected, even in the absence of any actual shift toward more self-interested behavior by physicians. Even if outward behavior does not change, a change in the motivations of the behavior, and in turn of perceptions by others of those motivations, may be important. If physicians are increasingly perceived by patients as motivated by self-interest rather than by a commitment to serving their patient, then even in the absence of a change in physicians' behavior, it is reasonable to expect an erosion in patient *trust* that physicians will act for their patients' best interests. Part of what is important to patients in health care is the reassurance that the professional *cares* about them and their plight. (This is one respect in which other health-care professionals, for example nurses, are often more important than physicians in patient care.) A change in a physician's motivations, or even in the patient's perceptions of those motivations, may be enough to affect the patient's belief about whether the physician "really cares" about him. This point should give pause to those who propose to test the effects of for-profits on the physician–patient relationship and on patient's trust by looking only at changes in physician's behavior.

FOR-PROFITS UNDERMINE MEDICAL EDUCATION

The charge that for-profits undermine medical education parallels the claim examined previously that for-profits exacerbate the problem of access to care. Medical education, like care for indigents, is in part funded through cross-subsidization, and for-profits are believed to be contributing to the demise of cross-subsidization. It is thought that not only will for-profits themselves refrain from providing medical education because to do so would not be profitable for them, but also that they will make it increasingly difficult for nonprofit institutions such as university hospitals to carry on medical education and still remain competitive.

Much of what was said regarding cross-subsidization of indigent care applies here as well. Even if the growth of for-profits is contributing to the crisis in funding for medical education it is difficult to estimate the magnitude of its contribution, and it is clear that other factors are at work as well. Faced with growing pressures for cost-containment, nonprofit institutions would presumably have strong incentives to reduce all "unprofitable" activities, including medical education, even in the absence of competition from for-profits. And here, as in the case of cross-subsidization for indigent care, whether one laments these developments or welcomes them will depend upon one's views on the efficiency and ethical acceptability of a system which in effect disguised the true costs of medical education and upon whether one thinks that the political process is likely to produce a workable alternative system for funding medical education through explicit public policy choices.

Furthermore, before a convincing answer can be given to the question of what obligations institutions or individuals have to help support medical education, several basic ethical issues must be resolved which the cross-subsidization system has effectively kept out of the public view. Perhaps most importantly, to what extent should medical education be subsidized by public resources?

To the extent that physicians benefit from the skills which they sell at their full market value there is a presumptive case for making them bear the costs of their own training. However, there are several countervailing considerations which may overcome this presumption. First, it can be argued that if medical education is publicly subsidized we will all benefit from a higher level of skills than would be possible under a system in which individuals had to bear the full costs of their training. Second, public subsidization makes it possible for persons from lower socioeconomic groups to become physicians and this is desirable, not only because it promotes equality of opportunity, but also because there is some reason to believe that physicians from the same socioeconomic background as their patients may be better able to communicate with those patients and to serve them effectively.

Third, it may also be that a strong system of medical education, like medical research, has some of the features of a public good. Medical education does not simply build economic assets for physicians. At both the graduate and postgraduate levels it also sets, transmits, and improves standards and methods of sound medical practice. Because the average patient is in a poor position to evaluate for him- or herself the quality of care provided by a particular physician, all patients benefit from a high-quality system of medical education that provides some assurance of the high quality of training and skills of the physicians produced by that system. If public subsidization of medical education facilitates training geared more toward the quality of patient care and less toward the economic value to physicians of the skills produced, that may be of benefit to patients, that is, the public.

While it would be unjustified to maintain that the growth of for-profits is a major source of the reported crisis in funding for medical education, it can perhaps be said that for-profits are one element in a complex array of changes which will test the strength of the public commitment to medical education and challenge the moral assumptions on which that commitment is based.

FOR-PROFITS AND THE POLITICAL POWER OF THE MEDICAL–INDUSTRIAL COMPLEX

The widespread view that the medical profession's dominance in the U.S. health-care system is waning has already been noted. One important aspect of the weakening of professional dominance is said to be the decreasing effectiveness of organized medicine's lobbying efforts in recent years. Whether or not one greets this development with enthusiasm or regret will depend, of course, upon the extent to which one believes that these efforts to influence public policy have promoted or impeded the public interest. However, both the supporters and the critics of professional dominance have voiced a concern that it may be replaced by the dominance of a few extremely wealthy—and politically powerful—giant health-care corporations forming a medical–industrial complex.[17] The fear is that a handful of the largest corporations might "capture" the regulators, molding public policy to their own needs through lobbying, campaign contributions, and use of the media to sway the electorate.

The real concern here should be the political effects of highly concentrated *corporate* power in health care—not simply the power of *for-profit* health-care corporations. While it is true that the hospital "industry" is becoming increasingly concentrated, it is important to point out that some of the largest hospital chains are owned or operated by large nonprofit corporations. Further, there is nothing to prevent large nonprofit corporations from using their wealth and power to influence public policy and little reason to believe that they will in general be less willing to do so than large for-profit corporations. At present, however, it is difficult to predict how concentrated the health-care sector will become or to what extent the disparate interest groups within and across health-care institutions can be welded together under corporate leadership to function as a unified influence on public policy.

The issue, then, is whether it may become necessary in the future to utilize regulation or some other form of societal control to neutralize or minimize the political effects of the economic power wielded by large health-care corporations, whether nonprofit or for-profit. Some possible, even if not politically likely, controls include limitations on campaign contributions and on political advertisements in the media, special laws designed to disqualify legislators or regulators with conflicts of interest, or limitations on the maximum size of corporations.

It has often been remarked that it is a hallmark of a profession to be self-regulating. In the case of the medical profession, the idea that the physician–patient relationship is fiduciary along with the belief that medicine is a service for healing and comfort rather than simply one commercial enterprise among others have buttressed the profession's claim that it can be trusted to regulate itself.

Until recently, it was widely assumed not only that the medical profession should regulate itself, but that it should also be chiefly responsible for regulating health care in general. This position rested on three main premises: (1) physicians and only physicians have the technical training and knowledge needed for informed control of their own professional activities, (2) physicians' professional activities are largely autonomous from other activities in health care, (3) the activities of other health-care professionals are almost exclusively dependent upon physicians' decision-making. The recognition that some of the most perplexing decisions concerning the use of medical treatments require complex moral, social, and legal judgments has undermined the first premise. (Decisions to forgo life-sustaining treatments for terminally ill or comatose patients are only the most obvious cases where medical judgment is not sufficient for guiding the physicians' own professional activities. These decisions require moral judgments because they rest on assumptions about the nature of individuals' rights and the quality and value of life.) The second and third premises also become dubious once it is seen that physicians' professional activities are increasingly dependent, not only upon decisions of other types of health-care professionals (such as biomedical engineers and laboratory and radiology technicians) who sometimes possess specialized knowledge which physicians lack, but also upon a complex web of institutional functions, including planning, investment, and allocation of resources.

Some of the same reasons that make it implausible to leave regulation of health care to physicians make it equally implausible to entrust it to corporations or groups of corporations. In particular, the vast commitment of public resources to health care grounds a legitimate public concern that the resources be used efficiently and fairly, and the growing list of ethical dilemmas concerning the uses of medical technology is no more amenable to the administrative expertise of the corporate manager than to the professional judgment of the physician. There is, however, one reason why the public is perhaps even less likely to tolerate self-regulation by health-care corporations than by the medical profession. If health care is perceived to be controlled by corporations—whether for-profit or non-profit—that are in many respects indistinguishable from other commercial enterprises, then the presumption in favor of self-regulation, which flourished under professional dominance, will erode. For if the key decision-makers in health care are perceived to be businessmen rather than fiduciaries committed to healing and comfort, an important barrier to societal regulation of all forms of health care will have fallen. Whether new forms of regulation will be needed to constrain the political influence of large health care corporations can only be determined after careful study not only of the impact that these organizations have on public policy, but also of the expected effectiveness of proposed regulations.

CONCLUSION

Any summary conclusion of our examination of the ethical issues in for-profit health care will inevitably oversimplify. The one continuing theme running through our analysis of the moral objections commonly voiced against for-profits is that those objections need to be both framed and evaluated more carefully than they usually are. In many instances these objections also rest on empirical claims for which the data are not yet available.

We have been generally critical of the argument that for-profits fail to do their fair share in providing health care to poor or unprofitable patients. That argument assumes that for-profits have special obligations to care for these patients, that a determinate content can now be given to that obligation, and that the obligation can be discharged without unreasonable sacrifice on the part of the for-profit. These assumptions are problematic. It is a mistake to focus on how for-profits exacerbate or ameliorate access. The debate could more profitably concentrate on the need for a coordinated societal response to the serious injustices in access to health care that now exist.

We have also been skeptical of the claim that for-profits represent unfair competition for nonprofits, though for-profits may have possible adverse effects on charitable motivations and a sense of community. We have again been critical of a common objection to for-profits, that they wrongly treat health care as a commodity rather than a right. It is only the view that all persons should have one *single* level of health care, not the recognition of a right to an adequate level of health care, that is incompatible with market provision of health care by for-profit institutions.

The arguments in each of the first three sections of the chapter ultimately raise deeper issues of great importance about the just distribution of health care that go beyond the for-profit/nonprofit debate. We have argued that potential adverse effects on medical education, like those on access, may indeed be worrisome, but the data on them are at this point very limited and they probably arise more from other forces such as cost-containment efforts than from for-profits. Similarly, although the possibility that a small number of large health-care corporations may come to wield disproportionate influence on public policy is a serious matter for concern and vigilance, it would be a mistake to assume that the potential for political abuse of economic power exists only with for-profit corporations, rather than with large institutions generally.

We believe that perhaps the most serious ethical concern with the growth of for-profits is their potential adverse effects on the physician–patient relationship and on the quality of care. Here too, potential conflicts of interest between patient and provider are not new. Indeed, they are fundamental to the physician–patient relationship in either for-profit or nonprofit settings. Moreover, other powerful forces besides the growth of for-profits, in particular cost-containment efforts and increased competition, are impinging on the physician–patient relationship. But the importance of the patient's trust in his physician, and the fragile balance between the physician's commitment to serve the patient and his natural concern with his own interests, give reason for serious continuing attention to this potential effect of for-profits.

6

MANAGED CARE: RATIONING WITHOUT JUSTICE, BUT NOT UNJUSTLY

Allen Buchanan

INTRODUCTION

Three ethical criticisms of managed care are often voiced: (1) by "skimming the cream" of the patient population, managed care organizations fail to discharge their obligations to improve access, or at least, to not worsen it; (2) managed care organizations engage in rationing, thereby depriving patients of care to which they are entitled; and (3) by pressuring physicians to ration care, managed care organizations interfere with physicians' fulfillment of their fiduciary obligations to provide the best care for each patient. This article argues that each of these criticisms is misconceived. The first rests on the false assumption that the health-care system includes a workable division of responsibility regarding access that assigns obligations concerning access to managed care organizations. The second and third criticisms wrongly assume that we in the United States have taken the first step toward assuring equitable access to care for all, articulating a standard for what counts as an "adequate level of care" to which all are entitled. These three misguided criticisms obscure the most fundamental ethical flaw of managed care: the fact that it operates in an institutional setting within which no connection can be made between the activity of rationing and the basic requirements of justice.

Originally published in *Journal of Health Politics, Policy and Law*. Vol. 23, No. 4, August 1998.

ETHICAL CRITICISMS OF MANAGED CARE

Managed care, the latest manifestation of efforts to privatize health care, is often passionately criticized on *ethical* grounds.[1] The ethical criticisms most frequently voiced are these: (1) by "skimming the cream" of the patient population, managed care organizations fail to discharge their obligations to improve (or at least not to worsen) the access problem; (2) in order to contain costs, managed care organizations engage in rationing techniques that withhold some types of beneficial care and that reduce the quality of care, depriving patients of care to which they are entitled; and (3) by pressuring physicians to ration care, managed care organizations interfere with physicians fulfilling their professional fiduciary obligation to provide the best care for each patient (Rodwin 1993, pp. 135–53; Council 1995; Emanuel and Dubler 1995; Spece, Shimm, and Buchanan 1996b, pp. 1–11).

I shall argue that each of these allegations is radically misconceived. The first criticism is misconceived because it rests on a false assumption: that the health-care system within which managed care operates includes a workable division of responsibility for achieving access to care for all, and that this division of responsibility assigns obligations concerning access to managed care organizations. The second and third criticisms are misguided because they wrongly assume that we in the United States have taken the first step toward ensuring equitable access to care for all, namely, articulating a standard for what counts as the "adequate level" or "decent minimum" of care to which all are entitled. Because the current U.S. system provides no basis for assigning obligations concerning access to managed care organizations, these organizations cannot be said to violate any obligations when they act in ways that reduce access. Since no authoritative standard has been determined for what constitutes the types and quality of care to which everyone could be said to be entitled, complaints that patients are treated unethically when they are denied care or when they receive care of less than the highest quality are groundless. As there is no authoritative standard for the care to which everyone is entitled, there is no benchmark for determining what the physician's fiduciary obligation to the patient is, once we acknowledge that in any system in which resources are not infinite, physicians cannot be expected to provide all of the highest quality care that is of any net benefit.

The three misguided criticisms stated earlier obscure the most fundamental ethical flaw of managed care: The fact that it operates in an institutional setting in which no connection can be made between the activity of rationing and the requirements of justice.

WHAT MANAGED CARE IS

For our purposes a simple characterization of managed care will suffice. A managed care organization *combines* health-care *insurance* and the *delivery* of a broad range of integrated health-care services for *populations* of plan enrollees, financing the services *prospectively* from a predicted, limited budget. At present the following cost-containment techniques are often identified with managed care: (1) payment limits (e.g., diagnosis-related groupings [DRGs] for Medicare hospital fees); (2) requirement of preauthorization for certain services (e.g., surgeries); (3) the use of primary care physicians as "gatekeepers" to control referral to specialists; (4) so-called de-skilling (using less highly trained providers for certain services than was customary during the pre-managed care, third-party fee-for-service era); and (5) financial incentives for physicians to limit utilization of care (e.g., year-end bonuses or holdbacks of payments that physicians receive only if they do not exceed specified utilization limits). In addition, managed care increasingly employs data from outcome (efficacy) studies to develop practice guidelines and for the ongoing assessment and refinement of diagnostic services and treatment services.

THE HISTORICAL RATIONALE FOR MANAGED CARE

Managed care is the result of a "payers' revolt" against the alarming escalation in the cost of health care in the United States under the third-party, fee-for-service system. The payers include employers in the private sector who provide health-care benefits for their employees, the federal government in the Medicare program, and federal and state governments in Medicaid. The initial stages of the managed care revolution occurred in the private sector, but government has begun to try to curb the increases in its health-care costs by utilizing the cost-containment measures developed in the private sector. For example, there are efforts to encourage Medicare and Medicaid patients to join health maintenance organizations (HMOs). Some analysts predict that the only solution to the projected severe underfunding of Medicare, as the population ages and the workforce shrinks, is to enroll all or most Medicare patients in managed care organizations.

It is extremely important to emphasize that the transition to managed care was primarily an effort at cost containment by the corporate purchasers of health care. Employers reached a point at which they were no longer willing to keep paying for services for their employees while the percentage of the gross domestic product (GDP) devoted to health care climbed toward 15 percent and the proportion of the cost of producing their goods and services devoted to paying premiums for their employees steadily rose.

In other words, the motivation for moving to managed care on the part of those whose efforts actually brought it about had nothing to do with addressing what might be called *the primary access problem*. By the primary access problem. I mean the fact that over 40 million people in the United States lack secure access to anything other than emergency care because they have no private health-care insurance and are not covered by any government program.

The only plausible—though somewhat tenuous and uncertain—connection between the payers' revolt that produced managed care and the primary access problem is this: By reducing the rate at which the cost of health care was rising, managed care may be preventing the access problem from worsening, by making insurance continue to be affordable for most of those who are now lucky enough to be insured. Even the most ardent defenders of managed care have not been able to make an empirical case for the claim that managed care will have any significant impact on, much less solve, the primary access problem.

Indeed, what is most remarkable about the vociferous popular debate about managed care—from an ethical point of view—is that the issue of access for the uninsured seems to have dropped off the public's radar screen entirely. If the primary access problem is mentioned at all, what is said is this: Unless the cost escalation is curbed, there is no hope of extending access to the uninsured; and managed care is the only realistic means of curbing the cost spiral.

This latter claim is astonishing, if it is understood as contributing in any way to the *justification* for the transition to managed care, in that it overlooks a simple but enormously important fact: There is simply no reason to expect that whatever cost savings do result from managed care will be used to make a significant contribution at all to ameliorating the primary access problem. As will become clearer as the analysis proceeds, we should not expect managed care cost savings to contribute to ameliorating the primary access problem because managed care has developed in a system in which there is (1) no social consensus on, or authoritative political determination of, what health-care services every citizen is entitled to (the "decent minimum" or "adequate level" of care) and (2) there are no institutional mechanisms capable of ensuring that resources saved through the cost-containment measures of managed care are utilized to ensure that all citizens have access to such an entitlement (Daniels 1986).

The chief reason why such institutional mechanisms are lacking is that the United States lacks something even more basic, something that virtually every other developed country has: a central government that takes ultimate responsibility for ensuring that every citizen has access to a decent minimum or adequate level of health care. Instead of this fundamental commitment, we in the United States have only an ideology: The naive belief (or cynical pretense) that everyone will have adequate access through a division of labor between government programs and private insurance, if both private and public entities fulfill their obligations. I argue, however, that without a politically effective societal consensus on what the right to health care includes, and without concrete institutional arrangements that embody a commitment to ensure that every citizen has access to the level of care included in the right, there is no reason to believe that the uncoordinated action of the private and public sectors will achieve a reasonable approximation of universal access.

WHY MANAGED CARE ORGANIZATIONS HAVE NO OBLIGATIONS OF JUSTICE TO ENSURE ACCESS

Although they seem oblivious to the fact, those who currently criticize managed care organizations for marketing strategies and benefit designs that "skim the cream" of the patient population and exclude those with costly health conditions are simply repeating a fundamental mistake that the opponents of the first wave of privatization made a decade ago. In the mid-1980s, privatization of health care in the United States took the form of the rapid growth of for-profit hospitals. Critics complained that for-profit hospitals were shunning uninsured or underinsured patients and that this had the effect of dumping such patients on already financially precarious public hospitals, thereby worsening the access problem.

That such behavior on the part of for-profits has made it harder for public hospitals to serve the medically indigent is probably true. But it does not follow that in behaving in this way, for-profit hospitals are violating their obligations to help ensure access to care. They would only be guilty of violating obligations to help ensure access if they had such obligations, but they do not.

To understand why they do not, it is important to draw a distinction between two models for how access to a decent minimum or adequate level of health care for all might be achieved through the combined operation of the private sector and government entities (Buchanan 1992, pp. 235–50).[2] According to the first model, a private health-care insurance market is expected to provide adequate care at affordable prices for a substantial portion (perhaps even a majority) of the total population, and government recognizes and acts on a commitment to fill whatever gaps in access remain. Private commercial entities, whether they are for-profit hospitals or managed care organizations, have no obligations to help ensure access. They are under no obligation to provide care that is not profitable for them to provide.

According to the second model, there is an institutionally prescribed *division of obligations to secure access* between the private and public sectors. Political processes at the highest level assign private-sector entities determinate obligations regarding access. In the first model, the role of government is to fill whatever gaps in access remain after the market has done its job, but commercial entities in the private sector have no obligations regarding access.[3] In the second model, private-sector entities are not simply agents in the market; they have special obligations to act in ways they would not act if they simply acted as agents in the market.

Those who charge that managed care organizations are violating ethical obligations when they engage in practices that exclude especially costly patients from coverage altogether (and thereby increase the financial strain on public providers) are implicitly assuming that in doing so, these organizations are not bearing their fair share of the burden of securing access for all. But this last assumption would only be true if the United States had adopted the second model, that is, if it actually had an institutional division of labor that assigned obligations concerning access to private commercial entities. It does not. Nor does it have a government that is willing to play the gap-filling role required by the first model (nor, apparently, is there a majority of citizens that is willing and able to demand that their representatives act so as to make government play that role).

In the absence of a political assignment of obligations to private-sector entities such as for-profit hospitals or managed care organizations, there is no more reason to assume that such entities have obligations regarding access than there is to assume that grocers have obligations to supply the poor with food or that home builders are obligated to furnish free housing (Brock and Buchanan 1986, pp. 224–49). It will not do to say that health care is unique. Food and shelter are also essential for life.

Of course, for-profit entities, like grocers, home builders, and anyone who has the resources to help the needy without excessive cost to themselves, may have what moral theorists traditionally have called "imperfect" obligations of charity (Buchanan 1987). Such obligations, unlike obligations of justice, are said to be indeterminate, with a large area of discretion for the benefactor to choose whom he will benefit and in what manner, and always within the limits of the provision that doing so is not "excessively costly." Under conditions of increasingly vigorous competition, private-sector commercial entities can plausibly argue that engaging in charity toward those who lack access may be an excessive cost. In other words, in a competitive environment, there is a predictable tendency for private agents to construe their imperfect obligations less and less generously. The simple but important point is that without an authoritative political assignment of determinate obligations of access to private-sector commercial entities, and without some effective system of sanctions to ensure each entity that its competitors are fulfilling their prescribed duties, we cannot say that the activities of managed organizations deprive anyone of what they are entitled to as a matter of the right to health care.

Moreover, unless a mixed private–public health-care system is an instance of one of the two models sketched earlier, there is no realistic hope that the combined operation of the public and private sectors will result in access to an "adequate level" or "decent minimum" of health care for all. The natural operation of a competitive market in health-care insurance (especially if, as in the United States, insurance is largely employment-based) will result in some of those who most need health care not being able to get it in the market. And if government fails to fulfill the gap-filling role, as it has in the United States, then some, perhaps many, will be without access to even a decent minimum of care.

It should be clear at this point that the chief *conceptual* mistake that prevents the U.S. public and policy-makers from dealing with the primary access problem (and from even framing the ethical issues of managed care in a coherent and fruitful way) is that we overlook the unpleasant fact that our system is neither an instance of model one nor of model two. My point is not that we have an access problem due to a purely conceptual mistake. Rather, what I am suggesting is that this conceptual mistake aids and abets both our unwillingness to confront the primary access problem and our confusion about what the real ethical problems of current arrangements are. This is nowhere clearer than in the muddled terms with which the debate over rationing in managed care is framed. The lack of (1) a societal agreement on what the entitlement to health care includes and of (2) concrete institutional arrangements for seeing that all have access to a decent minimum of care through the combined operations of the private and public sectors (the implementation of either model one or model two of a mixed private–public system) undercuts the very assumptions under which the current ethical debate about rationing in managed care is conducted. This fundamental point will become clearer as we examine the controversy over rationing in managed care.

RATIONING IN MANAGED CARE: RATIONING FOR COST CONTAINMENT, NOT FOR JUSTICE

We have just seen that by acting competitively, managed care organizations do not violate obligations of justice, even if their behavior worsens the access problem by shifting costs to public sector providers or by refusing to enroll individuals who would be very costly to treat. Frequently, however, a different allegation concerning rationing is leveled at managed care organizations: They are accused of acting unethically in their rationing practices toward those whom they *do* serve.

WHY THE DENIAL OF CARE IN MANAGED CARE IS NOT SUBSTANTIVELY UNJUST

There are three chief ways in which rationing practices may be unethical. Rationing practices are (1) *contractually unjust* if they violate the special rights of enrollees that are generated through the contract offering the plan; (2) *procedurally unjust* if there is discrimination (say, on the basis of sex or race), if the rules for limiting care are applied inconsistently, or if there are no reasonable institutional mechanisms for informing patients that rationing choices are being made and giving them opportunities to appeal decisions they believe to be unfair; and (3) *substantively unjust* if the principles of rationing upon which they rely are themselves unjust, even when applied consistently, without discrimination, and under conditions of adequate disclosure and due process.

Sometimes the complaint about managed care rationing practices is that they are contractually or procedurally unjust, but often it is stated or implied that they are substantively unjust. For example, there has been considerable public outrage (and several lawsuits) in response to the fact that some patients who might have benefited from autologous bone marrow transplant have been denied this treatment for breast cancer by their HMOs. In some cases, the complaint has been that denial of such care violates contractually generated rights. However, even here there is often the suggestion that contractual language concerning the provision of "comprehensive care" is to be interpreted ultimately by reference to the notion of an adequate level or decent minimum of care to which the individual is supposed to be entitled. The complaint about denial of care is then based on the assumption that the care denied falls within the adequate level or decent minimum to which each individual is entitled and that ultimately defines the "comprehensive care" that HMOs promise to deliver.

If such complaints about denial of care are understood as charges of substantive injustice, as opposed to procedural or contractual injustice, then they must rest upon an assumption that the form of treatment being denied is included in the array of services to which the individual is entitled, independently of the particular nature of the plan contract. But we have already seen that at present in the United States there is no authoritative standard for defining the scope of this entitlement. For this reason an individual who is denied some service cannot plausibly argue that the rationing practice of the organization commits an injustice by excluding a service that ought to be immune from exclusion. In the absence of an authoritative determination of what is included in the adequate level or decent minimum, virtually *no* service is in principle immune from exclusion.

It would be quite different if there were an authoritative political determination or even a rough but deep societal consensus on what the adequate level or decent minimum includes. Then disputes about whether a particular service may be denied would in principle be resolvable. But in the United States we have not settled on a standard because we have not been forced to do so as a prerequisite of trying to implement a commitment to provide universal access. Yet in the absence of a societal agreement about what services the individual is entitled to, we cannot say that a managed care organization rations unfairly when it refuses to pay for a particular form of care (unless doing so is contractually or procedurally unjust).

So, unless they are construed narrowly as disagreements about contractual rights or procedural injustice, charges that managed care wrongs patients by denying certain services are simply muddled.

This is not to say that procedural injustices and contractual injustices do not occur, or that when they do they are not serious ethical problems. Marketing schemes can oversell a plan, misleading potential enrollees about what they can reasonably expect by way of coverage. And both the contract between the payer and the managed care organization and the policy upon which the individual relies may be ambiguous or even intentionally misleading. Moreover, a fair interpretation of a contract or a policy must take into account the historical cultural context in which it exists, and it can be argued that until very recently, the U.S. context encouraged insured individuals to believe that they were entitled to "everything." Nevertheless, the further we proceed into the "managed care revolution," the less convincing it is to claim that enrollees have a reasonable expectation that there will be no limits on care. If contracts and policies are reasonably clear, if rationing policies are applied in a nondiscriminatory way, if marketing does not misrepresent coverage, and if a reasonable person should know that managed care means limits, there is no basis for inferring that injustice has occurred simply because a patient does not get some beneficial care or receives care of less than the highest quality. Efforts at ethical reform within the managed care system should focus on procedural and contractual injustices and on educating patients so that their expectations are realistic, not based on imagined substantive injustices.

WHY THE REDUCTION OF QUALITY OF CARE IN MANAGED CARE IS NOT IN ITSELF UNETHICAL

The situation is similar in the case of allegations that managed care is undermining the *quality* of care. The lack of an institutional commitment to securing access to an adequate level of care for all deprives us of any rational basis for saying that anyone is *wronged* by reductions in quality for the sake of cost containment, so long as contractual rights are respected and procedural justice is observed. For example, frequently there are complaints that managed care organizations are reducing the quality of care by so-called de-skilling—using less highly trained individuals to perform certain services (e.g., having nurses do some tasks physicians have customarily performed or using social workers to do what psychiatrists used to do). Or, to take another common example, there are complaints that some HMOs are using cheaper medications that have more side effects or that are less efficacious than the best drugs available for the condition in question (e.g., using older generation tricyclic antidepressants rather than the newer serotonin-uptake inhibitors).

Using a drug that is less efficacious or that has more side effects or using a provider with lesser skills may indeed reduce the quality of care. But it does not follow that there is anything unjust or in any way unethical about doing so. Rationing practices that reduce quality of care are only unethical if they are contractually unjust, procedurally unjust, or substantively unjust. Suppose for a moment that neither of our two examples of rationing-produced reductions in care quality involve violations of contractual obligations or of the requirements of procedural justice. Is there anything unethical per se about reducing quality to reduce costs?

The answer must be no, unless one of two assumptions is granted: (1) that every patient is entitled to the highest quality care that is technically feasible, regardless of cost; or (2) that these particular reductions in quality result in the care provided falling below the level of quality that is included in the adequate level or decent minimum of care to which every individual is entitled.

At this stage of the debate over health-care costs, the falsity of the first assumption should be obvious to everyone. Providing the highest quality of care for everyone all the time is neither politically feasible nor required by any reasonable theory of just health care. Only if one denies that resources are scarce (or fails to understand that there are other goods in life besides health care) would one assume that everyone is entitled to the highest quality of care that is technically feasible, without regard to cost.

So, if lower quality care is substantively unjust, it must be because it falls below the adequate level or decent minimum of care to which all are entitled. But as we have already seen, there is no societal consensus on what this is and political processes have yielded no authoritative determination of it. Of course, there may be some services that are so inexpensive and so efficacious in preventing or curing serious diseases that we can assume that they would be included in any reasonable societal consensus. But many reductions in quality wrought by managed care organizations will not fall within this uncontroversial core. For these latter quality reductions, there is no basis for saying that the organizations that effect them are acting wrongly, or that their enrollees are being deprived of something to which they are entitled.

WHY THE DENIAL OF CARE AND LOWER QUALITY ARE NOT INCOMPATIBLE WITH ETHICAL BEHAVIOR ON THE PART OF PROVIDERS

It is often said that participation in the rationing practices of managed care is incompatible with ethical behavior on the part of physicians (and nurses, etc.). The most vigorous critics seem to assume that it is unethical for physicians to provide anything other than all services that are expected to be of any benefit for the patient at the highest level of quality that is technically feasible.

This assumption, however, is indefensible. In any system, but especially in a system in which coverage is primarily financed by private employers, there must be limits on which services are provided and on the quality with which they are delivered. It is simply wishful thinking to assume that cost containment in managed care can succeed in controlling health-care costs without having a negative impact on coverage and quality. (It is worth noting that some managed care organizations have explicitly acknowledged that reductions in quality are sometimes justified by emphasizing that they seek to maximize *value*, where value is understood as a function of quality and cost.)

So, in itself the fact that managed care rationing denies services and lowers quality provides no basis for saying that these organizations are requiring physicians to act unethically. In the absence of an authoritative standard for what counts as adequate care, such behavior on the part of physicians would only be unethical if physicians were obligated to provide all beneficial care and to provide only care of the highest quality. Of course, some assume that physicians have this obligation simply by virtue of being medical professionals. But if a realistic appreciation of the need to control costs in health care is to count for anything, such an understanding of the role of physicians must be rejected. There is every reason to believe that effective cost containment can only be achieved if physicians refrain from insisting on the highest quality care that is expected to be of any benefit, regardless of costs and regardless of the ratio of costs to benefits.

If this is so, then the alternatives are stark but simple: Either we hold fast to the assumption that medical professionalism is incompatible with physicians providing anything less than the highest quality care in every case, but must conclude that a system that effectively controls costs has no place for medical professionals; or we rethink our conception of medical professionalism to make room for the idea that providing less than the highest quality of care is sometimes acceptable.

The former alternative is unacceptable. There is no reason why cost control in our health-care system should be held hostage to an indefensible "essentialist" conception of medical professionalism that, in effect, says that a physician cannot be a true physician or an ethical physician unless he ignores the fact that resources are scarce.[4] None of this is to deny that physicians face serious ethical challenges in managed care. It is only to reject the groundless claim that whenever physicians do not provide all beneficial care or provide less than the highest quality care, they act wrongly. Once this point is appreciated, it becomes clear just how debilitating the absence of a standard for adequate care is. In the absence of such a standard for what patients are entitled to there is no answer to the question, "Which denials of care and how much reduction in quality is acceptable?" And there is no answer to the question: "When does the physician's participation in efforts at cost containment violate his or her fiduciary obligation to the patient?"

A disclaimer is in order at this point. My contention is not that no standards of ethical behavior apply to the actions of physicians in managed care, nor that everything physicians are asked to do by managed care organizations is ethically permissible. I have only argued that the fact that physicians do not provide potentially beneficial care, or that they provide care that is not of the highest quality, does not in itself constitute a breach of their obligations. There are other ways that physicians can go wrong ethically in the managed care environment, however. For example, if physicians encourage their patients to believe that they are acting solely as advocates for the patient's best interests, but in fact make decisions that do not maximize the patient's interests, then they act wrongly. Similarly, given the pervasive and long-standing cultural expectation that physicians are to give their patients all reasonable information about alternatives for treatment, "gag clauses" that prohibit physicians from informing their patients of potentially beneficial treatments available elsewhere that are not provided by the patient's managed care organization are unethical.

THE POVERTY OF ETHICAL THEORY

At this point it might be objected that even if there is no societal consensus or authoritative political determination of what constitutes an adequate level of care, and no existing institutional division of responsibilities for access, an appropriate conception of the moral right to health care can tell us what we need to know. The problem, however, is that no available general ethical theory or theory of justice in health care can in itself tell us what the appropriate division of labor between private and public entities for securing equitable access to health care is in a particular society at a particular point in its history. Empirical premises are needed—premises predicting what will actually work and which concrete institutional arrangements will effectively implement the right to health care, as the various theories understand this right. Moreover, there is no reason to believe that there is only one set of institutional arrangements that would secure access for all. What is needed is not only a conception of justice but also a political choice among the feasible alternatives for implementing it (Health Care Study Group 1994; White 1995, pp. 290–91).

Similarly, no available general ethical theory or theory of justice in health care by itself can tell us what the concrete *content* of right to health care is for a particular society at a particular time. With the exception of libertarian theories (which deny that there is a right to health care), the most influential theories of distributive justice converge on the notion that the right to health care is a limited right—a right to a decent minimum or adequate level of care, not a right to all care that would be of any benefit (President's Commission 1983; Buchanan 1996a, pp. 349–51). However, none of these theories seems capable of articulating the content of this right with sufficient specificity to provide a basis for saying which denials of care and which reductions in quality of care fall below the adequate level, even if we could assume that we actually have an institutional division of obligations that assigns managed care organizations the task of providing an adequate level of care to their enrollees.

This point about the limitations of ethical theory can best be illustrated by reference to what many believe is the most thoroughly developed account of justice in health care, Norman Daniels's adaptation of Rawls's theory. According to Daniels, the right to health care is based on the right to equal opportunity. The distinctive contribution to equal opportunity that health care makes is to prevent, restore, or compensate for adverse departures from "normal species functioning" (Daniels 1985, pp. 26–31). Daniels's theory does give us some guidance in prioritizing various health-care services: generally speaking, those that are more effective in addressing the more serious adverse departures from normal species functioning are more important.

However, as I argued some time ago, and as Daniels now acknowledges, neither his theory of justice in health care nor Rawls's general theory of distributive justice can tell us how to prioritize among the needs of different individuals (Buchanan 1983; Daniels 1993). For example, these theories provide no answer to the question, "Should we devote all or most of our health-care resources to attempts to improve the conditions of those who are farthest from normal species functioning, or should some resources also be allocated for those whose departures from normal species functioning are not so serious?" In short, even the most systematic and best thought-out theory of the right to health care does not provide an answer to the question, "What is included in the adequate level or decent minimum of care to which all are entitled?"

It seems likely that ethical theory alone will not be able to provide a substantive account of what health care everyone is entitled to. Some ethical theories, such as Daniels's, may provide useful guidance on how to formulate an adequate level or decent minimum of care, but how generous the entitlement should be depends in part on the available resources in the society in question, and perhaps even on how much health care is generally valued compared to other goods. Above all, it is clear that in any pluralistic society there will be disagreements about the proper content of the right to health care that can only be resolved ultimately by procedurally just, democratic political processes, not by abstract theory. If this is so, then ethical theory alone cannot supply the standard by which we can judge whether rationing in managed care is substantively unjust, in the absence of sufficient political will and adequate political procedures for making that will effective. Without a societal commitment to a fairly concrete conception of the basic health-care entitlement, arrived at through fair political processes, and implemented through institutional arrangements that achieve a determinate division of responsibilities for ensuring that entitlement for all, ethical theory cannot tell us whether a particular denial of care wrongs the patient or whether a particular reduction in quality violates the physician's fiduciary obligation.

THE ILLUSION OF TECHNIQUE

In spite of the ethical complaints, managed care finds a number of supporters because it holds the promise of a technocratic solution to the problem of providing affordable, high-quality care. Managed care is not just a change in the structure of health-care organizations—it is an effort to reshape the very way in which medicine is practiced, making it more scientific by fostering greater reliance on population-based outcome studies to determine which treatment modalities are most effective. However, no amount of outcome data and no improvements in the efficiency of the organization and delivery of care can answer the question. "What is the decent minimum of care to which all are entitled?" This is an unavoidably ethical question. At most, reasoning about efficiency can tell us how best to achieve the decent minimum for all and can help us make informed judgments about how generous the minimum should be, in light of trade-offs for other socially desirable goods for which the same resources might be used.

Furthermore, to the extent that its techniques are rooted in cost–benefit or cost-effectiveness methodologies and focus on the health of populations, managed care is likely to exhibit an uncritical and unarticulated bias toward purely consequentialist (utilitarian) decision-making. But purely consequentialist decision-making can only reveal what maximizes utility for a given group (whether it is society as a whole or the enrollees of a managed care organization); and maximizing utility for the group may come at the price of depriving some individuals of even the most basic goods. The enthusiasm for technique that characterizes managed care thus not only fails to address the fundamental issue of what the standard for care should be; it may even encourage modes of reasoning that tacitly legitimate rationing practices that compromise the commitment to treating each individual as a legitimate subject of entitlements.

CONCLUSION

I began this essay by noting that the problems of managed care seem to have eclipsed the primary access problem in the United States—the fact that over 40 million people lack health insurance (along with at least another 20 million who are radically underinsured). Before we become excessively preoccupied with the ethical dilemmas of managed care, we should pause to note that all the parties to the controversy over managed care are the "haves"—the insured population that worries about denial of beneficial care, the payers who want to control costs, and the providers who fear losing their professional autonomy and forfeiting patient trust. Conspicuously absent from this triad are the millions of uninsured. If my analysis is correct, the "haves" cannot so easily escape the "have nots"—that is, the ethics of managed care will remain a confused muddle of blame-shifting until the primary access problem is addressed. For until a societal consensus emerges on what forms of health care at what level of quality all are entitled to, and until an authoritative and realistic division of responsibilities for access is institutionalized in our mixed private–public system, the ethical debate about rationing and quality of care *in* managed care will continue to be confused and sterile.

The ethical indignation over managed care, though sometimes conceptually confused, is both understandable, and—if properly redirected—potentially a force for progress. Given the expectations that the third-party fee-for-service system engendered, it is not surprising that people should tend to assume that if they have health-care insurance, they are entitled to "the best care," and that they should be deeply troubled by some of the reductions in coverage that are now occurring. If these negative sentiments can be informed by a recognition that the problem, ultimately, lies with the system, rather than with particular organizations or agents within it, they may eventually motivate systemic reform.

Instead of blaming managed care organizations for failing to fulfill obligations concerning access and quality that they do not have, excoriating them for giving patients less care than they are entitled to when what they are entitled to is wholly unclear, and accusing them of causing physicians to fail to discharge alleged fiduciary obligations that are incompatible with any reasonable hope of cost control, perhaps we should focus our energies on the primary access problem. What is most ethically problematic about managed care is not that it denies beneficial care, reduces quality, and pressures physicians to act as rationers. What is most ethically problematic about managed care is the system of which it is a part, for whose most basic ethical flaw it provides, and can provide, no remedy.

7

TRUST IN MANAGED CARE ORGANIZATIONS

Allen Buchanan

Two basic criticisms of managed care are that it erodes patient's trust in physicians and subjects physicians to incentives and pressures that compromise the physician's fiduciary obligation to the patient. In this article, I first distinguish between status trust and merit trust, and then argue (1) that the value of status trust in physicians is probably overrated and certainly underdocumented; (2) that erosion of status trust may not be detrimental if accompanied by an increase in well-founded merit trust; and (3) that under conditions of managed care the physician's commitment to traditional medical ethics cannot serve as an adequate basis for merit trust. Next, drawing on an analogy between managed care organizations and polities, I argue that (4) the most appropriate basis for merit trust in managed care is a conception of organizational legitimacy that includes procedural justice, empowerment of constructive criticism within the organization, and organizational accommodation of the noninstrumental commitment to patient's well-being that is distinctive of medical professionalism. I then explore the conditions necessary for robust competition for merit trust among managed care organizations and indicate the kinds of public policies needed to facilitate such competition. Finally, I show how the account of organization-based merit trust can accommodate the special fiduciary obligation of medical professionals, without indulging in the delusion that it is the physician's fiduciary obligation always to provide all care that is expected to be of any net benefit to the patient.

UNCRITICAL LAMENTATIONS OF LOST TRUST

The Goal: Optimal, Not Maximal Trust

It is a commonplace to complain that managed care is eroding patients' trust in physicians. Patients understandably may feel that managed care organizations' cost-control policies, especially when these include financial risk sharing with physicians, create powerful pressures that can result in physicians' doing what is good for the organizations rather than what is best for their patients.[1] It is also common to assume that this loss of trust is a bad thing. A patient's trust in her physician, we are told, has several benefits: It reduces the patient's anxiety (especially at times when the patient's illness, or fear of illness, makes her highly vulnerable); it can have a therapeutic effect; and it lowers decision costs for the patient because the trusting patient feels less compelled to consider alternative caregivers or to gather information to evaluate her physician's recommendations.

Simply to cite benefits of trust is inadequate, of course, because trust can have costs as well. Misplaced trust can result in iatrogenic injury or death, in both over- and underutilization of care, and in unnecessary expense. So a sound argument for the importance of maintaining patient's trust in physicians not only must provide good evidence for the benefits of trust (something that is rarely done), but also must carefully identify the costs of trust. A recent study, according to which there are 98,000 deaths a year resulting from medical mistakes, indicates that it may be an error simply to *assume* that the benefits of trust in physicians exceed the costs (Kohn, Corrigan, and Donaldson 2000).

Given that trust carries costs as well as benefits, what is needed is to achieve an optimal level of trust—a level at which the greatest *net* benefit accrues, not the maximal level of trust possible, because maximal trust will presumably carry unacceptable costs (Buchanan 1996b, pp. 125–27). The first step in evaluating the role of trust in managed care would be to do what has not been done: to document adequately the benefits *and* the costs of trust in physicians and to compare them.

I cannot undertake that daunting empirical task in this discussion. Instead, I will focus on a distinction between two types of trust that has largely been overlooked in the literature and then ask which type is most important in managed care and what sort of managed care organization would deserve this type of trust.[2]

Status Trust versus Merit Trust

Commentators who assume that trust in physicians is waning typically fail to consider the possibility that there is more than one type of trust and that loss of one type of trust may not mean loss of another type. It is important to distinguish between status trust and merit trust. Status trust attaches to members of a profession simply by virtue of their being identified as members of that profession. At least until recently, members of the clergy, physicians, and perhaps even teachers have enjoyed considerable status trust. If a person is identified as a member of an appropriate status group, he or she enjoys a presumption of trustworthiness quite apart from any perceived merit as an individual.[3] Long before managed care became a major force in health care delivery, Paul Starr (1982, pp. 379–92) noted that physicians in the United States enjoy less status trust than they formerly did (though he did not use the term "status trust"). So, even if the erosion of status trust has been augmented by managed care, it did not begin there.

Merit trust, in contrast, is trust that attaches to an individual because of his or her perceived merit, where merit is based on the individual's capacities and behavior. In the case of physicians, there are several dimensions of merit, technical competence, and commitment to patient welfare being the most obvious.[4]

Merit trust can either be *primary* or *derivative*. Merit trust in a particular physician is primary if the patient believes the physician is trustworthy because of her belief or perceptions about the competence and commitment of the physician as evidenced by the *physician's* behavior.[5] Merit trust is derivative if the patient believes the physician is trustworthy because of her belief or perceptions about the quality of the *organization* within which the physician practices.

Once these distinctions are noted, the claim that managed care is eroding trust appears to be too broad to be useful or testable. One must consider the possibility that managed care is eroding status trust, but also the possibility that it is making possible a shift toward a greater role for merit trust, especially derivative merit trust—trust of physicians derived from trust in the organizations in which they practice. One also must consider the possibility that such a shift would be, on balance, a good thing.

WHY STATUS IS NOT AN ADEQUATE BASIS FOR TRUST IN THE MANAGED CARE CONTEXT

Rational Trust

Like any kind of trust, status trust in physicians can be warranted or unwarranted. From the standpoint of the individual who presumes an individual is trustworthy simply because she is a physician, the rational bases of status trust may be unapparent or only dimly perceived. But to the extent that status trust in physicians is rational, it must be based on evidence that the process of selection, training, and acculturation for physicians equips them not only to be technically competent, but also to honor their commitment to patient welfare in the actual context in which they practice medicine. Increasingly that context is managed care. It is an interesting question whether recent revelations of the magnitude of medical errors will erode status trust in physicians to the extent that status trust is based on confidence in the technical competence of physicians as physicians. My concern here, however, is whether, given the selection, training, and acculturation processes for physicians, it is rational for patients to trust physicians, simply as physicians, to honor their commitment to patient welfare in the context of managed care.

If it is to be rationally grounded, status trust in managed care physicians as professionals who honor the commitment to patient welfare must be based on the following proposition:

Traditional medical ethics provides adequate resources for coping with the most important ethical issues that arise in managed care.

I shall argue that there is good reason to believe that this proposition T is false and, consequently, that status trust in managed care physicians, at least insofar as it focuses on the ethical behavior of physicians in that practice context, is not rationally grounded.

There are two chief areas of ethical concern in managed care. The first, and most obvious, is the ethics of rationing. "Rationing" here means withholding, on the grounds of cost, care that is reasonably expected to be of some net benefit for the patient.[6]

The second, less obvious area of ethical concern may be called the ethics of exit, voice, and loyalty (borrowing the title of Albert O. Hirshman's book [1970]). The ethics of exit, voice, and loyalty encompasses the ethical choices that confront an individual who is a member of an organization when her organizational role or the organization's policy dictates behavior that the individual finds ethically objectionable, either according to general ethical principles she espouses, or because of her conception of the ethical responsibilities conferred by her professional identity.

Apart from simply complying and ignoring her ethical objections, the individual confronted with this opposition between conscience and organizational requirements can respond in any of several ways: (1) leaving the organization (exit), (2) conscientious refusal to participate in the implementation of the policy or decision she deems unethical (the organizational analogue of civil disobedience), (3) constructive criticism of the policy (voice), (4) covert subversion of the policy (sabotage), or (5) whistle-blowing (going outside the organization to call the wrongdoing to the attention of the media and/or the legal authorities). Sound moral principles and sensitive moral judgment are needed to determine which response(s) is/are appropriate, and under which conditions.

Traditional medical ethics is singularly ill-equipped to provide substantive guidance in either of these two chief areas of ethical concern. It lacks resources for coping with the ethics of rationing because it denies the existence of scarcity;

it sheds little light on the ethics of exit, voice, and loyalty because it was developed for and takes as its paradigm a binary, non-organizational relationship between a single physician and a single patient.

Traditional medical ethics denies the existence of scarcity in the name of what it takes to be the constitutive ethical obligation of the medical professional: doing what is in the best interest of the patient. This fundamental obligation is understood in the context of a highly abstract and idealized picture of the setting in which the physician functions: The physician has a patient before her—only one patient—and knows what is in the patient's best medical interest. The physician's fiduciary obligation then is to do that which is medically best for this patient, as if there were no other patients and as if the cost of doing what is medically best for this patient were zero. Given this picture, allowing a treatment decision to be influenced by considerations of cost is assumed to be essentially contrary to the physician's most fundamental obligation. To the extent that this interest-maximizing conception of the physician's commitment to patient welfare is central to traditional medical ethics, the latter not only fails to provide guidance for the ethics of rationing, but also dismisses physician participation in rationing as an ethical impossibility.[7]

The same picture of the physician–patient relationship excludes guidance for the ethics of exit, voice, and loyalty because it portrays the physician as an isolated and fully autonomous individual, unconstrained by her role in an organization or by organizational policies. In a word, the physician is conceived as an agent with only one principal, rather than as an individual embedded in an organization that is understood as a complex web of principal–agent relationships (Buchanan 1996c).

If traditional medical ethics lacks the resources to cope with the two chief areas of ethical concern in managed care because it was not designed to guide individuals in organizations and denies the existence of scarcity, it is futile simply to exhort physicians to return to the traditional virtues of the physician. All that traditional medical ethics has to say about both areas of ethical concern is that the physician must "put the patient's interests first." The difficulty is that within the constraints of the traditional picture of the physician–patient encounter, this slogan gives no substantive guidance for how a physician can behave ethically in an environment in which not one patient but a population of patients are to be cared for within the constraints of a projected budget. Status trust, at least so far as it is grounded in the traditional medical ethics, is an unlikely candidate for trust in managed care.

Primary Merit Trust in Managed Care Physicians

At this point it might be argued that there is considerable evidence that regardless of whether status trust has eroded, many managed care patients sustain primary merit trust in their physicians. Especially when there are multiple contacts with the physician, patients tend to trust or not trust their physician depending upon whether she exhibits certain "caring behaviors." For example, physicians who maintain eye contact, do not interrupt patients, and who treat them as valuable sources of information about their own conditions may tend to be regarded as more trustworthy (Roter and Hall 1995; Mechanic and Meyer 2000).

It is almost certainly true that such "caring behaviors" have some value as indicators of the physician's commitment to patient's well-being. But there are two reasons to doubt that they can, by themselves, serve as an adequate basis for rational merit trust in physicians who practice in managed care. First, these behaviors can be engaged in deliberately for the sake of customer satisfaction, and some managed care organizations, like many commercial organizations that value customer satisfaction, may make it an explicit organizational policy to train their employees to enhance customer satisfaction by practicing these behaviors. But the appearance of caring is not the same as caring and satisfaction is not the same as trustworthiness. Second, and more important, even when such "caring behaviors" indicate a genuine commitment to the patient's well-being, it does not follow that this commitment will be effectively realized in the physician's treatment decisions. It may not if (1) the organizational structure and culture impose incentives on the physician that are of sufficient strength to override her concern for the patient's well-being when it comes to making decisions about utilization of care or if (2) organizational policy significantly narrows the range of situations in which physicians are free to act on their commitment to patient's well-being. Without information about these two factors, it would be less than rational for a patient to base her merit trust in the physician solely on the perception of "caring behaviors." To do so would be, in effect, to assume that the character of the organization has no significant effect on the physician's behavior.

Some contributors to the literature on the crisis of trust in managed care have suggested that trust can be maintained if organizational policies that impose financial risk on physicians create an "implicit rationing" arrangement in which there are no explicit rationing rules per se, so that patients do not perceive their physicians as rationers (Mechanic 1998, pp. 668–69). The limitations of this approach should now be apparent: It cannot provide a basis for well-founded, that is, rational, merit trust in physicians, even when combined with an accurate perception that the physician exhibits "caring behaviors." The patient's ignorance of organizational features that create incentives that may override the physician's concern for the patient or that limit the domain in which the physician can make decisions motivated by concern for the patient may contribute to trust, but it is no basis for well-founded trust.

TRUST FOUNDED ON LEGITIMACY

Given the limitations of status trust and of primary merit trust developed in ignorance of the ways in which organizational features can affect physician behavior, what is needed is a quite different basis for a quite different type of trust. I will present the broad outlines of a conception of the bases for merit trust in a managed care organization and then show how physicians working in such an organization might come to enjoy—and to deserve—merit trust derived in significant part from merit trust in the organization. The point is to develop a conception of well-founded merit trust, based on the conditions of managed care, rather than the picture of the physician–patient encounter that shapes traditional medical ethics.

I will argue that well-founded organizational merit trust must be grounded in an appropriate conception of the *legitimacy* of the organization, where legitimacy consists chiefly of three components: (1) The organization at least seriously reflects the most uncontroversial core elements of procedural justice, especially with respect to its rationing policies (Daniels and Sabin 1998); (2) The organization's structure and policies (a) empower its employees, including physicians, to voice constructive criticism of organizational policies and decisions and (b) clearly identify individuals in the organization who are held accountable for responding appropriately to constructive criticism; and (3) The organization's structure, policies, and culture (a) recognize the special responsibility of physicians as medical professionals who are assumed to have a noninstrumental commitment to patient's well-being and (b) reflect a proper appreciation of the distinctive technical expertise of physicians. Each of these three components of legitimacy will be explained in turn.

Procedural Justice

In general the case for relying primarily on procedural justice is strongest where there is no authoritative standard of substantive justice. The problem of rationing health care meets this description. The managed care revolution is based on a begrudging and belated recognition that adequate care or the care to which all (insured) individuals are entitled cannot be maximal care—that is, all the care, of the highest quality, that can reasonably be expected to be of any net benefit to the patient. However, there is no authoritative standard in our society for what level of care below the maximum counts as adequate care (Buchanan 1998). The most obvious explanation of why there is no authoritative societal standard (apart from the ingrained tendency to backslide into the delusion that adequate care is maximal care) is that our society has never had to develop one because it has never seriously attempted to provide universal access to care. Once the commitment to universal access is taken seriously—and once the fact of limited resources is acknowledged—the need to develop an authoritative standard for adequate care is inescapable.

It is not simply a societal authoritative standard for the content of "adequate care" that is lacking. At present no theory of distributive justice is capable of providing an operational standard for the health-care entitlement, though some theories can provide limited guidance (Buchanan 1984, pp. 62–64; Daniels 1996, pp. 317–32). Moreover, justice theorists disagree on even the most basic principles. In particular, contributors to the current debate over distributive justice are divided on the issue of "prioritism" (Parfit 1997; Norman 1999). Many theorists believe that the interests of the "worst-off" should be given special weight, but there is deep disagreement as to how much.

These theoretical disputes have direct consequences for concrete issues of rationing. For example, should we regard patients with advanced cancers that have been unresponsive to standard therapies as the "worst-off" and if so should society require managed care organizations to fund investigational "treatments" for them so long as there is even a very small probability of effectiveness? Different theories of justice may yield different answers to this and other questions about rationing. Furthermore, there is no guarantee that progress in theorizing about distributive justice will result in the articulation of a single standard for just health care. One possible outcome is an irreducible pluralism regarding distributive justice in health care. The most sophisticated theorizing about justice may only generate a range of reasonable candidates for what counts as the health-care entitlement, without being able to identify one uniquely just package of benefits. Given the lack of a societal authoritative standard for adequate care and given that ethical theory at present provides no such standard and may never do so, reliance upon procedural justice becomes all the more compelling.

Although there is also disagreement as to precisely what is included in the notion of procedural justice, there nevertheless is considerable consensus on the core elements. In the context of managed care, the following are plausible candidates for the main elements of procedural fairness regarding rationing policies:

1. Nondiscrimination—that is, the burden of cost-containment should not fall disproportionately on persons due to their race, ethnicity, gender, or age, or on the basis of other morally arbitrary characteristics;
2. Impartiality—that is, like cases should be treated alike; for example, physicians should not selectively bend or violate utilization limits for friends, colleagues, colleague's family members, and so forth;
3. Publicity of rules—that is, at least the most important rules defining rationing practices should be publicized to employees and enrollees;
4. Publicity of justifications for rules—that is, the organization should be prepared to provide public justifications for the priorities reflected in the rules that define its rationing practices;[8] and
5. Accessible, fair, and timely procedures for appeals of denial of coverage—fairness here often may require mechanisms for external review of contested denial-of-coverage decisions.

Items (3) and (4) warrant special comment. There are at least three distinct reasons why institutional policies affecting rationing should be publicized. First, as with all other institutional rules, publicity is a necessary condition for informed criticism, and informed criticism is necessary for continuing improvement. Second, some policies that affect rationing can create serious conflicts of interest for physicians and even if disclosure of conflicts of interest is not always a sufficient moral response to them, it is usually necessary. Legitimacy requires disclosure of financial incentives, especially risk sharing with physicians, not simply because the wrong incentives or the wrong magnitude of incentives can result in care that is clearly unacceptable according to any reasonable standard of adequacy, but also because the wrong incentives can undermine the effectiveness of even the best conceived, fairest policies. Third, as I shall argue later, a legitimate managed care organization is one that accommodates the distinctive fiduciary obligation of the physician, and disclosure of physician risk sharing is necessary if patients are to be able to judge whether this condition of legitimacy is met. Thus, condition (3) is to be understood as requiring disclosure of risk-sharing policies.

Condition (4) may seem to some an excessively demanding requirement. For one thing, the organizational leadership may be unable to agree on the principles that would best justify particular policies. It should not be assumed, however, that there must be a single principle or set of principles to serve as the justification of a particular policy. In some cases, the same policy will be supportable by more than one principle or set of principles, and, from the standpoint of compliance, this may even be a significant advantage, because different individuals may be motivated to comply for different reasons. More importantly, the attempt to supply a public justification of policies and decisions can have beneficial results. For example, suppose the organization justifies its decision to close a "well-baby" clinic in a particular neighborhood on the grounds that the clinic does not draw many patients and that the money used to sustain it could be better spent by establishing a hypertension screening program. Because the attempted justification includes certain putative factual premises (about the volume of patients at the well-baby clinic and the number of lives that will be saved by early detection and treatment of hypertension if the screening program is instituted), it can be challenged on empirical grounds, quite apart from any deep disagreement about values. Being based on the right "facts" is not sufficient for a rationing decision to be justifiable, but it is often necessary.

It will no doubt be objected that in some instances the distinction between procedural and substantive justice is blurry or hotly contested. For example, on some theories of distributive justice certain forms of age-related rationing will be discriminatory while according to other theories they will not.[9] My assumption is not that the requirements of procedural justice are either self-evident or uncontroversial, but only that there will often be more agreement on some of the broad outlines of procedural justice than on whether a rationing policy is consistent with providing all patients with the package of benefits that they are entitled to based on substantive principles of distributive justice. For example, individuals may differ as to whether the worst-off should be given priority or if so how much priority but nonetheless agree that a rationing policy that provides an effective regimen of cardiac drugs to whites but not to African Americans with the same health condition is discriminatory.

Organizational Empowerment for Constructive Criticism

This second component of organizational legitimacy overlaps with condition (5) of procedural justice, but extends beyond it. The structure of the organization, including not only its formal incentives and compensation schemes but also the more subtle ways in which organizational culture and practices reward or penalize members of the organization, must encourage constructive criticism of policy. There must be publicized and readily accessible channels for criticism, and the costs of criticism, including the time-costs, must be appropriately constrained.[10] Furthermore, it is not enough that every individual in the organization be empowered to criticize existing policies. In addition, some individuals must be held accountable for eliciting and responding to criticism as part of the process of ongoing assessment and improvement of policies.

Any well-functioning organization will include effective channels for constructive criticism. But there are additional reasons why managed care organizations should do so. I noted earlier that because this country has not made a sincere commitment to universal access, it has not faced the challenge of forging a societal consensus on what constitutes adequate health care. Managed care organizations that publicize their rationing policies and provide effective channels for criticizing them may contribute toward the process of evolving such a consensus, if only by making it clear that some rationing policies are unacceptable. Moreover, competition among managed care organizations on grounds of organizational merit may contribute further to a societal consensus on adequate care if it turns out that the winners in the competition for merit trust exhibit significant convergence in their rationing policies.

Organizational Accommodation of the Distinctive Character of Medical Professionalism

Procedural justice and empowerment of constructive criticism, though crucial, are not sufficient for legitimacy in managed care, especially if the legitimacy of the organization is to provide an important basis for rational merit trust in physicians.

In addition, the organization must reflect a proper appreciation of the distinctive character of the medical professional. First, organizational policies, especially policies regarding denial of care and appeals processes for denials, must give a proper place to the physician as a medical expert. In other words, policies should be explicitly designed so as to avoid situations in which nonmedical personnel will misapply their authority by acting as if they were qualified to make medical judgments. As in other complex organizations in which there is cooperation among persons with different kinds of expertise, the structure of the organization should reflect an awareness of the risk of what I elsewhere have called "expertise imperialism"—the tendency of experts to fail to recognize the bounds of their expertise (Buchanan 1996c, p. 426).

Second, the organization must carve out a niche for the physician as an individual who, by virtue of her professional identity, has a *noninstrumental* commitment to patient's well-being. This is not to say that physicians—and other health care providers, such as nurses—are the only professionals in managed care organizations. Administrators rightly may think of themselves as managerial professionals. Among the constituents of managerial professionalism are a commitment to efficiency, to stewardship of organizational resources, and to impartiality in the implementation of policies (Buchanan 1996c, p. 426). In addition, in organizations that provide services to the public, managerial professionals have a commitment to providing quality service for clients or customers. In most cases, discharging the obligation of organizational stewardship, as well as the manager's fiduciary obligations to the employer or stockholders, will require a commitment to client or customer service, but this will be a purely instrumental commitment, at least in the case of service organizations that are in a broad sense commercial. In other words, there is nothing in the concept of a managerial professional, at least in the sphere of what might broadly be called commercial organizations, that requires her to have a noninstrumental commitment to the well-being of those to whom the organization provides services.[11] Because managerial professionalism, unlike medical professionalism, does not include a noninstrumental commitment to service, the ethics of managed care cannot be reduced to even the most enlightened construal of business ethics.

It is essential to medical professionalism that the physician have a strong commitment to the well-being of her patients independently of any instrumental value of serving their interests and independently of any obligations she may have toward the organization or its principals. To warrant trust, and to confer derivative trust on the physicians it employs, a managed care organization must, therefore, create a space in which this defining commitment of medical professionalism can flourish. To do so, the organization must (1) assign to physicians a special responsibility for criticizing and helping to improve those organizational policies that affect patient welfare or impact patients' rights, and (2) empower physicians to be advocates for their patients. Both of these requirements flow from the distinctive noninstrumental service commitment of the medical professional.

To say that the physician should be an advocate for her patients is not to say that the physician must provide the best care that is technically feasible for each patient. We have already seen that literally maximizing each patient's interest is not possible in managed care, given that managed care must provide care to a population of patients within some predicted finite budget. Instead, proper advocacy will include other ways of expressing the noninstrumental commitment to patient's well-being and the recognition that this commitment, along with medical expertise, is the distinctive contribution that the physician brings to the organization. In particular, in cases in which organizational policy denies a patient care that can be reasonably expected to provide some net benefit, the physician should function as the patient's representative in the appeals process. Advocacy here encompasses at least two distinct functions: bearing a special responsibility either to present evidence that the treatment would be of exceptional benefit to this particular patient and that consequently it is necessary to make an exception to an generally appropriate rationing rule, or to challenge the appropriateness of the rationing rule itself. In addition, the physician must inform the patient if the care that is being denied is available elsewhere.[12] To enable the physician to honor her noninstrumental commitment to patient's well-being, the organization must not penalize the physician for being a vigorous advocate in appeals processes, or for disclosing that the care denied is available from other providers.

Managed Care Physicians as Critical Cooperators

I have already argued that it is a mistake to think that the traditional medical ethics can provide substantive guidance for physicians in managed care. What I now want to suggest is that the sort of ethics that is needed in managed care is one founded on a basic principle of reciprocity: If the organization reasonably approximates the conditions for legitimacy, then the physician has an obligation to try to be what might be called a "critical cooperator" in the organization.

If the managed care organization scores well on the three components of legitimacy (procedural justice, empowerment of constructive criticism, and accommodation of the distinctive commitment of medical professionalism), then being a saboteur, as opposed to a critical cooperator, is not a moral option for the physician. By a "saboteur," I mean a physician who covertly violates organizational policies on utilization, without voicing criticism through proper channels and without taking other appropriate steps to try to remedy what he takes to be unethical policies or decisions. The mentality of the saboteur is captured well in the following statement made by a specialist in internal medicine who admitted to me that he falsified diagnoses in order to secure coverage for his patients: "If they [the managed care policy makers] are going to practice medicine, then I'll practice insurance."

Sabotaging or gaming the organization's policies may be morally justifiable in some cases, just as covert noncompliance with the law sometimes is. But in general it is not morally justifiable if the organization provides fair and timely appeals procedures, encourages and supports constructive criticism of its policies and their applications in particular decisions, allows the physician to honor her distinctive noninstrumental commitment to patient well-being, and recognizes the physician's distinctive technical expertise.

The crucial point is that, in the context of a legitimate managed care organization, honoring the distinctive noninstrumental commitment to patient's well-being does not require fulfilling the traditional medical ethics requirement that the physician is to provide the best medical care for each patient all of the time. Furthermore, we now can appreciate that the traditional medical ethics focus on the slogan that the physician is always to act in the patient's best interest can be not only uninstructive in the context of managed care, but also destructive. Taken literally the slogan can serve as a rationalization for an abdication of responsibility on the part of the physician—an encouragement to be a saboteur rather than a critical cooperator. If the organization seriously approximates the conditions for legitimacy and evidences a capacity for and a commitment to improvement in legitimacy, the responsible physician will be a critical cooperator, contributing to the hard work of improvement rather than smugly acting the saboteur in the name of a commitment to maximizing the good of each patient—a commitment that she neither can nor should take literally.

Most managed care organizations will be neither clearly illegitimate nor perfectly legitimate. What is needed is a reconceptualization of the physician's ethics that encourages her to work to help bring the organization closer to legitimacy, rather than one that presumes at the outset that the organization's demand for the responsible use of resources for a population of patients is incompatible with an appropriate commitment to the individual patient.

It is worth emphasizing that the point is not that the physician should be an unconditional cooperator, but rather a critical cooperator. An account of the conditions for legitimacy is crucial, not just to ground the physician's duty to cooperate, but also to determine when she should not cooperate. Until an appreciation of the constituents of legitimacy is incorporated into medical ethics, physicians will lack a principled basis for deciding when they should and when they should not cooperate with organizational policy.[13]

This new ethics of managed care will require a cultural change in the medical profession. Many physicians have been acculturated to think that the good physician is an extreme individualist who is above "politics." Consequently, many would be offended by the political analogy I have used to develop the rationale for an ethics based on legitimacy rather than on the illusory ideal of maximizing the good of each patient. Nevertheless, unless physicians can replace or radically reinterpret their traditional ethics in a way that integrates it with a focus on organizational legitimacy, there will be little rational basis for trusting them in managed care. The legitimacy of managed care organizations will depend on how well physicians can function as critical cooperators within them. And whether managed care physicians can compensate for the loss of status trust by garnering merit trust will depend to a large extent upon whether their patients believe them to be working within legitimate organizations. Physicians can earn their patients' trust both by working within legitimate organizations and by refusing to work in organizations that fail to meet the standards of legitimacy.

I have argued that relying on status trust is a poor strategy for physicians working in managed care. Instead, I have argued, managed care physicians should recognize that to a large extent whether patients should trust them should depend on whether they trust the organization. I have also made the case that physicians should take seriously the idea that, given the realities of managed care, they can best serve their patients' legitimate interests by striving to create and sustain legitimate managed care organizations. Patients in managed care do not have a legitimate interest in maximal care, but rather in having a legitimate organization.

Legitimacy, Not Justice

The term "legitimacy" rather than "justice" is chosen to characterize the ethical quality conferred by satisfaction of the three fundamental constituents of legitimacy for two main reasons. First, as already noted, neither ethical theory nor social practice is currently capable of specifying a standard of adequate health care; consequently, we cannot say that an organization merits patients' trust if and only if it provides every patient with the health care that he or she is due as a matter of justice. Second, and more importantly, it is legitimacy, rather than justice, that is often the appropriate standard for evaluation, and in certain crucial respects managed care organizations are like polities.

What I am suggesting, and what others who have employed the notion of legitimacy with regard to managed care have intimated though not made explicit, is that in some ways normative political philosophy is a better resource for developing an ethics of managed care than traditional medical ethics. In normative political philosophy, a distinction is usually made between legitimacy and justice. A state or a government may be legitimate even though it is not fully just (even though one that is extremely unjust may lack legitimacy).

From the standpoint of each of the two main areas of ethical concern in managed care, legitimacy, rather than justice, is the appropriate evaluative concept. A physician working in a managed care organization cannot reasonably expect to agree in every case that organizational decisions or policies are just from the standpoint of substantive principles of justice. This is especially true with regard to rationing decisions, given the indeterminacy of what counts as adequate care, once we abandon the delusion that it is maximal care. Reasonable people may frequently disagree on the substantive justice of particular decisions and policies. Similarly, a citizen of a polity cannot reasonably expect that every law or policy will be just. Instead, what is reasonable for the citizen to expect is that political processes exhibit procedural fairness and that the government can be openly criticized and is accountable (and that laws or policies not be clearly and seriously unjust). Managed care organizations and polities are both concerned with the welfare of populations and must develop policies that employ collective resources responsibly, where this inevitably means making decisions that will impose costs on individuals as well as confer benefits.

The political analogy makes clear how completely off-target some popular criticisms of managed care are. Popular attacks on managed care, especially as presented in the media, often proceed as if the mere fact that a managed care organization denies a patient care that can reasonably be expected to produce a net benefit for her constitutes an injustice. This would be so only if at least one of three things were true: (1) having health insurance entitles one to maximal care; (2) insured patients are entitled to an adequate level of care and only maximal care is adequate; or (3) insured patients are entitled to have their physicians provide maximal care because they are entitled to being cared for by physicians who honor their fiduciary obligation to the patient and honoring the fiduciary obligation requires maximal care. But none of these assertions is true.

The first statement is false because it ignores the fact that health insurance policies have terms that limit coverage. The second is false because it denies the existence of scarcity and hence the inevitability of rationing. The third must be rejected because it begs the question of what the physician's obligations are in managed care, by taking literally a reading of the fiduciary obligation that is founded on a conception of medical practice that denies both the existence of scarcity and the fact that much medical care now is provided in a highly organizational context.

Just as it would be unreasonable for a citizen to expect that every political decision should serve his best interest, so it is unreasonable for a member of a managed care organization to expect that in every case health-care decisions will serve his best interest. Given that managed care organizations must provide care for populations of individuals and given the necessity of rationing, some decisions will be made—and *should* be made—that do not maximize the individual patient's interests.

"Trust" Redefined

"Trust" in the medical context is often defined as "the expectation that one's physician (or health-care organization) will act in one's interests" (Mechanic 1998, p. 661). We are now in a position to see how misleading, if not outright false, this common definition is. If the common definition is taken literally to mean that the expectation is that the physician will act to maximize one's interests, then trust in physicians is not only unwarranted (except possibly in the case when the physician has only one patient and no competing obligations to his family, himself, or anyone other than the patient); it is also not something that we should encourage. Patients should not expect that every decision will be made in their best interests as individuals anymore than citizens should expect the government to maximize their interests as individuals in all its decisions (or even in any of its decisions). What patients should expect is that the organization is legitimate, and this in turn will depend chiefly upon whether it satisfies the three conditions explained earlier (and is not clearly and seriously unjust in its decisions or policies). Similarly, what physicians should expect of their managed care organizations is not that the organization should never prevent them from providing the best technically feasible care to every patient, but that the organization should exhibit the constituents of legitimacy and make a good faith effort to fulfill its obligation of providing quality health care to a population of patients within a constrained budget.

I have just argued that trust in the context of managed care should not be understood as the expectation that one's physician or the organization should always act in one's interest, if this means in one's best interest. There is a kernel of truth in the common definition of trust, however, and the political analogy is useful to extract it. Regardless of differences in their particular interests, the citizens of a state are entitled to expect that public policy will act in everyone's interest in the sense of giving equal consideration to the basic, legitimate interests of all. Procedural justice, which includes nondiscrimination and impartiality, plays a crucial role in achieving this. But of course acting in every citizen's interest in this sense does not require, and indeed is not compatible with, maximizing every citizen's interests on every occasion. Similarly, every member of a managed care organization is entitled to equal consideration of her basic, legitimate interests in quality health care, and an organization is trustworthy to the extent that it acts in every patient's interest in this sense. But this is not to say that patients should expect decisions about their care to be determined according to what will maximize their (particular) interests or that physicians should expect that they will be permitted to make care decisions according to that maximalist standard.

POLICY IMPLICATIONS

Here I can only sketch some of the most important implications of the foregoing analysis of legitimacy-based trust for public policy regarding managed care. The chief implication is that public policy should stimulate managed care organizations to compete with one another for the merit trust of enrollees. Robust, informed merit competition is an appropriate goal for public policy because it would provide incentives for managed care organizations to strive to satisfy the conditions of legitimacy. As individuals who care about limiting health-care costs, we have an interest in robust price competition among managed care organizations; but as individuals who also care about quality health care and about achieving cost-containment in ethically acceptable ways, we have an interest in developing a system in which managed care organizations are rewarded by the market, not only for lower prices, but for legitimacy as well.

Robust competition for merit trust in the managed care market would require that the following conditions be satisfied: (1) consumers have access to information relevant to making reasonable comparative judgments about the legitimacy of competing organizations and (2) consumers are adequately motivated to get such information. Because of the peculiar reliance of the U.S. system on employment-based insurance, a third condition would also have to be met: (3) consumers are able to exert effective pressure on purchasers of insurance so that their judgments about the relative legitimacy of competing organizations will influence purchasing decisions. To foster informed competition for merit trust, public policy must address all three of these conditions.

The most obvious way to help satisfy condition (1) is to craft policies that provide effective incentives for managed care organizations to publicize their rationing policies and appeals processes and the justifications for them and to provide this information in a form that facilitates assessment of how well they satisfy the three constituents of legitimacy—procedural justice, empowerment of constructive criticism, and accommodation of the distinctive technical expertise and non-instrumental service commitment of medical professionals. It might be argued that the most serious hurdle to satisfying this publicity condition is that managed care organizations are likely to claim that this information is proprietary information to which their competitors should not have access. This is not a trivial problem, but neither is it an insoluble one. First, requiring all organizations to publicize policies relevant to the assessment of legitimacy would level the playing field and take much of the force out of the objection that publicity is incompatible with due regard for proprietary information. Second, an organization's appeals processes must be publicized to enrollees if they are to be effective, and if they are publicized to enrollees it will not be possible to prevent public access to them. Consequently, protection of proprietary information about appeals processes could only be achieved by the unacceptable policy of preventing enrollees from knowing about them. Furthermore, if patients are to be in a position to utilize appeals processes, they must know when they have been denied care, and this requires publicizing rationing policies. But again, if rationing policies are publicized to enrollees, competitors will not find it difficult to gain access to them as well. To summarize: If the only way to protect proprietary information is to undermine the effectiveness of appeals processes by making them inaccessible to the very individuals those processes are supposed to serve or by preventing those individuals from knowing when they have been denied care, then this a clear indication that the value of protecting proprietary information is far from absolute.

Promoting the satisfaction of condition (2) would require, at minimum, serious efforts to make the relevant information easily accessible and understandable to the public. In addition, a significant shift in patient attitudes may be required, if, as seems to be the case, most patients tend to gauge the trustworthiness of their physicians on the basis of their perception of "caring attitudes" in face-to-face interactions, rather than on perceptions of the character of the organization. For this reason, educational efforts may be required to get patients to take organizational legitimacy seriously as a basis for trust in their physicians.[14]

Condition (3) may be the most difficult of the three to satisfy, at least in the case of employee groups who are not highly skilled and cannot make their preferences felt by the threat of exiting the company that employs them. Legislation requiring employers to offer a significant range of alternative plans would ease this problem, but might prove difficult to craft and even more difficult to pass, given that offering more options would presumably be more costly to employers.

CONCLUSION

A common complaint about managed care is that it erodes patients' trust in physicians. I have argued that the debate about trust in managed care has been unfocused and unilluminating because of a failure to distinguish status trust from merit trust. I also have argued that the erosion of status trust may be not only unavoidable, but benign as well, to the extent that the status trust is based on the delusion that traditional medical ethics provides a firm foundation for ethical behavior on the part of physicians in managed care.

Instead of futile efforts to recover lost status trust, I have recommended a new basis for merit trust: the (well-founded) perception that one's physician is a member of a legitimate managed care organization. I also have tried to show how a proper conception of the physician as a critical cooperator in the organization (rather than a saboteur) accommodates the distinctive noninstrumental professional commitment to patient's well-being without encouraging the unrealistic and inappropriate expectation that every decision must maximally promote the patient's interests.

It might be objected that my view of trust is excessively rationalistic—in particular that it ignores the fact that what I have called primary merit trust in physicians has always been and will continue to be an important component of patient trust.[15] In other words, even if information about the legitimacy-conferring characteristics of managed care organizations becomes available, it may turn out that patients will continue to base their trust in their physicians chiefly on whether the physician listens to them, maintains eye contact, and engages in other "caring behaviors."

My reply is that nothing in my analysis suggests that primary merit trust in physicians will be or should be eliminated by a public policy designed to create the conditions for informed, robust competition among managed care organizations for merit trust. I would not wish to deny that the patient's perception of whether her physician exhibits "caring behaviors" will continue to be a major factor in whether the physician enjoys the patient's trust. Nor have I argued that the organization-derivative merit trust *should* entirely replace primary merit trust. My point, rather, is that regardless of whether primary merit trust in physicians can survive under the conditions of managed care, trust in the physician based on trust in the legitimacy of the organization in which she works is a necessary component of patient trust, if the latter is to be well-founded.

8

IS THERE A MEDICAL PROFESSION IN THE HOUSE?

Allen Buchanan

CONCERN OVER CONFLICT OF INTEREST

There is a growing awareness that the new conditions under which medicine is practiced in this country are creating or at least exacerbating conflicts of interest in the physician–patient relationship. On the one hand, private insurers and government agencies are exerting pressure on physicians to cut costs by reducing utilization of services. The result is that physicians increasingly practice under incentives for *underutilization of services*—that is, for utilizing fewer services or lesser quantities of given services than would be optimal from the standpoint of the patient's best interest.[1] On the other hand, hospital administrators and entrepreneurial physicians themselves are creating incentive structures designed to increase revenues even at the price of *overutilization of services*—that is, providing services that exceed what is optimal from the standpoint of the patient's best interest.[2] Whenever the incentive structure under which physicians practice either rewards or penalizes them for utilizing services that are not in the patient's best interest or for not utilizing services that are in the patient's best interest, a conflict of interest exists.

To the extent that private or government cost-containment measures employ incentives that serve to reduce *unnecessary* services—those that cannot reasonably be expected to produce any net benefit for the patient—they are morally uncontroversial and involve no conflict of interest. However, some of the cost-containment measures now employed by private insurers and government agencies provide incentives for physicians to reduce not just unnecessary (i.e., nonbeneficial) services, but also services that can reasonably be expected to provide a net benefit—sometimes a very significant benefit—to the patient.[3] Current cost-containment strategies give physicians an incentive to *ration* services, not simply to eliminate waste.

Underutilization (relative to the patient's best interest) can result in inadequate treatments that fail to relieve pain or to restore or preserve normal functioning, or failure to detect conditions that may later become untreatable or very difficult and costly to treat, and can shift costs to the patient or the patient's family (as when patients are discharged early from the hospital and must recuperate at home). Overutilization (again, relative to the patient's best interest) can lead to iatrogenic injuries, unnecessary discomfort, inconvenience and waste of the patient's time, increased out-of-pocket expenses (co-payments and deductibles), increased private insurance premiums, and more taxes to support government-reimbursed coverage such as Medicare and Medicaid.

A recurrent theme in the literature and in public discussions concerning conflict of interest in contemporary medical practice is the declaration that pressures for cost-containment and entrepreneurial behavior are eroding patient trust and undermining medicine as a profession.[4] Entrepreneurial behavior is especially troubling to some. They worry that when physicians are themselves motivated by the thirst for profit or are the virtual employees of those whose dominant concern is the bottom line, medicine becomes a mere business rather than a profession. It is this worry upon which I wish to focus in this chapter.

UNEXAMINED ASSUMPTIONS ABOUT THE NATURE, EXISTENCE, AND DESIRABILITY OF A MEDICAL PROFESSION

Instead of adding to what I believe to be rather inconclusive and speculative predictions about how entrepreneurial arrangements will or will not erode patient trust and extinguish professionalism, my objective is to uncover and critically examine certain highly problematic but rarely articulated assumptions that frame the debate about conflict of interest. The most fundamental assumptions are these: (1) the reduction of patients' trust in physicians as professionals is bad; (2) unless physicians are regarded as professionals, trust in them and the benefits it brings for patients will not exist; and (3) there currently is in this country a medical profession according to a conception of what a medical profession is that makes it desirable that there be such a profession. Together, these assumptions constitute what I shall call the "myth of professionalism."

To explicate and criticize these three fundamental framing assumptions, it is first necessary to clarify what is meant in this context by a profession and then to explain the *justification* or *rationale* for according a particular occupational group the status of a profession. In addition, it is necessary to distinguish clearly between the existence of a profession and belief in its existence, but in such a way as to take into account the fact that for this type of social entity, belief is partly constitutive of the entity itself. Finally, it is important to clarify the relationship between professionalism and trust. In particular, we must examine critically the assumption that the extinction of professionalism means the end of trust.[5] A secondary aim of this chapter is to show just how constraining the three major framing assumptions are. I shall argue that these assumptions seriously restrict the range of policy options for dealing with problems of conflict of interest in the context of increasing pressures for rationing and growing entrepreneurial activity. In brief, acceptance of the myth of medical professionalism tends to prevent us from dealing with—and indeed, even from adequately understanding—the problem of conflict of interest.

THE CONCEPT OF A PROFESSION AND THE JUSTIFICATION OF SOCIAL INEQUALITIES

The extensive literature on professions yields two distinct but overlapping conceptions of a profession. The first may be called the "ideal" conception. It includes the following elements:[6]

1. Special knowledge of a practical sort (whose application is the distinctive activity of the profession).[7]
2. A commitment to preserving and enhancing the special knowledge.
3. A commitment by the members of the profession to achieving excellence in the practice of the profession (in other words, practice of the profession is *not* motivated only by the desire to earn a living).
4. An intrinsic and dominant commitment to serving others on whose behalf the special knowledge is applied. (To say that the commitment is intrinsic is to say that it is not exclusively instrumental, that is, derived from other motives, such as the desire for personal gain. The commitment is dominant in the sense that, at least in many cases, it overrides other desires or commitments with which it may come into conflict.) This element may be referred to as the *service commitment*.
5. Effective collective self-regulation by the professional group, including the articulation of standards of competence for the profession, measures for inculcating in individual members the commitment to these standards,

> *and* sanctions (including expulsion from the professional group) for ensuring compliance with them.[8]

It is worth noting that at least in the case of the medical profession, and perhaps in all of the so-called caring professions (e.g., nursing and social work), elements 4 and 5 may not be clearly distinguishable. If serving the needs and interests of others is essential to the characteristic activity of the profession, then an intrinsic commitment to performing the characteristic activity well (element 4) already includes an effective disposition to put the patient's (or client's) interest first. If the professional allowed her own interests to interfere with providing appropriate care for the patient (or client), this would be a departure from excellent performance. In other words, excellent performance requires that the activity be directed toward some goals and not others. Accordingly, a commitment to excellence in performing the activity—at least this kind of activity—includes a commitment to putting the patient's interest first. In that sense, the commitment to excellence and the service commitment, according to the ideal conception of a medical profession, are not distinct.[9]

Some have equated what I have referred to as the service commitment with *altruism*.[10] In this context, however, the term "altruism" is misleading unless it is qualified with the adjective "limited" (or "particularized"). Sometimes altruism is understood as a rather *general* disposition to act so as to serve the interests of others (other people generally), and to do so even when this means *sacrificing* one's own interests. The service commitment differs from altruism so understood in two ways. First, it does not imply a general disposition, that is, a disposition to serve the interests of all persons or even of all persons in need of medical care, but rather only a disposition to put the interests *of one's patients* first. Second, the service commitment need not (usually) involve sacrificing one's own interests, and we need not think of the professional as one who, by virtue of superior moral will, ruthlessly suppresses his own most basic interests (at least as far as his most important interests are concerned, as the notion of sacrifice suggests). Instead, the service commitment is better understood as *limited* (as opposed to generalized) *altruism* that is substantial, though not necessarily literally self-sacrificing. To put it in a slightly different way, the service commitment focuses attention on the interests of certain others, not all others. The professional, by striving to perform the characteristic activity with excellence, focuses on the interests of the patient, since the characteristic activity is the application of his special knowledge for the purpose of serving *those* interests, not his own. What (generalized) altruism and the service commitment, or limited altruism of the professional, have in common is that both involve *not* being guided primarily by the goal of maximizing self-interest.

This first conception of what a profession is may be called the ideal conception because it is normative, not purely descriptive. Even if it could be shown that most physicians do not exhibit some or all of the characteristics listed in elements 1 through 5, it would not follow that the concept of a medical profession is vacuous or nonsensical. Instead, one might conclude that there are few "true" medical professionals. Similarly, the concept of a virtuous person or of a good carpenter is an ideal rather than a purely descriptive concept: It expresses a norm, a prescription, about how things should be, not simply about how they are. In other words, the ideal conception functions as a standard for evaluating the behavior of physicians: Those who conform to it are said to be professionals (or "true" or "genuine" professionals); those who do not are condemned for unprofessional conduct or for not being ("true") professionals.

The second conception of a profession I wish to distinguish is what may be called the "sociological" conception—the conception that is most prevalent in sociological analyses of the professions. It incorporates all the elements of the ideal conception, but in a way that wavers between pure description of the actual characteristics of those whom we call professionals and a report of the social perception of the occupational group in question, at least under conditions in which the "professionalism" of the group is not widely called into question. For example, according to the sociological conception of a profession, members of the group in question avow a commitment to service and are generally thought of as actually having such a commitment, at least when there is not a "legitimation crisis" with respect to the public's attitude toward the profession.

The sociological conception also includes another element, which is purely descriptive:

6. Special status for members of the group (public acknowledgment of worth, marks of prestige, etc.) and special privileges, including financial advantages (such as public subsidies for training and education and insulation from economic competition) and a significant sphere of autonomy, that is, substantial freedom from external regulation of the characteristic activity.[11]

It is crucial to point out that at least some components of this sixth element are quite separable, at least in principle, from the preceding five. In particular, there is no obvious connection between elements 1 through 5, on the one hand, and the favored economic position of medical professionals, on the other.

Professions are *social constructs*, not facts of nature. As such, they are appropriate subjects for critical appraisal. It makes sense to evaluate them and, indeed, to ask whether it is a good thing that they exist. Indeed, professions, at least as far as they exhibit the features listed in item 6, are *socially constructed inequalities*. And with respect to any socially constructed inequality, it is appropriate to ask: What is the justification for this unequal treatment? Why should some occupational groups (such as physicians) and not others (such as automobile mechanics or butchers) receive special status, reap exceptional financial rewards, and be accorded an exceptional degree of freedom from external regulation in their activities?[12]

Two different putative justifications may be distinguished: (1) *the simple appeal to expertise* and (2) *the social cost–benefit justification.* The former is at best capable of justifying only one aspect of that socially constructed inequality we call the medical profession: the relative freedom from external regulation. The idea is simply (indeed, as we shall see, simplistic) that only those who possess special expertise are qualified to exercise control over how the expertise is employed.

It is, of course, true that physicians possess special expertise.[13] But this is true of every specialized—that is, skilled—occupational group. Yet we do not generally assume that possession of a special skill exempts an occupational group from external regulation. Nor does the fact that the special skill of physicians is highly technical seem to be a good reason for allowing them to be free from external regulation in its exercise. A number of other occupational groups, including accountants, air traffic controllers, ships' captains, and mining and petroleum engineers, possess technical skills, yet they are not exempt from external regulation. Nor does the fact that a technically skilled occupational group works directly with people, in the service of their needs, seem to be a good reason for excluding external regulation: Financial advisors do just that, yet they are subject to external regulations in the form of legal obligations under the law of agency and fiduciary law.

Generally speaking, the question of regulating a group's characteristic activity arises only where the activity has the potential for seriously affecting the interests of others who are not in a position to protect themselves adequately. The physician–patient relationship—which, like other principal–agent relationships, is characterized by an asymmetry of knowledge and capabilities—creates just such a situation. The patient seeks a physician because the physician has knowledge and capabilities that the patient lacks.[14] But, as is also the case in other principal–agent relationships, the very asymmetry of knowledge or capabilities which makes it attractive for one person to engage another as his agent also creates the potential for a divergence between the agent's and the principal's interests and hence introduces "agency risk"—the risk that the agent will use his superior knowledge and ability to pursue his own interests (or the interests of others) at the expense of the principal's.

In attempting to justify its relative freedom from external regulation, the medical profession implicitly claims that patients in general are *not* able to provide adequate protection for themselves and that some other party must do so. But once it is assumed that some sort of regulation by another party is necessary, the question arises: Who should the regulator be? Surely the agent is not the most obvious candidate. Simply put, the agent—that is, the one who is placed so as to exploit the asymmetry of knowledge and capability that characterizes the principal–agent relationship—is the *least* obvious candidate for the regulator, assuming that some form of regulation is necessary. But if the physician as agent—the source of the risk that makes regulation desirable—is not the most obvious choice for the regulator, why should the collectivity of agents, the medical profession, be allowed to perform this function?

Self-regulation, whether individual or collective, generally is not the most plausible option for regulation. Indeed, a presumption against self-regulation is expressed in a wide range of our social institutions and practices, from the use of *civilian* review boards for complaints against the police, to government regulation of certain industries, to the system of checks and balances of constitutional government itself. In short, the mere fact that a group possesses special technical knowledge does not by itself defeat this presumption in the case of many other groups. So there must be something more than a simple appeal to (technical) expertise if the medical profession's relative freedom from external regulation is to be justified. The simple argument from expertise does not do the job.

What the simple argument from expertise overlooks is that effective regulation is to a large extent procedural or structural rather than content-specific, or substantive. It is no doubt true that in formulating substantive standards of performance for a certain activity, external regulators must rely to a greater or lesser extent on advice from those who possess the special technical expertise. But once this crucial substantive input is available, an external authority can impose reasonable structural and procedural regulations. For example, effective regulation of railroad engineers or airplane pilots requires input from engineers and pilots regarding the types and levels of particular skills that are desirable and the training programs needed for them. But an external authority can then use this information to formulate, publicize, and enforce licensing and relicensing requirements designed to ensure that those who work as pilots and engineers initially possess and continue to maintain the skills in question.

Furthermore, even if reliance on those who possess the technical skills is necessary for formulating substantive standards, this is only one aspect of effective regulation. Another crucial point that the simple argument from expertise overlooks is that some central aspects of effective regulation have nothing whatsoever to do with technical skills or with standards for their maintenance. Much regulation has to do, instead, with eliminating or reducing situations and relationships that involve potentially dangerous conflicts of interest.

All regulation prohibiting or controlling self-dealing and self-referral practices is of this nature. In many cases, the situations and relationships in which conflicts of interests occur can be identified, and a measure to prevent or control them can be intelligently devised, without relying in any substantial way on the special expertise of those who are to be regulated. An example from the case at hand—the activity of medical professionals—will make this simple but significant point clearer.

One does not have to be an internist to understand that a situation in which internists refer their patients to their own diagnostic laboratories involves a conflict of interest. The conflict is between the service commitment of the physician to doing solely what is in the best interest of the patient and his own financial interest in securing additional revenue from referring the patient to a facility that the physician owns. The danger inherent in this conflict of interest is that the physician's referral will not be based solely on his judgment of what is best for the patient. A number of studies indicate that this danger is not merely speculative: Physicians who are owners of facilities to which they refer patients order the procedures in question much more frequently than nonowner physicians, and these higher rates of referral are *not* explained by higher incidences of the conditions in question in the populations that the owner physicians treat.[15] The most stark example of such a conflict is an arrangement whereby the diagnostic facility pays the physician a fee for each patient he refers. Such arrangements have now been legally prohibited. But it is worth noting that self-regulation by the profession did not prevent them from flourishing before they were outlawed.[16]

The special expertise of physicians is not needed either to understand that such practices involve a conflict of interest or to appreciate the evidence that the physician's financial interest corrupts her clinical judgment. (In the latter case, all that is required is a basic grasp of the relevant data concerning rates of referral and rates of normal versus abnormal results from diagnostic procedures.) Further, the special expertise of physicians is not essential for determining whether the best strategy for coping with such a conflict of interest is to prohibit such self-referral arrangements. Whether prohibition is advisable depends on what the facts are—in particular, on whether prohibition would adversely affect the availability of such facilities by removing the incentive for physicians to invest in them. A sound prediction of whether the needed capital would come from sources other than the referring physicians themselves may require some technical expertise, but the expertise is economic, not medical.

To summarize the argument thus far: The attempt to justify the medical profession's special exemption from external regulation by a simple appeal to the special expertise of physicians fails. Two important aspects of effective regulation are less directly tied to special expertise than the simple argument from expertise assumes. First, much important regulation designed to ensure that technical standards are initially met and maintained is procedural or structural rather than substantive or content-specific. Second, some important regulation is a response to conflicts of interest and neither the identification of situations involving conflicts of interest, nor the development of policies to minimize these conflicts need involve the special expertise of physicians to such an extent that external regulation is not feasible.

It is worth emphasizing that even if the simple appeal to expertise succeeded in justifying the profession's relative freedom from external regulation, this would not suffice to show that the full range of inequalities involved in the existence of the profession is justified. In particular, it is not at all obvious that proper recognition of the special expertise of physicians requires that they be accorded such a favorable and secure economic niche.

A second, more promising justification for the medical profession as a socially constructed inequality is *the cost–benefit justification*. Again, the basic idea is simple. The special status, exceptionally advantageous economic position, and relative freedom from regulation enjoyed by the profession are *costs* to society, but they are worth bearing because they are more than compensated for by the *benefits* that these arrangements secure for society. These benefits include the preservation, advancement, and transmission of valuable practical knowledge, effective collective self-regulation by the profession, and the profession's inculcation of the service commitment in its members. The inequalities are justified because the benefits to society associated with them outweigh the costs.

As we shall see, the success of the cost–benefit argument depends on two problematic assumptions: (1) that the benefits to society in question are adequately provided (e.g., is collective self-regulation by the profession adequate? Is the service commitment sufficiently pervasive and effective?) and (2) that there is no less costly (and morally acceptable) arrangement that does not involve these inequalities and that would provide the same benefits.

A variation on the cost–benefit justification is suggested by sociological discussions of the medical profession. It may be called the "social bargain model." The fundamental idea is that society grants special status, financial advantage, and exceptional freedom from external regulation to an occupational group *in exchange* for some significant expected benefits for society, benefits that either cannot be attained in any other way or that can be achieved most cheaply and effectively by this exchange. As with the cost–benefit justification, the benefits in question are indicated in the other five characteristics of a profession. In exchange for elevated social status, financial advantage, and substantial autonomy, the members of a profession are expected to preserve and enhance the special knowledge applied in their distinctive activity, to cultivate an intrinsic attachment to excellence in the performance of the activity, to be motivated predominantly by the desire to further the interests of those on whose behalf they act, and, perhaps most important, to exercise collective self-regulation. Presumably, the rationale for allowing the group a substantial degree of autonomy in exchange for collective self-regulation is the assumption that self-regulation will be more cost-effective than external regulation.

To some, the social bargain model may be more attractive than the cost–benefit justification. It carries with it resonances of a long distinguished tradition in the justification of inequalities: that of the social contract. The social bargain model also has the advantage of making especially vivid the idea that the profession is a social creation, not an unalterable fact of nature, for one implication of the bargain metaphor is that the bargain may periodically be reevaluated and renegotiated or even not renewed.

The dangers of the social exchange model are, however, considerable. If taken too literally, it presents a falsely democratic picture of the way social institutions come about (by "society deciding to do such and such"). A literal construal of the model also mistakenly suggests that the social inequalities in question were created by someone's deliberate choice, rather than emerging from complex interactions of agents and groups pursuing much more concrete and limited purposes.[17] The cost–benefit justification has the advantage of avoiding these dangers. Nonetheless, partly because it makes the question of the medical profession's legitimacy more vivid and because it so clearly conveys the idea that the profession is a socially constructed inequality, I will, in the remainder of the chapter, frequently use the metaphor of a social bargain. However, all of what I say concerning the social bargain model will apply to the less rhetorically potent cost–benefit justification.

The social bargain model has explanatory import: It helps explain the distinctive features of professions by seeing them as elements in an exchange between an occupational group and society. But it also has *normative* significance: The social bargain model articulates the conditions under which the special status and exceptional autonomy of some occupational groups are *justified* according to a public standard of justification that appeals to the common good. Our focus will be on the justificatory function of the social bargain model.

It is worth emphasizing *why* it is appropriate to ask for a justification of the elevated status, favored financial position, and relative autonomy of the medical profession. The answer, in brief, is that a profession is a *social construct*, not an unalterable fact of nature. It is a particular kind of institution or social arrangement, one alternative among others. More important, it is a *socially constructed inequality*, an arrangement involving benefits for one group that are not generally available to other members of society. As such, it is appropriate to ask for a justification for it. In other words, those who endorse the continuation of a socially constructed inequality bear the burden of justification. Even if inequalities per se do not require a justification, socially produced—that is, institutional—inequalities do. The social bargain model is one attempt to justify the socially constructed inequalities inherent in a profession.

Many analysts have emphasized one aspect of item 6, the favored financial position of professionals, that is in special need of justification. More specifically, they focus on the fact that professional organizations characteristically attempt to carve out a *sheltered economic niche*—to limit competition and keep income levels high.

The social bargain or exchange model explains, at least in principle, why such behavior might be tolerated, in spite of the fact that it is costly to society. According to the social bargain model, the only justification for allowing professionals to carve out a sheltered niche for themselves is the assumption that by doing so they *insulate* themselves from the more severe economic pressures that might undermine the commitment to excellence and to serving their clients' or patients' interests.[18] The idea is that if physicians are more or less guaranteed a comfortable and stable financial position, most will not succumb to venal impulses. (Interestingly enough, even one of the most acerbic critics of the medical profession, George Bernard Shaw, apparently accepted this assumption uncritically. He attributed venal behavior on the part of many of the physicians of his day to their poverty.)[19]

As we shall see later, there are actually two assumptions here that require more critical attention than they usually receive. The first is that a privileged economic position is an effective obstacle to corruption. The second is that the actual level of economic well-being currently available to medical professionals in this country is necessary to achieve whatever insulation against incentives for venality can be secured by according physicians a privileged and secure economic position. Even if (as seems highly unlikely) the first assumption is true as a broad generalization, it is an altogether different question as to whether the actual favored economic position of physicians in this country is optimal, from the standpoint of providing insulation against temptation, or whether it includes what we may call "surplus inequalities." There is the danger that if the economic rewards of being a physician are too high, the profession may attract the wrong sort of people—those whose primary interest is in money. Thus, if there are surplus inequalities, the assurance of a favored economic position would erode rather than encourage the service commitment. In other words, it is one thing to say that the physician lives comfortably enough so that the howling of the wolf at his door does not distract him from serving his patients' interests; it is quite another to say that physicians should be able to expect an income that is four times the average income of their fellow citizens.[20]

THE COSTS OF THE BARGAIN

In what follows, I offer what I hope is a comprehensive classification of the most serious costs of granting professional status to practitioners of medicine in our society under present conditions. Whether these costs are *excessive*—that is, whether, in the aggregate the cost of the social bargain exceed the benefits—is very difficult to determine. My aim in this chapter is only to show that the wisdom of the social bargain today is seriously in doubt. I offer no rigorous calculation purporting to *prove* that the bargain is a bad one from the social perspective.

Nevertheless, it is worth emphasizing where the burden of argument should lie in this matter. Given that the recognition of a particular occupational group as a profession ipso facto involves the granting of special status, privileges, and autonomy to that group, a convincing case must be made that such preferential treatment is justified. My contention is that a convincing case has not been made, and that for that reason the wisdom of the social bargain, and hence the legitimacy of the special status, privileges, and relative freedom from external regulation of practitioners of medicine, are in doubt.

The major costs of having a medical profession under current conditions can be classified under three main headings: (1) the costs of granting the authority for self-regulation (and of the correlative freedom from external regulation), (2) the costs of allowing or enabling the profession to construct for its members a sheltered economic niche, and (3) the costs of the public's trust in professionals qua professionals. I take up each of these classes of costs in turn.

The first class of costs is well known to economic analysts of the medical profession and to historians of organized medicine. A number of scholars have described the ways in which the medical profession has used its authority to maintain standards of excellence in order to stifle competition and keep the incomes of practitioners of orthodox medicine high.[21]

The profession's control over licensure is perhaps the most obvious example: Historically, organized medicine has steadfastly refused to require periodic demonstrations of competence to practice (unlike, say, airplane pilot licensing regulations). Instead, it has tended to erect barriers to licensure excluding alternative forms of medicine, some of which were not shown to be less efficacious than orthodox medicine, and to allow those who clear the initial hurdle to continue practicing even though it is known that some will lose their competence at some point after entering the profession. Other things being equal, a system of licensure with a high entry barrier and no comparable periodic relicensing requirements clearly functions better to protect from competition those who succeed in entering than to protect the public by ensuring that standards of excellence are maintained.[22]

Moreover, continuing medical education requirements are almost universally recognized as both inadequate and subject to serious abuses. Physicians can receive credit for simply attending any of a wide range of conferences (of greatly varying quality) and merely sitting in the audience. Indeed, in some cases, physicians simply sign the attendance sheet the first day of the conference and then attend either sporadically or not at all, while receiving full credit for the entire conference. No examinations to demonstrate mastery of the material supposedly acquired in continuing medical education are required.

It will not do to reply, in defense of this system, that the continued competence of licensed physicians is adequately ensured by malpractice litigation and monitoring by state medical licensure boards. For one thing, most cases of malpractice are not even detected by patients, much less litigated or settled out of court.[23] For another, state medical licensure boards, which are physician dominated, have received a great deal of criticism for repeated failures to revoke licenses even from extremely incompetent and even dangerous physicians. Moreover, even if a state board of medical licensure takes the highly unusual step of revoking the license of a physician who has exhibited a pattern of malpractice, the physician can sometimes continue to practice in another state. Finally, even if malpractice litigation and revocation of license were much more effective than they apparently are, it would still be difficult to understand why serious periodic relicensing requirements (as for airline pilots) would not also be advisable.

By the very nature of the case, it is difficult to form even rough estimates of the social costs resulting from orthodox medicine's monopoly on licensure and, until very recently, its near monopoly on certification for reimbursement by government and private insurers. It is hard to know what magnitudes of cost savings or gains in medical outcomes *might* have occurred had alternative types of services and forms of practice been allowed to develop. We *do* know that some types of services and some forms of practice that finally gained legitimacy despite dogged resistance and outright persecution by organized medicine, such as midwifery and prepaid group practice (HMOs), have provided significant benefits.[24] And hence we know that society was deprived of these benefits during the many years in which organized medicine succeeded in suppressing them.

Defenders of the medical profession would be quick to point out that the question is not whether the profession's control over licensure and reimbursement has resulted in the exclusion of some high-quality and/or lower cost alternatives. The question, rather, is whether, on balance, the profession's self-regulation has adequately protected the public. If the price of preventing quacks from inflicting themselves on the unwary is the mistaken suppression of some unobjectionable (or even superior) types of services or forms of practice, then this is a necessary, though regrettable, cost.

This defense of the status quo is inadequate for two reasons. First, the question is not simply whether the profession's self-regulation has adequately protected the public, but rather whether self-regulation, with all the social costs it entails, has provided the *least costly* method of ensuring an adequate level of protection. Pointing out that this system, like any other, is imperfect and that we must expect some "false positives" in the workings of any system designed to suppress quackery does not answer that question.

If, as I have already suggested, the burden of argument lies with any group whose activities seriously affect the well-being of others under conditions of conflict of interest, but that nonetheless claims that it ought to receive special authority for self-regulation and special exemption from external regulation, then this means that the medical profession or its defenders must show not only that the profession's actual record on self-regulation has been adequate, but also that self-regulation is more efficient than external regulation alternatives. This burden of argument certainly has not been borne.

Second, and more important, the most obvious objection to the way the medical profession has performed the task of self-regulation, as noted earlier, is independent of the question of whether the profession has done an acceptable job, on balance, of developing appropriate standards for distinguishing good medicine from quackery. That objection is that *regardless of the content* of the standards (i.e., regardless of what is counted as good medicine and what as quackery), the public would be better served by a system of periodic relicensing than by one that imposes high (and very narrow) barriers to entry at the beginning of a career and then allows those who clear them to continued to practice for the rest of their lives without a serious attempt to ensure that they are even continuing to meet the original standards, much less whatever new standards become appropriate in the light of advances in medical technique and knowledge.

So far, I have simply noted what several generations of sociologists and historians of medicine have documented: That the authority for self-regulation granted to medicine as a profession has often been exercised, especially in establishing licensing requirements, in ways that serve better to further the interests of physicians than to protect patients. The chief function of licensing requirements, at least in principle, is to articulate and enforce technical standards of competence. But there is another important function of self-regulation whose performance has been even more defective, if anything: The articulation and enforcement of ethical standards, especially these regarding conflict of interest in the physician–patient relationship.

As a broad generalization it is fair to say that organized medicine in the United States from before the beginning of this century through the present has tended to abdicate its responsibility for *effective, collective self-regulation* regarding conflict of interest. With few exceptions, the profession has not articulated clear standards of conduct regarding conflict of interest and establishing effective institutional sanctions to ensure an acceptable level of compliance. Instead, it has usually relied on rather vague ethical norms (often only after public disapproval has become widespread and the threat of government regulation has become imminent) and on appeals to the conscience and judgment of individual physicians rather than to collective mechanisms for compliance.

One of the best treatments of this failure of collective ethical self-regulation is found in Marc A. Rodwin's major work on conflict of interest in medicine, *Medicine, Money, and Morals: Physicians' Conflicts of Interest.*[25] Rodwin skillfully traces the history of organized medicine's responses to one of the most prominent conflicts of interest—physician self-referral in its various guises—from the 1890s to 1992. Rodwin documents the fact that the two most prominent medical organizations, the American Medical Association (AMA) and the American College of Surgeons, have for long periods entirely evaded the problem of self-referral, and that when they have taken positions on the issue, they have only announced vague and ambiguous exhortations while relying on individual physicians to interpret and apply them to their own conduct.

Rodwin aptly characterizes this approach as "subjective." Perhaps more important, the dominant approach of organized medicine to these crucial ethical problems may be characterized as *individualistic*, as opposed to *institutional* or collective, and *voluntary*, as opposed to *sanctioned*. Organized medicine has not only opposed *government* regulation of self-referral, it has also refused to undertake serious efforts at collective *self*-regulation.

Rather than using its organizational resources to articulate collectively endorsed, substantive standards and to provide institutional sanctions to ensure that physicians comply with them, the profession has narrowed its role to that of offering rather general principles for the purely voluntary consideration of individual practitioners. Especially after the mid-1950s, the AMA backed away from anything resembling clear prohibitions against self-referral, asserting that a physician could dispense drugs and devices he prescribed so long as, in his own judgment, this was "in the best interests of the patient."

Similarly, in 1961, the AMA held that physician ownership of pharmacies was permissible "as long as there is no exploitation of the patient." Again, since no provision was made for authoritative, substantive guidance on what counted as exploitation and what did not, and since no measures were developed for collective sanctions to ensure compliance with the vague prohibition against exploitation, the approach was voluntary, individualistic, and nearly vacuous.[26] The same approach was followed in 1976 when the AMA chose not to develop specific guidelines concerning conflicts of interest arising from physicians' investment in diagnostic technology. Instead, it approved of physician ownership of such facilities, saying only that "physician ownership of equipment should not involve abuse or exploitation of the physician–patient relationship."[27] Issuing the stamp of approval to practices that clearly involve conflicts of interest, while merely announcing the rather uncontroversial proposition that physicians ought not to exploit patients (or, presumably, to murder or rob them), hardly counts as self-regulation in any sense that could satisfy the normatively adequate conception of a profession.

At present, the AMA's Principles of Ethics include no reference whatsoever to conflicts of interest arising from self-referral practices. To the extent that it has made any official pronouncements on the issue, it has spoken equivocally. In 1989, the AMA's Council on Ethical and Judicial Affairs stated a presumption against self-referral (but noted that there were cases in which self-referral was ethical). However, once again, no mechanism for enforcement was mentioned, and forty-three state medical associations failed to recommend that their members comply with the AMA's presumption against self-referral. (Indeed, it is hard to know exactly what it means to comply with a presumption whose exceptions are left so vague.)

Even this rather anemic response to the public outcry about self-referral was thought to be too restrictive by many physicians. The reaction against it culminated in June 1992, when the AMA's House of Delegates passed a resolution that contradicted the Judicial Council's position. The resolution stated that self-referral was ethical so long as physicians disclosed their ownership of facilities to which they referred. Again, enforcement mechanisms were not even suggested, and the problem of developing adequate procedures for disclosure was not addressed. Given mounting public pressure, the House of Delegates reversed itself several months later and condemned self-referral except to meet a special medical need or if the only way a center could be established were by the involvement of referring doctors.[28]

To the extent that the profession has relied chiefly on an individualistic, subjective, and voluntary approach to problems of conflict of interest, it has failed to discharge one of the chief functions of self-regulation: The development of ethical policies specific enough to provide substantive practical guidance, with collective sanctions to ensure a reasonable level of compliance. Yet, as we have seen, this self-regulatory function is essential to the social bargain that elevates an occupational group to the status of a profession.[29]

The second major class of costs of the professionalism consists of the costs of providing a sheltered economic niche for members of the profession. It is important to note that the much higher than average incomes of physicians cannot be explained simply as the result of average rates of return on the individual physician's investment in his or her own education and training, comparable to average rates of return on other investments in our society. Since physician education and training is heavily subsidized by public funding, physicians' incomes cannot be explained simply as returns on their own investment.[30]

It was observed earlier that, according to the social bargain model, the chief justification for the privileged economic position of physicians is that it supposedly reduces the temptation to behave venally. Another way to put this is to say that according to physicians, a privileged economic position is supposed to lower the physician's costs of focusing on the interests of his patients. If a physician is assured a high income, then he "need not weigh economic benefits to himself when considering treatment recommendations for his individual patients."[31] In the simplest economic terms, society buys the service commitment, the commitment of the physician to put the patient's interests first, by allowing physicians a favored economic position.

One result, of course, is that higher incomes for physicians mean higher health-care costs overall—higher costs than would exist if physicians' incomes were determined solely by the operation of the market and normal rates of return on investment. This is the first and most obvious cost of providing medical professionals with a sheltered economic niche.

Until quite recently, physicians' income from professional activity was generated almost exclusively by third-party, fee-for-service payments. This system's incentives ensured a high degree of convergence between the financial interests of the physician and the patient's interests as a consumer of health care. (It is crucial to remember here that by the "patient" we mean only those individuals who are in need of health care *and who are insured.*) At least where co-payments or deductibles are low, the physician can assure himself that in ordering all services that can be expected to produce any net benefit for the patient, he is serving the patient's best interest and his own financial interest as well. Under such a system of payment, the angelic voice of the conscience of the physician as fiduciary and the insistent whine of self-interest become one.

Moreover, since the level of fees was not determined by competition but according to the so-called reasonable and customary standard, which was largely determined by the providers themselves, regardless of their actual costs, the fee-for-service system turned out to be a very expensive way to ensure a privileged economic position for physicians. It became increasingly clear over the past decade that the price of ensuring this congruence of the patient's best interest and the physician's self-interest—the social cost of making the service commitment cheap for physicians—is unacceptably expensive health care. Indeed, the whole gamut of recent restrictions on straightforward fee-for-service payment, from diagnosis-related groups to the myriad constraints on utilization imposed by various managed-care practice plans, can be seen as a renegotiation of the fee-for-service system "bargain" for ensuring high incomes for physicians.

The demise of unconstrained fee-for-service reimbursement has not, however, resulted in a decline in average physician income.[32] Physicians have found other ways of keeping their incomes much higher than average, including, most conspicuously, investment in health-care facilities—laboratories; dialysis, radiation, and imaging centers; outpatient surgical centers; and ancillary services of various sorts. And there can be no doubt that physicians are exceptionally well placed to reap high profits from such investment opportunities, in part because the higher economic position they have traditionally been assured, including the public subsidization of their education and training, has equipped them with more resources for investment than the average individual investor and greater knowledge about where to invest.

The question of whether the favorable economic position of physicians is a good bargain for society is correspondingly transformed. The issue now is whether the enhancement of physician altruism that physicians' higher economic status is supposed to produce is worth the cost to society associated with these new entrepreneurial sources of physician income. Those who argue that the new entrepreneurism exacerbates conflicts of interest in the physician–patient relationship—for example, when physicians refer patients to facilities that they own—doubt that it is a good bargain.

So far, I have only raised questions about whether the costs of ensuring physicians' high incomes in order to encourage the service commitment (limited altruism) to patients exceed the benefits. A more radical challenge to this element of the social bargain model is to cast doubt on the assumption that high incomes do in fact produce an exceptional level of the service commitment in physicians—that is, a service commitment that is deeper and more pervasive than that found in the population at large or in the population of those in occupations providing services to others.

There is, in fact, considerable evidence that, contrary to the myth of medical professionalism, physicians are not significantly more altruistic toward those they serve than many others whose altruism is not encouraged by exceptional incomes.[33] One need not adduce evidence that at least *some* physicians are more self-seeking than the average person—the all too familiar instances of Medicaid fraud, sexual molestation of patients, and so on. The relevant questions, rather, are these: (1) What evidence is there that physicians, as a class, are more likely to forego the pursuit of self-interest and cleave steadfastly to the interests of those they serve, if such evidence exists? (2) What additional evidence is there that this extraordinary (limited) altruism results (at least in part) from their being assured a favored economic niche? and (3) Is the additional level of service commitment thus secured worth the cost?

If, as I have already noted, the burden of argument is on those who would try to justify the favored economic position of physicians as the price we must pay for physicians' (alleged) exceptional (limited) altruism, then the first step is to marshal convincing evidence regarding statement (1) (the claim that physicians as a class really do possess the service commitment to an exceptional extent). Until this is done, the second and third questions cannot be answered. And unless the first question is answered affirmatively, they are irrelevant anyway.

To my knowledge, no empirical evidence that physicians as a class possess the service commitment to an exceptional extent (as compared with other service providers, including auto mechanics, roof repairers, etc.) has been presented. It is, of course, the business of a profession to encourage the belief that its members are especially altruistic to those they serve, and I suspect that the indignation that the mere request for such evidence brings in some quarters is a good indication that, in achieving this objective, the medical profession has been quite successful. But it is important to distinguish between the inadequately supported beliefs that compose the myth of professionalism and genuine evidence that professionals are especially altruistic.

There is considerable evidence that many, indeed perhaps most, physicians are not exceptionally altruistic individuals. This evidence surfaces once we reflect on some major patterns that emerge from the choices that physicians make *as individuals* (apart from the activities of organized medicine). First, individual physicians have a great deal of freedom to choose where they will practice. The resulting pattern of geographical distribution—or rather maldistribution—is hardly what one would predict if physicians as a class were imbued with an extra dose of altruism. On the contrary, there is persistent maldistribution of physicians. As Uwe Rheinhardt points out:

> Careful empirical research has established scientifically what was known to any cab driver all along: physicians, like everyone else, like to locate in pleasant areas where money is to be had. Thus our favorite areas have been vastly over-doctored, while other areas, notably the inner cities, have been sorely under-served.[34]

A second indication that physicians are not exceptionally altruistic is the maldistribution of physicians across specialties. A number of recent studies contradict any assumption that patient need is a good predictor of the choices medical students in the United States make regarding specialties when applying for residencies; and some recent studies indicate that expected financial gain is an important, even dominant consideration in such choices.[35] If physicians were exceptionally altruistic human beings, or even individuals who placed the health interests of others whom they could serve above the maximization of their own interests, we would expect a different distribution of physicians among specialties.

It is worth emphasizing that these are only two of many forms of evidence drawn from the behavior of individual physicians, that physicians are not exceptionally altruistic. If we concentrate on the behavior of organized medicine, there is perhaps even less reason to attribute exceptional altruism. Indeed, it is difficult to imagine how any impartial person familiar with the history of organized medicine in this country could sincerely conclude that it exhibits the triumph of altruism over self-interest.

A third bit of evidence that at least casts doubt on the assumption that physicians as a class are exceptionally altruistic is the fact that many physicians refuse to accept Medicaid patients because Medicaid reimbursement rates are lower than private insurance reimbursement rates. This phenomenon is in some ways more directly pertinent to evaluating the extent of the service commitment, since it indicates that significant numbers of physicians are willing to put their own financial interests ahead of the medical interests of patients in a very concrete way. Such physicians sometimes refuse to care for individuals who arrive at the physician's place of practice needing care. This is a more dramatic and direct example of not putting the patient's interests first than a situation in which a physician simply chooses not to go into a specialty in which practitioners are desperately needed or chooses not to locate in an underserved area.

Fourth, the studies cited earlier concerning the much higher rates of referral by doctors who own diagnostic facilities provides compelling evidence that the service commitment in these practitioners is far from robust. In the absence of any data to show that they are referring more because more referrals are medically indicated in their patient populations, the only reasonable explanation of their higher referral rates is that these physicians are pursuing their own financial interests rather than the best interests of their patients.

Of the evidence cited thus far, the self-referral studies bear most directly on the question of the extent of the service commitment. However, the cumulative import of all four areas of evidence (not to mention well-documented cases of Medicaid and Medicare fraud and other, more egregious abuses of the fiduciary relationship) is to cast serious doubt on the assumption that the service commitment in physicians is so deep and pervasive as to justify the exceptionally favored economic positions they occupy. And again, it is important to note that even if it could be shown that some degree of special economic reward did something to facilitate the service commitment, it would not follow that the extremely high level of reward that now exists is required to secure this benefit for society. For it is one thing to say that physicians will be better able to honor the service commitment if they are not poor or are financially comfortable and quite another to say that they must be rich.

So far, I have raised questions about whether the benefit of the service commitment is worth the economic costs of the favored economic position of physicians. Two other costs of providing medical practitioners with a secure and elevated financial position must be noted. The first is the creation of organized medicine as a powerful political force. The second, an effect of the way in which this political force has been deployed, is the barrier that the medical profession in this country has erected in response to repeated efforts to extend access to care to those who are unserved or underserved.

A prominent and dramatic theme in the history of organized medicine in the United States is the profession's largely successful efforts to block national health insurance, which many believe to be the only workable reform that would have a chance of making a truly significant impact on the access problem.[36] Organized medicine has traditionally seen national health insurance, as well as more radical proposals for extending access, as a threat both to physicians' income and status and to the profession's relative freedom from external regulation.

Despite strong initial opposition from organized medicine, Medicare and Medicaid were established in the mid-1960s. However, the price of securing them became another major barrier to universal access: Reimbursement rates for Medicare were set at such generous levels that the extension of publicly funded access to other populations became politically unfeasible.[37]

Here we see another significant—and perhaps largely unanticipated—cost of the social bargain: The creation of a highly concentrated, well-educated, and financially powerful political force, willing and able to place severe constraints on society's capacity to carry out major social reforms. The social "bargain" that allows practitioners of medicine to secure a sheltered economic niche also empowers the profession as a formidable political lobby—a class of individuals with exceptional resources and prestige, united by a common interest in maintaining and preserving these advantages. Moreover, if medical practitioners enjoy status trust and are thought to be exceptionally altruistic, this is likely to enhance the effectiveness of their lobbying efforts by fostering the perception that when they speak out on public issues, they have the common good, rather than their own good as an interest group, at heart.

According to some theories of social justice, the mere fact that any group, including the medical profession, enjoys such exceptional political power is itself a serious social cost—an infringement on the principle of political equality.[38] But even those who hold less egalitarian conceptions of justice must admit that the profession's tendency to use its resources to impede solutions to the access problem is a major cost of according physicians a favored economic position. It is also a cost that is *not* taken into account in the public understanding of the social bargain that is supposed to legitimate the existence of the profession. Once it is added to the reckoning, the desirability of the bargain, and hence the legitimacy of the medical profession, become all the more doubtful.

The third and final category of costs of professionalism consists of the costs of trust. Here, it is important to distinguish clearly between two sorts of trust. According to what I shall call "status trust," the individual practitioner is deemed worthy of at least significant patient trust simply by virtue of being a member of the professional group—independent of evidence of his own conduct. The second sort of trust is what might be called "individually merited trust"—trust based on evidence about the actual conduct of the individual in question.

Some of the most prominent defenders of medical professionalism have explicitly held not only that the trust of patients in physicians is beneficial but also that what I have called status trust is a necessary concomitant of the social recognition of an occupational group as a profession.

> The sheer fact of having been socially "certified" as professionals means that clients [or patients] will typically take it for granted that professionals are [to be trusted].[39]

Defenders of the medical profession often stress the beneficial therapeutic effects of status trust. But before we can assume that anything that erodes status trust—including entrepreneurial or rationing behavior by physicians—is undesirable, we must first consider whether status trust provides a *net* benefit. And to do this, we must consider the costs of status trust, not just the benefits. We must attempt to compare whatever therapeutic benefits status trust provides with the costs associated with status trust, not in an ideal world in which status trust is justified by a profession that satisfies the normatively adequate conception of a profession, but in our real world.

If the argument thus far is correct, then it is far from clear that the actual medical profession in this country (as opposed to its idealized image, as portrayed in the myth of professionalism) possesses all the features it would have to have in order to be legitimated according to the social bargain model. In particular, there is at least serious doubt about its performance of the essential function of self-regulation. In addition, the burden of argument has not been borne to show that the elevated status and advantageous economic position of medical practitioners are both effective and necessary for securing the service commitment.

These same considerations cast serious doubt on the rationality of status trust. For status trust, if it can be rationally grounded at all, must be supportable by evidence that the profession is doing an adequate job of self-regulation, especially with regard to conflicts between the professional's and the patient's or client's interest, and that its members can be counted on to resist temptations that others would find irresistible.

The costs of status trust are many and significant. In some cases, patients wrongly assume that simply because an individual is a physician, his referrals or prescriptions for treatment are appropriate, or at least that they are motivated solely by concern for the patient's interest rather than by the desire for revenue. The results of such misplaced status trust range from death and disfigurement to merely unnecessary treatment and additional costs.

A more subtle but nevertheless significant cost of status trust is the inhibition that many patients apparently feel about questioning their physician. If the tacit assumption is that the physician is to be trusted as one whose motives are pure—simply because he is a physician, independently of having done anything to earn one's trust—then one may understandably be reluctant to ask certain pertinent questions.

For example, suppose one knows that one's physician is an owner of the laboratory to which he refers one for a test. How easy would it be for most of us to ask him if he is referring us there because it provides the best service for the money or because it is to his financial benefit to do so?

At least in some cases, such a query—and indeed any questioning of a physician's clinical recommendations—will be greeted with righteous indignation, if not hostility, from physicians who have been socialized to expect status trust.[40]

To the extent that status trust prevails, it is likely that many patients will find it difficult to raise questions that may challenge the physician's dedication to putting the patient's interest first. But if this is so, then status trust can seriously impede certain otherwise plausible strategies for dealing with conflict of interest. In particular, simply posting an announcement in the waiting room disclosing that the physician is the owner of the laboratory to which he refers patients will not be likely to empower patients to protect themselves.

As was noted at the beginning of this chapter, a number of prominent physicians bemoan the erosion of trust in medical professionals. What they fail to consider is the possibility that the erosion of misplaced status trust may be essential for developing realistic responses to the problem of conflict of interest. Instead of relying primarily on the service commitment of medical professionals and the supposed self-regulation of the profession, it is more reasonable to consider the entire range of possible arrangements for dealing with conflicts of interest.

Among the possibilities worth considering—but that we are not likely to take seriously if we cleave to the unsupported dogma that the medical profession is a self-regulating cadre of exceptional altruists—is the proposal that the law of agency, which applies to other principal–agent relationships, should be extended and adapted to provide protection against conflict of interest in medicine.[41] For example, federal or state legislatures could impose fiduciary standards on physicians in the same way they have already done for government officials, corporate directors and officers, lawyers, trustees, and certain financial specialists (often called "financial professionals"), including money managers and investment brokers. Self-referral, or certain forms of it, might be prohibited by such statutory fiduciary standards. Alternatively, or in addition, courts might award strict liability damages if patients are harmed when a physician engages in self-referral.[42]

Another possibility that emerges once the myth of professionalism is dissipated is that the resources of principal–agent theory should be utilized to protect patients from the adverse effects of conflicts of interest.[43] Contractual or other arrangements might be devised to ensure a closer congruence between the physician's and the patient's interest, for example, by financially rewarding exemplary physician decision-making. Alternatively, or in addition, arrangements external to the physician–patient relationship might also be employed to reduce agency risk to patients.

Indeed, three instances of the latter approach are already being employed with growing frequency. The first is the practice of seeking second opinions, with the implied threat of terminating the relationship. The second is the use of advance directives for medical care. As I have argued at length elsewhere, advance directives, as public documents rather than confidential instructions to one's physician, serve to avoid or cope with potential failures in the physician–patient relationship, understood as a principal–agent relationship.[44] This is clearest in the case of a proxy advance directive, a legal document that creates a *secondary* principal–agent relationship (between the patient and his proxy). Some patients may be led to create this secondary principal–agent relationship out of apprehension that the physician will not honor their wishes concerning termination of treatment. Similarly, if patients were thoroughly assured that their physicians would honor their wishes once they become incompetent, there would be little need for a witnessed, public document recording the patient's instructions, as opposed to a personal, confidential communication to the physician. The third method that is being employed with increasing frequency is the case manager approach. The use of a case manager, who tracks the patient throughout the complexity of a multi-specialty course of treatment is an admission that the physician–patient relationship (or rather a series of such relationships) can put the patient at risk.

It is revealing to note that some physicians oppose all of these methods for reducing agency risk in the physician–patient relationship, contending that they signal a failure to trust the physician as professional. That is undoubtedly so. And that is precisely the point. To dismiss them and other related proposals that do not rely exclusively on physician altruism and existing collective self-regulation on the grounds that they are incompatible with professionalism is simply to beg the question of to what the alternatives are for protecting patients from conflicts of interest.

None of these approaches is exclusive of the others or exhaustive of the alternatives. The point is that one of the hidden costs of the recognition of medicine as a profession, at least so far as this carries with it widespread status trust, is the foreclosure of options for dealing with conflict of interest.

Some might protest that the imposition of legal fiduciary standards or the use of financial incentives to reduce conflict of interest would transform a profession into a mere business and *thereby* extinguish trust. This objection wrongly equates all trust with status trust and hence mistakenly assumes that if physicians are not regarded as professionals their patients will have no basis for trusting them. However, the erosion of status trust, even its total disappearance, need not mean the end of trust in the physician–patient relationship. Even if physicians came to be regarded not as professionals but as people in the business of providing health care (or rather certain forms of health care, since much health care is provided by nonphysicians), this would not mean that trust would not be an important element in the interaction between physicians and patients. It would merely mean that trust would have a different basis. Nor would the disappearance of medicine as a profession necessarily mean the end of the provision of medical care within a framework of moral norms.

In recent years, social scientists and legal theorists alike have increasingly emphasized the vital role of trust and of moral norms at the very heart of the market exchanges that purveyors of the myth of professionalism have portrayed as "mere business." Of particular importance is the recognition that the complex exchanges that characterize many contemporary business activities flourish only within a framework of trust built up by compliance over time with norms of reciprocity and fairness.[45]

CONCLUSIONS

The main conclusions of our investigation can be summarized briefly:

1. The most plausible justifications for according certain occupational groups (and not others) the status of a profession are (a) that the benefits to society of this socially constructed inequality exceed the costs (and that this way of securing the benefits is the least costly morally acceptable alternative) or (b) that such recognition can be viewed as the outcome of a social bargain.
2. According to the latter justification, in exchange for certain social benefits, including exceptionally altruistic behavior and cost-effective self-regulation by a group that applies special knowledge on behalf of those lacking this knowledge, society grants special status, a favored and secure economic position, and considerable freedom from external regulation.
3. A profession is a social construct and, more precisely, a socially constructed inequality whose justification depends on whether the benefits of having the profession exceed the costs or upon whether the social bargain is fair and mutually advantageous.
4. Whether the costs do exceed the benefits, or whether the bargain is fair and mutually advantageous, depends on whether there is convincing evidence that the elevated status and favored economic position of physicians in fact promote an exceptional service commitment in the members of the profession, and on whether there is convincing evidence that the profession is exercising collective self-regulation that is not only adequate but superior to other forms of control.
5. At present, convincing evidence for an exceptional service commitment or for adequate collective self-regulation is lacking. Nor is it clear that there is good reason to think that the extremely high level of financial reward available to physicians in this country is necessary for securing whatever depth and extent of service commitment in fact exists. Those who wish to legitimate the socially constructed inequality known as the medical profession have not produced convincing evidence of a deep and pervasive service commitment. Moreover, neither the history of organized medicine nor the patterns of career choices of individual physicians support the hypothesis of exceptional physician altruism toward patients. Furthermore, for the most part, the past century of organized medicine's history exhibits an abdication of the responsibility for effective collective self-regulation. On the one hand, the exercise of self-regulatory authority in medical licensure has been a qualified success at best, imposing strenuous initial barriers to entry that historically have kept physicians' incomes high while excluding some forms of practice and certain types of services that could have produced valuable

benefits. At the same time, licensing regulation has failed to ensure the continued competence of licensed physicians.

6. While there is little hard evidence that the favored economic position of the medical profession has enhanced altruism toward patients by insulating them from crass economic concerns, there can be no doubt that it has imposed other significant costs on society. Among the most important of these are higher health care costs, political inequality resulting from the empowering of an articulate and rich medical political lobby, and major impediments to implementing reforms in the health care system that would enhance access to care for those currently unserved or underserved. In addition, the chief argument for according physicians a favored economic position is most compelling if it is construed as a justification for ensuring them a comfortable living; it cannot justify the extremely favored economic position physicians actually achieve in this country. On the contrary, there is the danger that the exceptionally high economic prospects enjoyed by U.S. physicians may attract those in whom the service commitment is not the dominating motivation.
7. If one element of the normatively adequate—or, as we might also say, the legitimating—conception of a profession is effective collective self-regulation, including sanctions to ensure compliance with authoritative, contentful norms, then the American medical profession does not exemplify such a conception. It follows that in the sense in which the medical profession could be said to be legitimate—that is, a justified, socially constructed inequality—there is no medical profession in this country. There is, instead a privileged occupational group whose defenders wrongly present it as exemplifying the normatively adequate conception of a profession.
8. Even if there is, strictly speaking, no medical profession in this country (in the legitimating or normatively adequate sense), there is still, to some extent, the public belief that there is a profession. One aspect of this belief—the allegiance to the myth of professionalism—is status trust: the assumption that a physician is entitled to significant trust simply because he is a member of the medical profession. The prevalence of status trust may have therapeutic benefits in some instances, but it also has serious social costs.
9. Among the social costs of the recognition of medicine as a profession, and of the concomitant status trust in physicians, is an inability to consider objectively the full range of options for coping with conflicts of interest.

It is worth emphasizing that I have *not* argued that the medical profession should be abolished or that the professional status of physicians should be revoked. Instead, I have only argued that the legitimacy of a profession, as a socially constructed inequality, requires a convincing showing that having a medical profession is a good bargain for society and that this burden of justification *has not* been borne. Strictly speaking, nothing in my analysis demonstrates that it is *impossible* to provide convincing evidence that the existence of the profession is a good social bargain. However, in arguing that the burden of justification has not been borne, I have, I believe, shown that providing the needed evidence will be hard indeed.

There are, it seems, three possible responses to my analysis. First, one might attempt to show that, despite appearances to the contrary, granting professional status to medical practitioners is a good social bargain. Second, proposals might be offered for improving the performance of the profession (especially with respect to collective self-regulation) so that the bargain would become a good one. Third, one might opt for a serious departure from the model of professionalism, and in particular from reliance on self-regulation, by developing other means for controlling conflicts of interest, including external regulation. My main objective in this chapter is to challenge the legitimacy of the profession so as to get these three options on the table.

Whether pursuing the third option would amount to the abolition of the medical profession depends on how malleable the concept of a medical profession is. We do speak of lawyers and financial advisers as professionals even though they are subject to much more substantial external regulation, especially with regard to conflict of interest, than physicians are.

The implications of these conclusions for the current debate about rationing, medical entrepreneurism, and professionalism are significant. The much-lamented erosion of professionalism in medicine may be better characterized as the disintegration of the myth of professionalism. We might well welcome this process of disillusionment as a recognition that the time has come for renegotiating the social bargain, if not for refusing to perpetuate it.

Early in this chapter, I distinguished between the ideal or normative conception of the medical profession and the sociological conception. The chief difference between the two is the sociological conception's emphasis on the special status, favored economic position, and relative freedom from external regulation of the medical profession. It is these features—these socially constructed inequalities—that call for justification. It is these features that cast doubt on the legitimacy of the profession if a convincing justification for its existence is not forthcoming. What must have struck the reader by now is how *separable* these problematic features are from the laudable characteristics that constitute the ideal conception of the profession. Indeed, from the standpoint of common sense, these two sets of features are not only separable but also conflicting, the danger being that the high status and exceptional economic reward of being a physician in this country undoubtedly will attract some people to the profession who are motivated by self-interest rather than the desire to serve others.

We have seen that the cost–benefit and social bargain justifications attempt—rather unconvincingly—to forge a necessary connection between the special advantages of the profession and the characteristics of the ideal conception, in particular, the service commitment and the commitment to excellent performance of the special activity of the profession. Once we realize the tenuousness of this connection, we may well conclude that our way of thinking about the medical profession requires a major revision. We should jettison the idea that it is somehow in the nature of the medical profession that this group should enjoy high status, economic privilege, and relative freedom from external regulation. We should then ask physicians and ourselves the following questions: How did we come to regard these problematic social inequalities as inextricably linked with an otherwise admirable conception of the profession? Why should we assume that a steadfast and overriding commitment to serve others can—much less must—be combined with high status and economic privilege? To what extent does this assumption reflect a particularly American cultural interpretation of the idea of a medical profession? Might it be the case that a society gets the medical profession it deserves?[46]

9

SPECIFYING THE CONTENT OF THE HUMAN RIGHT TO HEALTH CARE

Kristen Hessler and Allen Buchanan

Recent writing on the human right to health care is characterized by two trends. First, human rights scholars and health professionals emphasize that health is a complex good, promoted and protected by much more than services provided by medical professionals.[1] This has prompted recognition that the human right to health care is not confined to entitlements to medical care alone. Second, and relatedly, some writers have attempted to delineate a universal, determinate standard defining the precise scope and content of the human right to health care (Toebes 1999). We argue in this chapter that, whereas the first trend is an important step forward, the second is misguided.

We proceed by first exploring the meaning of a human right to health care, considered in the context of the importance of health as a component of general well-being. We then consider some arguments against the claim that health care is a human right, and we show that those arguments fail. We then briefly survey three different accounts of health care as a human right. On the basis of those accounts, we demonstrate that a human right to health care is necessarily vague, and that the appropriate forum for specifying its content is through appropriate democratic political procedures, and not by moral or political theory alone.

HUMAN RIGHTS

"Human rights" are those moral rights that all people possess. International human rights documents, like the Universal Declaration of Human Rights, reflect the efforts of the international community to make the protection of these rights binding under international law. As the rights of all persons as such, human rights are importantly egalitarian. Hence, the first article of the Universal Declaration of Human Rights proclaims, "All human beings are born free and equal in dignity and rights," and the preamble of each document comprising the International Bill of Rights states that "recognition of the inherent dignity and of the equal and inalienable rights of all members of the human family is the foundation of freedom, justice and peace in the world." More substantially, international human rights documents enumerate specific rights that all persons have, including rights to life, rights to be free from torture or arbitrary arrest, to marry, and to start a family.

Two features may be taken as essential to all human rights claims. First, the claim that health care is a human right is much stronger than the claim that health care is a good thing, or that it is desirable that all people have health care. One does not have a right to all those things that might increase one's well-being; for instance, one does not have a human right to possess a sense of humor. Rather, human rights are moral entitlements: "*A* has a right to *X*" means "*A* is morally entitled to *X*." As such, *A*'s possessing human rights entails that some other agent, or group of agents, has obligations to *X*. These obligations may include providing *A* with *X*, or, more minimally, refraining from depriving *A* of *X*. Second, human rights are universal rights, in the sense that they "are held by people simply as people" (Nickel 1987, p. 3). Thus, at a sufficiently abstract level of description at least, the human rights attributable to any one person will be attributable to all people.

RIGHT TO HEALTH CARE, RIGHT TO HEALTH

In the United States, discussions about a right to health care often are focused explicitly on rights to medical care—that is, services provided by medical professionals to individuals (Toebes 1999, p. 246). However, in a global context, it is clear that such services are only a small component of the health-related services that make a difference to people's health. Public-health services are at least as important as medical services, and in many places much more important, to improving the health of large numbers of people.[2] Even more general factors like poverty and fertility rates affect the health of entire populations.[3]

Unsurprisingly, poorer countries fare worse on all sorts of health measures than do richer ones. One obvious reason for this is that richer countries have more money to spend on medical care, but no less important is the fact that citizens of richer countries have better access to healthy environments and adequate nutrition. The broad range of factors that influence the health of individuals and entire populations indicates that health is a complex good.

This raises a thorny terminological issue in human rights literature. Given the complexity of health, many have thought that the right to health care is too narrow and have favored using the term "right to health" instead. Support for this usage comes from the major human rights documents, which more often assert a "right to health" than a "right to health care." For example, the International Covenant on Economic, Social, and Cultural Rights includes the "right of everyone to the enjoyment of the highest attainable standard of physical and mental health,"[4] whereas the Universal Declaration of Human Rights embeds a right specifically to medical care within a broader right to health and well-being.[5] However, the problem with asserting a right to health, as opposed to asserting a right to health care, is that it seems too demanding. A *right to health care* implies, on its face, a right to certain services; by contrast, a *right to health* seems to imply a right to be healthy, which is an impossible standard. Some severely ill or impaired individuals will never be healthy, no matter how many resources are expended on them. Moreover, seriously pursuing health for everyone would be so draining on social resources as to leave little, if any, room for the pursuit of other social goals.

However, despite this objection, there are two reasons to search for an acceptable interpretation of the "right to health" rather than to reject the term entirely. One is that, as we mentioned, major human rights treaties assert a right to health. It would be a serious cost to reject all articles in human rights treaties that assert a right to health, especially if an acceptable understanding of that locution were available. Second, given that it is undeniable that factors other than access to medical care have a significant impact on health, the notion of a right to health is valuable. A right to health *care* seems too narrow to cover factors like healthy environmental conditions or good sanitation facilities. This suggests that the "right to health" may be a useful label for a wider category than that of rights to medical care. Such an understanding is consistent with current usage of these terms, as many human rights treaties assert specific rights to certain kinds of medical care or public-health services as a part of the general right to health.

There are two ways to understand a right to health as including the right to health care. One is to see the right to health as shorthand for a longer list of specific entitlements, including the subset of entitlements that comprise the right to health care. To a certain extent, we accept this description. We use the term "right to health care" in this chapter to refer to rights to services rendered by health-care professionals to individuals or to populations. Thus, the right to health care includes curative and preventive services provided to individuals—such as therapy for illness, health screenings, and prenatal care—as well as population-based services like immunizations. The right to health care, on our understanding, does not include rights to clean water, adequate sanitation, or the careful placement of toxic waste. In this sense, the right to health care picks out a subset of the entitlements that comprise the broader right to health.

However, this should not blind us to the other, more foundational, way of understanding the right to health as including the right to health care. The right to health asserts that the basic human interest in health is so important as to justify asserting a social obligation to satisfy that interest. It is because health is so important to human beings that rights to health care are so important. However, it is also with an eye on the importance of the basic human interest in health that we see that, in some circumstances, health care is less important than other contributors to health, like sanitation or clean water. In this way, rights to health care and rights to healthy environments are best seen as parts of the right to health, in the sense that they are different kinds of claims that are both justified by reference to the basic human interest in health.

ARGUMENTS AGAINST A HUMAN RIGHT TO HEALTH CARE

Typically, arguments against a right to health care are only one application of more general arguments against the whole category of social and economic rights. Maurice Cranston argues, for example, that civil and political rights are universal human rights, but that social and economic rights are not. The major difference, in his view, is that civil and political rights can be implemented very easily, via simple legislation; but social and economic rights cannot. "The traditional 'political and civil rights' can…be readily secured by legislation; and generally they can be secured by fairly simple legislation. Since those rights are for the most part rights against government interference with a man's activities, a large part of the legislation needed has to do no more than restrain the government's own executive arm" (Cranston 1973, p. 66). Because social and economic rights require expenditures that many poor nations cannot afford, Cranston believes they are not universal human rights at all.

However, Cranston is mistaken in his characterization of civil and political rights. The issue of limited public resources arises for civil and political rights as well as for social and economic rights.[6] The implementation and enforcement of civil and political rights cost money. As one observer noted: "The need for expenditure is clearly evident in rights such as that to a fair hearing before an independent and impartial court; funds will be required not only for the buildings and personnel which constitute a court system but also for the provision of legal aid and interpreters where these are required" (McBride 1997, p. 128). Further, it would be difficult to disagree with the Human Rights Committee's assertions that the prohibition of torture entails positive obligations to supervise the treatment of prisoners and to establish complaint procedures, and that upholding the right to free assembly requires states to ensure that demonstrations are not suppressed

(McBride 1997, pp. 128–29).[7] This shows that expenditures of money must be made in implementing civil and political rights, as in implementing social and economic rights. If one is willing to recognize civil and political human rights as human rights, then the fact that social and economic rights require state expenditures does not imply that they are not human rights.

Cranston has another objection to social and economic rights. This is that such rights are not of "paramount importance," or morally urgent. According to Cranston, "A human right is something of which no one may be deprived without a grave affront to justice" (Cranston 1973, p. 68). In Cranston's view, civil and political rights, like the right against torture, pass the test of paramount importance: "[T]he use of torture at the pleasure of a despot is precisely the kind of thing which declarations of the Rights of Man are meant to outlaw, and which the United Nations at its inception was expected to banish from the earth. This is a matter of moral urgency, which is far removed from questions of holidays with pay" (Cranston 1973, p. 71). Holidays with pay, and other social and economic rights like rights to health care, are in Cranston's view merely goals, and not matters of moral urgency. Thus, in his view, they are by definition not universal human rights.

Cranston spells out this objection in two different ways. First, he argues that the difference between civil and political human rights on the one hand, and economic and social rights on the other, is analogous to the distinction between duty and charity. In his view, no one can be morally obligated to provide *charity* for another (indeed, this is what makes it charity); but because economic and social rights are really just charity for the worst-off, no one can be obligated to uphold them, and therefore they are not really rights at all. The problem with this formulation of Cranston's objection is that he does not *argue* for his characterization of social and economic rights as charity. Cranston cannot simply label them charity, for that would be begging the question (Buchanan 1987). As we have seen, government expenditure is as necessary for civil and political rights as for social and economic rights, so the fact that government expenditure is required to achieve social and economic rights cannot hold up as a justification for labeling them charitable goals as opposed to human rights.

The second and related development of Cranston's second objection is that there is no readily identifiable duty-holder who is responsible for upholding social and economic rights, and therefore that these are not really rights at all.

> They [economic and social rights] are rights to be given things, things such as a decent income, schools, and social services. But who is called upon to do the giving? Whose duty is it? When the authors of the United Nations Covenant on Economic and Social Rights assert that "everyone has the right to social security," are they saying that everyone ought to subscribe to some form of worldwide social security system from which each in turn may benefit in case of need? If something of this kind is meant, why do the United Nations Covenants

make no provision for instituting such a system? And if no such system exists, where is the obligation, and where the right? (Cranston 1973, p. 69)

The problem with this argument is that Cranston seems to assume that there can be no rights to anything that cannot readily be provided by identifiable parties. But surely this does not distinguish neatly between civil and political rights and social and economic rights. To ensure the enjoyment of civil and political rights, stable, rights-respecting institutions must be developed and staffed by individuals trained to uphold them and to hear grievances. In many places, such institutions do not currently exist and cannot be established overnight (or via "simple legislation", McBride 1997, pp. 129–34). But more importantly, it is simply false that no rights exist to goods that cannot be immediately provided. There is no incoherence in understanding human rights as entitlements to be progressively achieved. This concession does not give up on the project of human rights; it merely implies that enjoyment of human rights will not be achieved quickly.

JUSTIFYING A HUMAN RIGHT TO HEALTH CARE

As we have seen, Cranston failed to establish that human rights must consist of only civil and political rights. Civil and political rights are neither costless nor obviously more "morally urgent" than other human rights. However, though Cranston has not given us good reason to deny the existence of a human right to health care, we have yet to see a positive argument that health care is a human right.

To assert the existence of a human right to health care is to make a very strong moral claim: that everyone in the world, regardless of nationality, culture, country of citizenship, or any other distinguishing feature, can claim a moral entitlement to certain medical services and public-health measures. In the sections that follow we discuss several ways of justifying this claim, paying particular attention to how each account specifies the scope and content of the human right to health care. In evaluating these accounts, we focus on two main questions. First: Does the account securely justify the existence of a human right to health care? Second: Does the account provide us with the theoretical resources to determine in practice what kinds of health care must be provided to secure enjoyment of the human right to health care?[8]

Health Care as a Basic Need

One account of human rights is that they are generated by a set of basic needs shared by all people. The universality of human rights on this view derives from the universality of human needs. The main difficulty with this approach is that "basic needs" are difficult to define. The most basic human needs are those things essential to survival. However, if we take this to imply that the human rights to health care is an entitlement to all and only that health care necessary for survival, we will find that this account is both too narrow and too broad. It is too narrow because health care is important not just for saving or extending lives in dire situations, but also for making people healthier, or more comfortable, or for removing barriers to important opportunities. It is too broad because it is literally impossible to provide all people with all health care they need to survive. Given the great cost of some medical care, especially very advanced technology like kidney dialysis machines or organ transplants, and even the expense of public health, limitations on resources will severely constrain the fulfillment of a right to health care, if that right is understood as the right to all care needed to survive.

To be plausible, then, a basic needs justification of human rights requires qualification. David Ozar's account of "basic needs" identifies such needs as those necessary for minimal security. His definition of "minimal security" is "the condition of a person who has sufficient resources to assure survival not only in the present moment and for one additional moment into the future, but for several more moments into the future as well, so that it is reasonable and possible for the person to devote some part of his or her energy and attention to ends other than survival" (Ozar 1983, p. 302). This is a morally significant threshold, in Ozar's view, because without the freedom to attend to ends other than survival, a person cannot live a life that fulfils distinctively human capacities. Basic needs are those which, when satisfied, would place one at or above the level of minimal security. Basic health care, then, is "such health care as will place a person at the level of minimal security with regard to health care" (Ozar 1983, p. 307).

Exactly what sorts of health care count as basic, on this account? Ozar indicates that this category includes such things as emergency medical care, treatment to prevent illnesses from becoming life-threatening, and some care for conditions that are not life-threatening, like physical therapy or the relief of pain.[9] Notice that these descriptions are vague and suggestive. This is true for at least three reasons. First, as Ozar notes, the development of medical technology continues to result in new treatments becoming available. This has the result that any specific list of basic health-care services must be dated (Ozar 1983, p. 304). Second, the threats to people's health vary from place to place: Malaria is a serious health problem in many places, but not in Tucson, Arizona. So both the treatment for malaria and prevention are basic health needs in some areas but not in others.

These first two sources of indeterminacy about the content of the human right to health care are in principle resolvable. However, the category of basic health care is still fuzzy, even given Ozar's analysis. As he points out, his analysis does not tell us whether American citizens have a right to what he calls "life-maintaining care"—which maintains "the lives of persons who, according to our best judgments about their conditions, have lost the capacity to ever maintain their lives without assistance" (Ozar 1983, p. 308). We could add that Ozar's analysis does not tell us whether those who suffer from kidney disease have rights to publicly funded dialysis, or whether all children have a right to some set of immunizations. This third source of indeterminacy about the content of the right to health care indicates that the concept of basic health care is not well-defined enough to specify the content of the human right to health care.

A more basic question is whether Ozar's account securely justifies the existence of a human right to health care in the first place. According to his account, people have human rights to those things necessary for minimal security—that is, to those things necessary to assure survival for several "moments" into the future. It does seem plausible that guaranteed access to some health care is necessary to assure my survival in the event that I am the victim of some fairly common mishap: an accident, for example, or a bout of malaria. However, to assure my survival for some significant time, much health care might be required; for example, I might need a heart transplant. But surely the right to health care does not require everyone to receive heart transplants as needed. Because donor hearts are scarce, and because a social guarantee of a heart transplant for everyone as needed would be prohibitively expensive, it would be impossible to guarantee heart transplants to all who need them to survive for a significant time. From this we can conclude that the right to health care is not really the right to anything necessary to ensure anyone's survival for a significant time.[10] If that is so, then we have good reason to reject Ozar's account as too broad.[11]

Health Care and Human Dignity

The view that human rights are those moral entitlements that respect human dignity is implied by the language in some prominent human rights documents. The International Covenant on Civil and Political Rights, for example, asserts that "[human] rights derive from the inherent dignity of the human person." Similarly, the United Nations' Charter asserts that one of the UN's missions is "to reaffirm faith in fundamental human rights, in the dignity and worth of the human person, in the equal rights of men and women and nations large and small." Jack Donnelly endorses this view: "Human rights are 'needed' for human dignity, rather than health, and violations of human rights are denials of one's humanity rather than deprivations of needs. We have human rights not to the requisites for health, but to those things 'needed' for a truly human life" (Donnelly 1985, p. 31; 1989, p. 17).

This view avoids the problem of having to come up with a plausible list of basic human needs. However, the real work of this approach is to generate a compelling characterization of human dignity, and its material conditions, in order to get a sense of the scope of human rights. Thus, we might understand "human dignity" as "conditions fitting or suitable for human beings." Unfortunately, this understanding is so close to the meaning of human rights—"the moral entitlements of all human beings as such"—that it sheds little or no light on the concept of a human right. It is probably as a consequence of this fact that Donnelly is led to assert that "human rights doctrines rest on something very much like an equation of having human rights and being human" (Donnelly 1985, p. 33). The defects of this kind of analysis for our purposes are obvious; starting with the concept of human dignity does not set us very far along the road toward justifying the claim that health care is a human right, not to mention toward ascertaining what kinds of health care are necessary for fulfilling that right. The appeal to human dignity has a broad resonance, but this is purchased by its vagueness.

Health Care as a Basic Right

Henry Shue (1996, p. 19) has argued that certain human rights are basic, in the sense that their enjoyment is necessary for the enjoyment of any other right: For example, if one does not enjoy the right to physical security (in Shue's phraseology: the right "not to be subjected to murder, torture, mayhem, rape or assault") (Shue 1996, p. 23), then it is impossible for one to enjoy other, nonbasic rights like the right freely to assemble. Shue writes (1996, p. 67): "[T]he substance of a basic right can have its status only because, and so only if, its enjoyment is a constituent part of the enjoyment of every other right, as...enjoying not being assaulted is a component part of the enjoyment of anything else, such as assembling for a meeting." Shue argues for three main categories of basic rights: rights to security; rights to subsistence; and certain liberty rights, including rights to political participation. He includes health care and public health as components of the basic right to subsistence. Thus, Shuc places health care and public-health measures in a privileged class of human rights—basic rights—which in his view deserve first attention. If Shue's arguments are good ones, then anyone who accepts human rights at all should accept that health care, including public-health measures, is a human right of particular importance.

However, Shue's arguments support a much wider class of basic rights than he realizes. Basic rights are those whose enjoyment is necessary to the enjoyment of any other rights. According to this account, health care is a basic right because it, like freedom from assault, is necessary for the enjoyment of any other right. In the argument quoted earlier, Shue states that basic rights are *constituent parts* of nonbasic rights: One does not enjoy the right to assemble, for example, if one does not enjoy the right not to be beaten for joining certain assemblies. But consider his argument that political participation is a basic right. In his view, the content of the basic right to political participation includes "genuine influence upon the fundamental choices among the social institutions and the social policies that control security and subsistence and, where the person is directly affected, genuine influence upon the operation of institutions and the implementation of policy" (Shue 1996, p. 71). In support of his claim that participation is a basic right, he argues:

> It is not possible to enjoy full rights to security or to subsistence without also having rights to participate effectively in the control of security and subsistence. A right is the basis for a certain kind of demand: a demand the fulfillment of which ought to be socially guaranteed. Without channels through which the demand can be made known to those who ought to be guaranteeing its fulfillment, when it is in fact being ignored, one cannot exercise this right. (p. 75)

In this argument we see that the sense in which a basic right must be necessary to the enjoyment of all other rights is not as narrow as it might have appeared at first. For enjoying a right to effective political participation is not *logically* a constituent of enjoying rights to security and subsistence; if participation is required for the enjoyment of all other human rights it is because of empirical facts about the tendencies of nonparticipatory governments to ignore the interests of their citizens.

Moreover, we can show in a different way that, on Shue's view, the scope of basic rights must be vast indeed. Shue (1996) argues that the right to participation is no mere formal requirement; rather, "for a right to the liberty of participation to be of any consequence, the participation must be effective and exert some influence upon outcomes" (p. 71). However, the conditions for effective political participation are themselves extensive. For example, surely some kind of education is necessary to render people's participation effective, as are free deliberation among citizens, which requires a free press and rights to free speech and free association. Indeed, the class of basic rights threatens, on this kind of expansion, to include nearly all human rights.

In this way, basic rights are much more extensive, by his own argument, than Shue realizes. The more extensive the class of basic rights becomes, the less that class can accurately be described as a set of core rights deserving first priority among all human rights. Instead, we begin to see a complex interdependency among the entire corpus of rights, with no clear priority attached to one small subclass of rights. While this view of human rights might support the claim that health care is a human right because it is a basic right, we would need arguments different from Shue's to bear out that claim.

Finally, if we could show that some health care is necessary for the enjoyment of other rights, we would still be left with problems determining the content of the human right to health care. It is a reasonable assumption that healthy people have an advantage when it comes to enjoying their human rights; but this does not tell us how to decide which health-care services to provide when we face a limited budget, nor how to balance health against other necessary conditions for enjoying other human rights, nor even which aspects of health are most important to enjoying other human rights. So the thesis that health care is necessary to securing people's abilities to enjoy other human rights does not eliminate the need to specify further the content of the human right to health care.

JUSTIFYING THE HUMAN RIGHT TO HEALTH CARE

As we have seen, neither the basic needs approach, nor Shue's basic rights approach, nor the human dignity approach to human rights provides a clear account of a human right to health care that offers some guidance for understanding its content. We suggest instead that human rights should be understood as moral claims grounded in *basic human interests*. These are interests that are universally shared by all (or nearly all) human beings, and they are the kinds of interests that justify assigning obligations to others, or to society generally, to secure or protect those interests. The interest in developing a sense of humor, though it may be important to human well-being for some individuals, and may at least be beneficial for most, is not as important for well-being as adequate food, shelter, or access to immunizations. Because some interests are so important for virtually all human beings, they ground obligations on others to help see that they are satisfied. Ultimately, what grounds human rights, including the corresponding obligations, is something fundamental to morality: equal consideration for all persons.

We can say, on this account, that health care is a human right because being healthy is a universal interest, common to all people, that grounds duties in others. The basic human interest in health grounds negative duties—duties not to make anyone sick—and, especially for governments, positive duties—duties to protect and/or to promote the health of others.

One advantage of this account is that it places all human rights on the same footing. People have a human right to health care because they have a basic interest in health, which justifies assigning responsibilities to society to ensure that this interest is met. Similarly, people have a basic interest in security, and in being able to express freely their deeply held views. Both interests are components of overall well-being. Thus, when different human rights conflict, this view refers us back to consider how the interests that ground the conflicting rights contribute to human well-being. This provides at least the possibility of a principled method for resolving such conflicts.

However, the specification problem still looms. The fact that the human right to health care is grounded in the basic human interest in health does not imply anything about the specific content of the right to health care. For example, it does not specify whether that right includes a right to access to abortions, or how to decide which health services to provide when resources are limited. We address this question in the next section.

THE CONTENT OF THE RIGHT TO HEALTH CARE IN INTERNATIONAL LAW

The vagueness of the right to health care creates some difficulty for implementing the right to health care—that is, for ensuring that people enjoy this right. If it is not clear what the content of a human right is, implementing that right through international human rights law, and monitoring nations' compliance, will be correspondingly difficult. In response to this problem, some observers have attempted to specify the scope and content of the right to health care for legal purposes. Brigit Toebes, for example, concludes her extensive study on the human right to health in international law with an account of its core content:

> Irrespective of their available resources, States have to provide access to maternal and child health care, including family planning; immunisation against the major infectious diseases; appropriate treatment of common diseases and injuries; essential drugs; and adequate supply of safe water and basic sanitation. In addition, they are to assure freedom from serious environmental health threats. (Toebes 1999)

Toebes's aim is to give an account of the content of the human right to health care that is universally applicable to all nations. However, in pursuing this goal, she ignores several important parameters of difference among nations. First, Toebes ignores the particular circumstances of individual states in her prescription for which health-related services they should provide. Her qualifier—that states (nations) are obligated to provide health care as she defines it, "[i]rrespective of their available resources"—is much too strong. On her view, states would be considered in violation of human rights legal standards if they could not afford to provide all the services that she includes in the right to health care. But surely there is something perverse about a system that would criminalize states essentially for their poverty. If all states had something like a fair share of the world's resources, then requiring them to spend some fixed sum (at least) on health-care provision might be justifiable. But without such attention to global distributive justice, disregarding a nation's available resources is inexcusable.

Second, Toebes's specification of the content of the human right to health care ignores the fact that different health-related problems in different countries may well require different health services. Any attempt to specify a single, universal standard for the human right to health care must depend on the premise that all health problems in all countries can be equally well addressed by the universal package of health services. But a very limited set of services is all that most nations can ensure, and no very limited set of services can adequately address the diverse health needs of different nations.

Third, Toebes also ignores cultural differences that might be relevant to the implementation of a right to health care. For example, the International Conference on Population and Development was boycotted by several Moslem nations because the draft statement issued by the UN in preparation for the conference included access to family planning as a strategy for population control. In reporting on this boycott, David Thomasma notes that at its root is a fundamental objection to the preparatory statement, namely that "the very idea of intervening in reproduction to control population growth is seen as Western-influenced scientific bigotry—blasphemy even—that denies the power of God. This is a fundamental objection to scientific advancement and to the objectification of human processes for manipulation and control" (Thomasma 1997, p. 297). If Thomasma's analysis of the boycott is correct, this is an example of the cultural differences among nations that affect how human rights should be implemented within nations.

These differences among states—differences in resource levels, health-related problems, and culture—combine to recommend *against* the project of incorporating into international human rights law a universal, determinate specification of the content of the human right to health care. However, to implement and enforce the human right to health care in international law, we need some account of how it should be specified. Without such an account, we are threatened by two undesirable consequences: Either states will be free to claim almost any arrangement as a fulfillment of the human right to health care, or the international monitoring bodies will be tempted to enforce one single standard on all states, regardless of their differences.

Currently, the content of human rights in international law is specified mainly through the operation of international institutions, with some contribution from national governments. For example, one international institution that contributes to this process is the Human Rights Committee, a UN organization that monitors the reports of state representatives and nongovernmental organizations (like Amnesty International) on human rights enjoyment within those countries that have ratified the International Covenant on Civil and Political Rights (ICCPR). As a part of this process, countries are permitted to present their understandings of the content of human rights, and the UN committee issues judgments on how well particular nations have implemented human rights. This process contributes to the specification of human rights law, for in making its judgments the committee must clarify its understanding of the provisions of the ICCPR.

Whereas specifying human rights is an essential process in human rights implementation, we should ask whether the authority for specifying such rights properly lies with international institutions, or whether it should lie elsewhere, or whether there should be a division of labor regarding the tasks of specification. The most obvious justification for granting this authority to international institutions is that large segments of human rights are best viewed as rights against the state. Rights against torture and arbitrary imprisonment, as well as rights to health care, impose obligations on the state. Accordingly, states should not be allowed to specify the content of human rights for themselves, for this would allow them to judge the extent of their own obligations. On this view, the best human rights protection must come from supranational institutions.

However, if all human rights are specified through international institutions, it is unlikely that the local differences that we mentioned earlier—which include differences in levels of resources, existing health problems, and culture—will be taken adequately into account. Our discussion of the vagueness of the human right to health care has thus led us to an institutional question relating to all human rights: What institutions can specify the content of human rights in such a way that differences among states are taken adequately into account?

We propose that the virtues of democratic governments suggest that they are better suited than international institutions in protecting the human rights of their own citizens than are international institutions, and also that they might be able to do so in a way that adequately accommodates local differences. Briefly, those virtues are as follows: First, through contested elections, democratic procedures allow people to assert their interests in the political arena. Moreover, through majoritarian decision procedures, democratic government embodies equal consideration for the interests of all citizens (Christiano 1994). Therefore, insofar as human rights are grounded in basic human interests, there is an important connection between democratic politics and human rights.

Second, democracy is (at least in theory) the system of government that is most closely allied with the interests of the governed; to the extent that this ideal is realized in practice, democratic governments have little impetus to violate the human rights of their citizens. Third, participatory political procedures are most likely to bring out the knowledge that citizens have of their particular human rights problems, and of solutions that would make the most sense for those problems. These virtues provide grounds for exempting democratic governments from the general authority of international institutions to interpret human rights law. On our view, then, states that function democratically should have some authority to interpret human rights law for implementation within their borders.

Democratic states should not have absolute interpretive authority, however, even regarding the human rights of their own citizens. One reason is that human rights, while vague, are not meaningless. The human right to health care asserts that all people have the right to health care sufficient for their health and well-being. While this broad statement leaves many particular questions unanswered, it is determinate enough to provide the grounds for criticizing a system in which only members of a certain class, or race, have access to any health-related services. Some situations clearly violate human rights, even in their vague form. For that reason, international human rights bodies should have a role to play in supervising the implementation of human rights in both democratic and non-democratic states.

At this point, one might raise the objection that this account seems circular. The appearance of circularity is suggested by the fact that we have argued that human rights require interpretation in order to be implemented and enforced, but also that the international community should supervise the implementation of human rights even within democratic countries. To do this, it would seem that international institutions would have to solve the specification problem. However, if they could do so, then there would be no need for specifying human rights at the national level through democratic institutions.

Our reply to this objection is to note the restricted way in which international institutions should supervise the implementation of human rights within democratic countries. We suggest that the role of international institutions should be limited to two functions. First, they should specify *minimal* conditions for effective democratic procedures within states. These conditions must be designed to ensure that democratic procedures work as they should, so they will include a well-functioning electoral system, wide freedom of speech and association, and the like. Second, international institutions should review national healthcare situations and point out any obviously inadequate policies. For neither of these tasks must the specification problem be solved; therefore, objection that our account is circular is unfounded.

CONCLUSION

We conclude by acknowledging two limitations of our argument in this chapter. First, a thorough treatment of the human right to health care must acknowledge problems of international distributive justice. In our presentation here we have worked within the assumption that nations have widely diverse levels of resources, such that some nations do not have enough resources to spend on their legitimate needs. We have relied on this assumption for the limited purpose of pointing out the fruitlessness of holding poor nations responsible for providing the same protections for all human rights that richer nations are capable of providing.

However, two reasons exist to go beyond this assumption in the search for a complete theory of human rights and their correlative obligations. First, on many plausible theories of distributive justice, the radical inequality of the international distribution of resources is seriously unjust. Second, to the extent that the human right to health care has determinate content, it justifies holding the international community responsible for providing health care adequate for the health and well-being of populations whose governments are too poor to do so. Both of these premises would lead to an examination of *international* duties for human rights protection.

Moreover, the human right to health care exists within a framework of human rights more generally. Accordingly, research on the human right to health care should shed light on how to make sense of the human right to health care within that framework. The most illuminating research is likely to involve sustained attention to the basic human interest in health. Important questions in this area include how that interest can be satisfied in different circumstances, and how that interest is related to other basic human interests that ground other human rights. Understanding human rights as grounded in basic human interests provides a framework for understanding the interdependence among health care and other human rights, and for beginning to provide an account of how to make implementation decisions about these rights, even when they conflict.

10

RESPONSIBILITY FOR GLOBAL HEALTH

Allen Buchanan and Matthew Decamp

There are several reasons for the current prominence of global health issues. Among the most important is the growing awareness that some risks to health are global in scope and can only be countered by global cooperation. In addition, human rights discourse and, more generally, the articulation of a coherent cosmopolitan ethical perspective that acknowledges the importance of all persons, regardless of where they live, provide a normative basis for taking global health seriously as a moral issue. In this chapter we begin the task of translating the vague commitment to doing something to improve global health into a coherent set of more determinate obligations. One chief conclusion of our inquiry is that the responsibilities of states regarding global health are both more determinate and more extensive than is usually assumed. We also argue, however, that institutional innovation will be needed to achieve a more comprehensive, fair distribution of concrete responsibilities regarding global health and to provide effective mechanisms for holding various state and non-state actors accountable for fulfilling them.

INTRODUCTION

Growing Concern about Global Health

"Global health" is becoming a fashionable term among scholars, human rights activists, state officials, leaders of international and transnational organizations, and others.[1] Until recently, health as a matter of collective concern largely implied national health. When the health problems of people in other countries became a public issue, it was usually within the confines of the notion of disaster relief, short-term responses to acute health crises caused by natural disasters, or wars. Global health is a relatively new category of moral concern, empirical investigation, and institutional action.

There are several reasons for the current prominence of global health issues. First, there is a widening recognition that some major risks to health are global in three senses: Their adverse impact on health is potentially worldwide, the conditions for their occurrence include various transnational dependencies that are lumped together under the rubric of globalization, and an effective response to them requires cooperation on a global scale. Examples of major health risks that are global in each of these three senses include emerging infections, pollution of the oceans, depletion of the ozone layer, global warming, nuclear terrorism, and bioterrorism. Second, due to the revolution in information technologies and the emergence of transnational epistemic communities equipped with powerful empirical methodologies for measuring and explaining health and disease, we now know more about the health problems of people in other countries than ever before. We also now have greater institutional resources, both within wealthier states and through international and transnational organizations, for applying this new knowledge to ameliorate global health problems. Finally, human rights discourse and, more generally, the articulation of a cosmopolitan ethical perspective, provide a normative basis for taking global health seriously as a moral issue.[2]

An Inadequate Response: Duty Dumping

Having reliable information about the nature and causes of global health problems, the capacity to ameliorate them, and a cosmopolitan ethical perspective that regards the need to ameliorate them as urgent is not sufficient, however. It is also necessary to move from the judgment that these problems must be addressed to concrete conclusions about who should do what to solve them. Call this the Problem of Concrete Responsibilities.

One response to the Problem of Concrete Responsibilities is what might be called Duty Dumping. To "dump" a duty in global health means to ascribe obligations to individuals or institutions, holding them accountable for the adverse health effects of their policies, without offering adequate justification for why particular obligations should be imposed on particular individuals or institutions. The thought might be that the putative obligation is too onerous or that it has been assigned to the wrong entity. In either case, Duty Dumping occurs when critics assign duties or obligations without good—or sometimes, without any—reason. However, we do not use Duty Dumping to signify *only* a mistake in assigning duties; in the complex area of global health, such errors might be expected. Instead, we reserve the term for errors of a particularly egregious sort that would be easily rejected in other contexts. Duty Dumping is both morally unjustified and potentially counterproductive for the overall goal of improving global health.

A prominent example of Duty Dumping is the claim that pharmaceutical companies that produce antiretroviral HIV/AIDS drugs have a duty to supply these drugs to all of those who could benefit from them at prices they can afford. The claim here is not just that it would be a good thing for drug companies to do this, nor simply that they have a moral obligation to do *something* to make their medicines more affordable to the worst off. Instead, those who criticize these private corporations often imply something much stronger: that the companies are acting wrongly if they do not do *whatever* it takes to make the drugs affordable to all who need them. In this case, the assigned obligation seems too demanding. Analogously, two decades ago in the United States, it was often said that for-profit hospitals ought to provide free care for the medically indigent and that, if they did not do so, they were guilty of acting unjustly.[3] Duty Dumping seems to proceed on something like a "can implies ought" principle or a principle to the effect that the producers of health-care goods or services have a determinate obligation to provide them to those who cannot pay. But such a principle cannot withstand scrutiny. There is no more reason to believe that drug companies are responsible for providing drugs to all who need them or that for-profit hospitals are to provide care to all that need it, than there is to believe that grocers have an obligation to ensure that no one goes without sufficient food.

Duty Dumping may be an effective political strategy, but it is unprincipled, evasive, and in the end most likely counterproductive. It may well be true that drug companies ought to do something to make their drugs more affordable. In the language of traditional moral theory, perhaps they have an imperfect duty of beneficence—a moral obligation to do something to help some of the needy. Whether they should do this by lowering their drug prices or by engaging in some other form of beneficence (say, funding scholarships to train people from poor countries to become doctors or scientists) is another matter.

Duty Dumping is not only morally unjustifiable; it also is a powerful mechanism for the evasion of responsibility. The analogy with the problem of securing access to care for the indigent in the United States is illuminating: The obligation to make basic health care affordable in the United States is a societal obligation; therefore, the lack of affordable basic health care is a moral failing of the citizens of the United States. To pretend that for-profit hospitals are the villains conveniently diverts attention from our failure to fulfill our obligations. Similarly, to focus exclusively or even primarily on the supposed obligations of drug companies is to divert attention from a whole range of responsibilities for responding to the HIV/AIDS crisis. From a cosmopolitan moral standpoint, all of us, as individuals, whether we happen to be leaders of corporations or not, have a moral obligation to help ensure that all persons have access to institutions that protect their basic human rights.[4] From the perspective of the principle of humanity or benevolence, we also have an obligation to relieve the sufferings of others. From either of these vantage points, we might all have moral obligations for responding to the HIV/AIDS crisis. This includes the major multinational pharmaceutical companies, but it is substantially different because it recognizes our collective obligation, rather than dumping this obligation solely on these companies (as if only they were responsible for the HIV/AIDS crisis). It is one thing to say that an appropriate collective effort to ensure that HIV/AIDS medications are affordable will include specific obligations on the part of drug companies; it is quite another to pretend that such specific obligations already exist.

Because of their own lack of resources and inability to participate effectively in political processes, however, many individuals are not in a position to do much to act on this obligation. Those of us who are fortunate enough to have resources beyond what we need for a decent and fulfilling life, and who have the freedom to organize with others to influence political processes, have many opportunities to fulfill our obligations regarding human rights and benevolence. Perhaps most important, we have the capacity—if we can muster the will—to work together to create an effective specification of responsibilities.

Duty Dumping is also a short-sighted and inherently conservative response to global health problems. The problem is not simply that it leaves the root causes of both illness and lack of access to health care untouched, though that is bad enough. In addition, by focusing arbitrarily on unpopular private organizations (such as big drug companies), it gives political cover to institutions that do have determinate responsibilities for health and which are failing to fulfill them. Chief among these, we shall argue, are states.[5]

A satisfactory account of determinate responsibilities for ameliorating the most serious global health problems will have to do three things. First, it should correctly identify whatever reasonably determinate responsibilities for health already exist in our world (rather than simply foisting imagined determinate responsibilities on whatever resource-rich agents are conveniently at hand-Duty Dumping). Second, it should recognize "responsibility gaps"; that is, it should acknowledge that, in many cases, determinate responsibilities will have to be *created* through the development of new institutions or through modifying existing institutions. Third, it must make clear that the responsibility for holding powerful agents accountable for the determinate responsibilities they already have, and for creating institutions that assign new determinate responsibilities, lies with all of us—but especially with those who have surplus personal resources and political clout.

We have noted that from a cosmopolitan standpoint there are two sources of moral concern about global health: the obligation to help ensure that every person has access to institutions that protect their basic human rights (including the human right to health, and other rights, such as rights against discrimination, which have implications for health), and the so-called imperfect obligation of humanity or benevolence. Both of these moral obligations are indeterminate—taken by themselves, they provide insufficient guidance for ameliorating the complex problems of global health. Taking them seriously requires a commitment to collective action to construct a moral division of labor that is both fair and effective. In most cases, successful collective action requires institutions.

Consider first the imperfect obligation of humanity, or benevolence. Because of the impact of health status on human well-being, those who act from the duty of humanity will naturally be concerned about improving health, whether by efforts to help ensure that the sick receive medical care or through the amelioration of social and economic conditions that adversely affect health. However, if they act alone, individuals cannot do much to alleviate large-scale health problems. Instead of continuing to act independently and inefficiently, they can and should create institutions for health-care research and for the provision of services, thereby coordinating their efforts and achieving great efficiencies of scale, as well as the benefits of the division of labor. Such institutions will assign various determinate duties to a range of individuals occupying various institutional roles; they will create determinate duties, not simply identify preexisting determinate duties.

How is this different than Duty Dumping? Consider again the case of HIV/AIDS medications. We have already noted that it is a mistake to assume that drug companies already have determinate obligations to ensure that such medicines are available to all who could benefit from them. It might be possible, however, to create determinate obligations on the part of drug companies. For example, one way might be to modify existing intellectual property rules. As a condition of receiving drug patents—a form of intellectual property right of particular import to the pharmaceutical industry—drug companies might be required to contribute a certain percentage of future sales to a global fund for subsidizing purchases of medications by the health services of poor countries. This hypothetical example is not offered as a policy proposal, but rather as an illustration of the difference between the unprincipled attribution of determinate responsibilities (Duty Dumping) and a collective effort—in this case, new legislation regarding intellectual property rules to create determinate obligations.

Acting conscientiously on the obligation to help ensure that all have access to just institutions also requires collective *institutional* action, for at least two reasons. First, in some cases institutions are needed to give determinate shape to abstract principles of justice, through legitimate processes for selecting particular "justice-regimes" from among a range of feasible alternatives. For example, even if it is true that justice requires some form of private property, there are many alternative private property rights regimes. Yet to reap the benefits a property rights regime can produce, a society must have some way of settling on one particular arrangement, and the process of choosing a particular arrangement must itself accord with principles of justice. Within the constraints of a constitution, democratic institutions are needed to specify a particular property rights regime as one important element of the establishment of justice.

Second, institutions are needed to create or collect resources needed for the provision of justice and for ensuring that the costs of providing justice are distributed fairly.[6] For example, if a particular society, through its institutional processes, recognizes that all its members have a right to a "decent minimum" or "adequate level" of health care, it will also need institutions for raising the revenues needed to secure this right for all and for ensuring that the costs of doing so are distributed fairly. Finally, institutions are often needed to enforce the fulfillment of the duties that institutions create.

Once these various roles of institutions are understood, it becomes clear that whenever human needs are not fulfilled this need not be the result of someone's failure to fulfill a determinate duty; it could be primarily a failure of collective action. To revert to an earlier example, the fact that millions of people are dying whose lives could be prolonged by antiretroviral drugs does not necessarily show that any particular party has failed to perform a determinate duty. Instead, it may indicate a deeper failure of many people to undertake collective action to establish the sorts of institutions that make the ascription of determinate duties both morally justifiable and efficacious.

In the next section, we begin the task of identifying the most important existing determinate responsibilities regarding global health by outlining some of the main responsibilities of states. On our view, it is important to begin with the responsibilities of states both because state behavior plays a larger role in the burden of disease than is usually recognized and because at present, states are the primary agents of distributive justice. Then, in the following section, we consider, also in a preliminary way, the responsibilities of some of the most important non-state actors, including global corporations and certain types of global governance institutions, such as the World Trade Organization (WTO) and the World Bank.

Our inquiry will focus on responsibilities for ameliorating the most serious health problems of the world's worst-off people. Apart from the fact that this is literally a life and death matter, and for that reason morally urgent, there is another reason to concentrate on the most serious health problems of those who have the least resources for addressing them. This commitment can be seen as the focus of an "overlapping consensus" among quite disparate views of justice, ranging from strict egalitarianism to an extreme prioritarianism, according to which only the well-being or resources of the worst-off count from the perspective of distributive justice. This is a signal advantage because it allows us to make some progress on the Problem of Concrete Responsibilities without having first to determine which of a number of competing conceptions of justice is correct.[7]

THE RESPONSIBILITIES OF STATES

The recognition that some health problems occur globally and may require supranational responses should not blind us to the fact that, in our world, states are not only the primary agents of justice, but also the institutions that have the greatest impact on the health of individuals. Even if it were true, as libertarian political theorists argue, that there are no positive general moral rights, states would still have significant responsibilities for ameliorating those health problems that are caused by the injustices they commit or support—responsibilities that they are not now fulfilling.

The Responsibilities of States: Justice and Membership in the State System

The first responsibility of states regarding global health is to avoid committing acts of injustice that have health-harming effects. This general obligation implies more determinate obligations. Among the most important of these are the obligation to refrain from fighting unjust wars abroad and using violence for oppression at home. In addition, states have a moral obligation to put an end to the common practice—especially among some of the wealthiest countries—of equipping and training the military forces of states that are likely to use this power unjustly, whether against their own people or others.

Another important source of rather determinate obligations of states is their participation in the state system. A key aspect of participation in the state system is the practice of recognizing the legitimacy of other states. States routinely contribute to massive health problems in other countries by recognizing the legitimacy of governments that either fail to fulfill their responsibilities regarding the health of their citizens or deprive them of the resources they might otherwise use for securing health care or the better living conditions that are essential for health.

Under the current state system, international recognition of the legitimacy of a government confers two eminently abusable rights: the right to dispose of the country's natural resources and the right to borrow from individual countries or international agencies such as the World Bank.[8] The first right enables corrupt government officials to enrich themselves with wealth that properly belongs to the people and could be used by them to ameliorate their health problems, in part by raising their standard of living. The second right enables state leaders to incur crushing national debts that make it harder for their people to lift themselves from poverty and reap the health benefits of a higher standard of living.

The traditional criterion for legitimacy in the state system is normatively vacuous. The Principle of Effectivity asserts that the basis for conferring the rights of sovereignty, including the right to dispose of resources and the right to borrow, is simply the ability to exercise control over a relatively stable population within a given territory.[9] On this criterion, human rights-violating, kleptocratic regimes that pillage their people's resources and exacerbate their poverty by incurring debts to fund projects that benefit only ruling elite are legitimate, so long as they achieve control. Furthermore, until recently, the recognition of legitimacy has largely been an all or nothing affair because sovereignty has been regarded as indivisible. However, both the normatively-vacuous conception of sovereignty and the assumption that sovereignty is unitary are now being challenged.[10]

States have a moral responsibility not to be accomplices in injustices by conferring predictably abusable rights on bad governments. The question is whether effective international institutions can be devised that reward responsible governments with the full range of sovereign rights and withhold certain rights from those governments that seriously abuse them. If the effective fulfillment of this responsibility requires the creation of new international institutions that "unbundle" the rights of sovereignty and confer rights only when they can be expected to be exercised responsibly, then states have a higher order responsibility to contribute to their creation.

If more states did a better job of fulfilling their obligations to refrain from committing injustices and from supporting states that commit injustices, the positive impact on health would be enormous. Consider only the obligation not to engage in unjust wars and not to supply weapons and training to states that are likely to engage in unjust wars or use their military forces unjustly against there own people. In the last six years, around 3.9 million people have died in Congo as a result of the war raging there. It is estimated that for every violent death in Congo's war zone, there are sixty-two "non-violent" deaths—from starvation, disease, and exposure.[11] This is only one instance of the devastating direct and indirect health effects of war.

To summarize, even if there were no such thing as positive human rights (such as the right to an adequate standard of living, the right to basic health care, the right to basic education), states would still have rather determinate moral obligations to act in ways that would greatly ameliorate the health problems of the world's worst-off people. Simply by refraining from unjust violence and from supporting unjust governments, states could do much to improve global health.

The Responsibilities of States: Primary Guarantors of their Own Citizens' Human Rights

So far we have made the case that states have determinate responsibilities whose fulfillment would do much to ameliorate some of the most serious threats to health simply by appealing to relatively uncontroversial standards of justice. Once we expand the moral framework to include states' responsibilities for protecting the human rights of their own citizens, the scope of their responsibilities increases considerably.

The primary "addressees" of human rights claims are states.[12] This is so, not only because historically states have been the major violators of human rights, but also because, for better or worse, they are best equipped to specify and apply determinate human rights norms and to achieve the conditions of distributive justice upon which the effectiveness of individuals' rights depends. International and regional human rights institutions have a valuable role to play in specifying the minimal human rights standards that all states should meet; and in providing venues and frameworks of discourse in which domestic and transnational forces can exert pressure on states to live up to them.

Unfortunately, the connection between human rights and health, though important, has not received the attention it deserves from moral theorists. There are at least two ways in which the connection might be made. On the one hand, a right to health could itself be included among the human rights. On the other, one could think of health as precondition for the enjoyment of various human rights. Let us consider each approach briefly and try to ascertain their implications for the Problem of Concrete Responsibilities.

The Idea of a Human Right to Health

Human rights are best understood as high-priority minimal moral entitlements of all persons and as implying both fairly determinate obligations on the parts of states (their primary "addressees") and more indeterminate obligations on individuals to work with others to promote the protection of these rights, if they have the opportunity and resources to do so.[13] In order to integrate global health issues into the human rights framework, the first question to ask is whether the human right in question is a right to health care or to health. The attraction of focusing on a right to health, rather than to health care is obvious: Health depends upon many factors, health care being only one of them—and, in the larger scheme of things—not the most important of them.

However, the idea of a right to health is not without difficulties. First, there is the problem of settling on a defensible definition of what health is. Among the most basic sources of disagreement here is the division between more "objectivist" and more "social constructivist" conceptions of health and disease. Second, if the notion of health is understood too ambitiously, satisfying the right to health for all will not be possible, simply because there are some people whose health is so poor that they could not be made healthy even if cost were not an issue. The third difficulty is that cost *is* an issue. However, the right to health as a human right is to be understood, it must—as with other human rights—be understood as a moral minimum, not a maximum. Health is not the only good. For one thing, there are other human rights and protecting them requires that not all of our resources be used to satisfy the right to health. In addition, as most moral theories recognize, there are limits on what we owe to others. For these reasons, any approach to global health that relies on the idea of a human right to health must first develop a defensible conception of the limited character of the right. Unless this is done, it will not be possible to make headway on the problem of determining specific responsibilities for seeing that all enjoy the right, if only because the whole idea will be dismissed as unrealistically demanding or as imposing unacceptable restrictions on individuals' freedom and property rights.

Nonetheless, the lack of a fully developed theory of the human right to health is not such a serious problem if our focus is on the most serious health problems of the world's most vulnerable people. Their health problems are undeniable and severe, regardless of which of a broad range of competing conceptions of health and disease one adopts. Furthermore, whatever the full content of the human right to health turns out to be, it is clear that many states are not ensuring that this right is enjoyed by all of their citizens.

At present, the most significant mechanisms for ensuring compliance with human rights standards are domestic. More specifically, individual states that ratify human rights conventions increasingly incorporate them into their domestic legal systems over time, thereby giving individuals and groups standing to appeal to the courts when they believe their rights are being infringed upon.

However, so long as the idea of a human right to health is left vague and therefore subject to the charge that it implies ever-expanding obligations, there is little hope that it will be incorporated in a meaningful way into domestic legal systems. This pitfall can only be avoided by building a broad international consensus on a conception of the human right to health that is sufficiently determinate to allay the worry about an over-expansive entitlement, while avoiding an overly specified right that would not do justice to cultural differences and differences in the resources available to various states.[14]

One way of achieving this goal would be to articulate a minimal conception of the human right to health that consists mainly of two elements. The first is a set of operationalizable standards for what might be called the "negative" right to health, a specification of the responsibilities of states to remove barriers to access to existing health-care resources, to eliminate discrimination in health services, and to ensure that the health needs of all citizens are taken into account both in the development of health services and in the pursuit of policies of economic development that can have serious health effects. The second is a set of operationalizable standards for ensuring that all citizens enjoy a core set of "positive" health entitlements, including, for example, such relatively uncontroversial items as clean drinking water, basic sanitation and shelter, as well as access to basic perinatal care and immunization for the most serious infectious diseases. In both cases, the standards must be operationalizable in the sense that appropriate international and transnational organizations must be able to make publicly defensible judgments as to whether states are complying with them. The chief responsibility for seeing that this two-pronged strategy is successfully executed lies with the leaders of international and transnational human rights organizations and with individuals who are in a position to work with others to influence their own governments to cooperate with these organizations.

Health as a Precondition for the Enjoyment of Human Rights

On some accounts, health is not a human right, but rather something that is nonetheless of critical moral importance because it is a necessary condition for the enjoyment of human rights. To advocate human rights without making a commitment to achieving all the conditions for their effective exercise is morally incoherent.

To a large extent, this second approach to global health converges with that according to which health is a human right. Ensuring that the burden of disease does not undercut the effective exercise of human rights does not require equality of health (however that might be defined) nor that all health needs be met. Instead, it requires a collective effort to forge an international consensus on a core set of health entitlements (both "negative" and "positive") that generally protect individuals against the most serious health problems and that are sufficiently concrete to allow states to be held accountable for providing them, either through their own judicial institutions or through formal or informal pressures from international and transnational organizations.

In some cases, states will not be capable of achieving these basic health entitlements for some or even most of their citizens. The most extreme example is that of literally "failed states," in which civil order no longer exists and there is no government capable of providing any services, including those that are important for health. In other cases, there may be a minimally functioning state, but it lacks some capacities that are critical for providing adequate levels of the core public health and health-care services. When this occurs, the people of wealthier states have an obligation to work together to provide aid to help every state discharge its obligations regarding the health of its citizens.

The effective fulfillment of this obligation will generally require the world's wealthier people to act through the institutions of their own states, by pressuring their political leaders to create international institutions that fairly distribute the burden of providing aid, devise benchmarks for progress, and provide incentives for donors to carry through on pledges of support. An example of this type of international institution might be the Global Fund to fight AIDS, tuberculosis, and malaria.

THE RESPONSIBILITIES OF NON-STATE ACTORS

An Obligation Not to Cause Harm?

We argued earlier that states have rather direct and relatively uncontroversial obligations that would, if fulfilled, avoid serious harms to health. It might be thought that every organization, whether private or public, has an obligation not to act in ways that are harmful to people's health. However, the notion of acting in ways that are harmful to people's health is so all-encompassing as to be incapable of providing moral guidance. It covers both cases where the causal connection is sufficiently clear and robust to warrant the attribution of responsibility and those in which it is not.

Where the agent in question is itself a significant causal factor in the production of the harm, the attribution of responsibility may be unproblematic. In some cases, there clearly are obligations not to cause harm that non-state actors violate with disastrous consequences for the health of some individuals. For example, a company may dump large quantities of toxic chemicals into a major river, causing death or serious illness not just in one country, but in several.

However, in morality, as in the law, merely making a contribution to the production of a harm is not sufficient for the attribution of responsibility. One difficulty is that some harms result from the cumulative effects of the actions of many individuals, none of which can reasonably be held responsible for the harm. Thus, when global health problems, such as the pollution of the oceans, result from the cumulative effects of the actions of millions of agents, including individuals, corporations, and governments, the attribution of concrete responsibilities on the basis of causality is not possible. Although much more could be done and ought to be done to hold corporations and governments legally liable for harms to health when appropriate standards for liability apply, it is a mistake to rest the case for addressing global health problems on the reduction of moral responsibility to the obligation not to cause harm. To do so not only requires an indefensible understanding of the relationship between causality and responsibility; it also overlooks the responsibility of a wide range of actors to work together to develop institutions that create morally defensible assignments of concrete responsibilities.

Accordingly, in the discussion of the responsibilities of non-state actors that follows, we will focus chiefly on grounds for responsibility other than the more obvious cases in which an agent's actions play an important and direct role in the causation of health-related harms.

"Global Governance Institutions"

Like the term "global health," the phrase "global governance institutions" is currently in vogue. It is used to refer to a quite heterogeneous collection of different international organizations, from "government networks" comprised of high-level bureaucrats from many nations (including judges and regulatory networks[15]) to the World Trade Organization and the United Nations Security Council. Since there are such great differences among these organizations, we should not expect them all to have the same causal role in global health nor the same responsibilities. For this reason, we do not attempt even to begin the daunting task of providing a theory of responsibility for all "global governance institutions." Instead, we only aim to articulate some of the different grounds for attributing responsibilities regarding global health to them.

Consistency with the Public Goals of the Institution

In some cases, global governance institutions expressly or tacitly assume responsibilities for global health. One example is the World Health Organization (WHO). Less obviously, the WTO recognizes the importance of its activities for global health and welfare in several of its formal statements. A brief tract intended to explain the functions of the organization to the general public states that the WTO's "goal is to improve the welfare of the peoples of its member countries,"[16] and in a joint report with the WHO, the WTO affirms "human health as important in the highest degree."[17]

Consider the WTO's Agreement on Trade-Related Aspects of Intellectual Property (TRIPS), which was negotiated and agreed upon in the Uruguay Rounds of 1986–1994.[18] A strong case can be made that this agreement, far from promoting health as being of "the highest-importance," in fact creates a new obstacle to the amelioration of some global health problems, by raising the prices and slowing the introduction of generic drugs in developing countries. When an organization acts in ways that are inconsistent with its own public commitments to global health, the attribution of responsibility is relatively unproblematic.

Of course, it might also be argued that whether or not it explicitly includes health concerns within its public mission statement, the WTO has come to have responsibilities for health in the process pursuing its primary goal of liberalizing trade. If the predictable consequences of liberalized trade in certain contexts include working conditions that endanger the health of workers, thereby endangering their human rights, then the organization that is the chief instrument for liberalizing trade is obligated to take these consequences into account in its policies and to cooperate with other actors to ameliorate them. Unlike the simple appeal to special responsibilities for health that organizations sometimes assume, this argument requires much more in terms of elaborating responsibility in the complex causal web connecting liberalized trade policies to the endangering of human rights at the individual level. Given that there can be disagreement about the facts that are relevant to the attribution of responsibilities, a credible identification of the special responsibilities of particular organizations may require reliance on the expertise of "epistemic communities," mobilized through the operation of international organizations such as the International Labor Organization (ILO) or various transnational human rights organizations.

Global Corporations

The responsibilities of global corporations for global health fall into three main categories: (1) obligations to avoid actions and policies that in themselves are significant causal factors in harms to health; (2) obligations not to support governments engaged in unjust activities that are harmful to the health of their citizens or others; and (3) obligations not to impede the health-promoting efforts of states, labor organizations, and legitimate international and transnational organizations that have more direct responsibilities regarding global health.

As we have already noted, the moral basis of the first class of obligations is relatively straightforward. The main problem is not the attribution of responsibility, but rather how to achieve accountability. In developing countries, the state regulatory agencies charged with holding global corporations responsible for the harms are often too inadequately resourced to be effective. In more developed countries, they are often staffed by people who previously worked in, and still have connections with, the very industries they are supposed to regulate. Or the agencies are ordered to go soft on enforcement by higher government officials who seek political support from powerful corporations.

The second class of obligations is extremely important. Like states, global corporations can and often do help corrupt governments stay in power, with disastrous effects on the health and general welfare of individuals. And like states, global corporations can have powerful incentives to provide such support. However, as the case of Apartheid South Africa demonstrates, under certain conditions these incentives can be countered by a sustained global campaign to expose the role of corporations in supporting unjust governments and mobilize public pressure and state action against it.

When corporations explicitly embrace a role in helping to ameliorate a global health problem, as some drug companies have done, they assume new responsibilities and ought to be held accountable for fulfilling them. Apart from such self-assigned responsibilities, the extent to which global corporations have obligations to promote health is debatable. However, it is much less difficult to argue that they at least have the obligation not to impede the efforts of others to ameliorate the most serious health problems of the world's worst off. For example, a global corporation violates this obligation when it blocks the formation of labor unions committed to ameliorating hazards in the workplace. Similarly, even though it is problematic to say that drug companies have an obligation to provide essential medicines at prices that even the poorest people can afford, it is clear that they have an obligation not to exert pressure on governments to ratify intellectual property agreements that increase their profits at the expense of preventing poorer countries from having access to less expensive generic drugs.

CONCLUSION

Global health is increasingly becoming the object of interdisciplinary empirical research, institutional action, and moral concern. If this convergence of factors is to result in a significant amelioration of the most serious health problems of the world's most vulnerable people, the abstract commitment to "improving global health" must be translated into concrete responsibilities for action. We have argued that the needed work of specification requires a systematic understanding of the different roles and capacities of a broad range of private and public institutions, with a sensitivity to the different grounds for attributing responsibility. One important result of our inquiry is that the responsibilities of states are much more extensive than is usually assumed. Instead of focusing only on the obligations of wealthier states to transfer resources to poorer ones, we should recognize the full range of state activities—from making war, to according legitimacy to corrupt governments—that are harmful to health and prevent individuals from achieving a standard of living that makes better health possible.

NOTES

Chapter 1

1. Ronald Dworkin, *Taking Rights Seriously* (Cambridge, MA: Harvard University Press, 1977), pp. 184–205.

2. It is not my purpose in this article to articulate the main factors that should determine the content of the decent minimum. For an attempt to do so, see *Securing Access to Health Care*, Report of the President's Commission for the Study of Ethical Problems in Medicine and Biomedical and Behavioral Research (Washington, D.C., U.S. Government Printing Office, 1983), especially chapter. 1.

3. "Is There a Right to a Decent Minimum of Health Care?" in *Securing Access to Health Care*, Appendix Two.

4. Norman Daniels, "Health-Care Needs and Distributive Justice," *Philosophy & Public Affairs* 10, no. 2 (Spring 1981): 146–79.

5. For an exploration of various arguments for a duty of beneficence and an examination of the relationship between justice and beneficence, in general and in health care, see Allen E. Buchanan, "Philosophical Foundations of Beneficence," *Beneficence and Health Care*, Earl E. Shelp (ed.) (Dordrecht, Holland: Reidel Publishing Co., 1982).

Chapter 2

1. This was reported to the author in a personal communication with the director of the oncology unit.

2. The discussion of utilitarianism, and some material on libertarianism and on Rawls's theory, is drawn from Buchanan's essay "Justice: A Philosophical Review" with permission from D. Reidel Publishing Co.

3. This statement may be misleading because Nozick's view is more extreme than that of some who are frequently labeled libertarians, such as F. A. Heyek, who admit that enforced contributions to provide a minimal welfare safety net are sometimes justifiable.

4. It would be a mistake, however, to conclude that the idea of an adequate level has no useful policy implications. See M. A. Baily, "Rationing Health Care: Defining the Adequate Level."

5. The argument is drawn from Buchanan (1987), with permission of the journal *Ethics.*

Chapter 3

This essay is a revision of one prepared for a Blue Cross/Blue Shield project on the ethics of insurance. I am indebted to the following individuals for their valuable comments on an earlier draft of this essay: Norman Daniels, Albert Jonsen, and Paul Menzel.

1. For discussions of ethical issues arising from the new emphasis on competition, see "Money, Medicine, and Markets," Baruch A. Brody (ed.), *Journal of Medicine and Philosophy*, 12: February (1987), pp. 1–99.

2. See Dan W. Brock and Allen Buchanan, "Ethical Issues in For-Profit Health Care," in *For-Profit Enterprise in Health Care*, Bradford M. Gray (ed.) (Washington, D.C.: National Academy Press, 1986), pp. 224–49.

3. See Tom L. Beauchamp and Norman E. Bowie (eds.), *Ethical Theory and Business*, 2nd ed. (Englewood Cliffs, N.J.: Prentice-Hall, 1983).

4. Norman Daniels, *Just Health Care* (Cambridge: Cambridge University Press, 1985), pp. 11–17 and 114–39.

5. Brock and Buchanan, "Ethical Issues in For-Profit Health Care," pp. 227–28.

6. President's Commission for the Study of Ethical Problems in Medicine and Biomedical and Behavioral Research, *Securing Access to Health Care*, vol. 1: *Report* (Washington, D.C.: Government Printing Office, 1983), p. 14.

7. Ibid., p. 23.

8. Ibid., pp. 22–23.

9. Allen Buchanan, "Competition, Charity, and the Right to Health Care," *The Restraint of Liberty*, Thomas Attig et al. (ed.) (Bowling Green, Ohio: Bowling Green State University, Applied Philosophy Program, 1985), pp. 129–43.

10. Gray, *For-Profit Enterprise in Health Care*, pp. 97–99. Pamela J. Farley, "Who Are the Uninsured?" *Milbank Quarterly* 63: 3 (1985), pp. 476–503. For a discussion of the difficulty of specifying an adequate level of care, see President's Commission, *Securing Access to Health Care*, pp. 35–43.

11. It might be thought that the public subsidies for health care research and medical education would generate special obligations for providers. For a refutation of this claim see Brock and Buchanan, "Ethical Issues in For-Profit Health Care," pp. 228–29.

12. For an analysis of the concept of charity and of distinctions between justice and charity, see Allen Buchanan, "Justice and Charity," *Ethics* 97: 3 (1987), pp. 558–75.

13. In the case of the Blue Cross/Blue Shield system the prominence of a self-imposed ethical mission may be explained by the fact that the founders of the organization emerged from a physician-dominated hospital environment in which professionals acknowledged a duty to serve the needy even at some cost to themselves. (Odin W. Andersen, *Blue Cross since 1929: Accountability and the Public Trust* [Cambridge, Mass.: Ballinger, 1975], pp. 20–21, 29, 40–41, 104–5).

14. Even self-imposed ethical duties, however, are not wholly immune to ethical criticism. For example, a charitable organization might rightly be criticized for having racist policies. This point is due to Norman Daniels.

15. Perhaps the most widely discussed version of the competitive approach is Alain Enthoven's Consumer-Choice Health Plan, described in Alain Enthoven, *Health Plan: The Only Practical Solution to the Soaring Cost of Medical Care* (Reading, Mass.: Addison-Wesley, 1980).

Chapter 4

1. Nicholas Van de Walle, "Privatization in Developing Countries: A Review of the Issues" in *World Development*, 17: 5 (1989); Joseph L. Scarpaci, "Dismantling Public Health Services in Authoritarian Chile" in Joseph L. Scarpaci (ed.), *Health Services Privatization in Industrial Societies* (New Brunswick, New Jersey: Rutgers University Press, 1989); Paul Sigmund, "Chile: Privatization, Preprivatization, Hyperprivatization" in Ezra Suleiman and John Waterbury (ed.), *The Political Economy of Public Sector Reform and Privatization* (Boulder: Westview Press, 1990); R. Korte, Heide Richter, F. Merkle and H. Gorgen, "Financing Health Services in Sub-Saharan Africa: Options for Decision Makers During Adjustment" in *Social Science and Medicine*, 34: 1(1992); "Editorial: Accessibility, Ethics and Equity in Health Care" in *Social Science and Medicine*, 36: 12 (1993); Donald W. Light, "Escaping the Traps of Postwar Western Medicine" in *European Journal of Public Health*, 3(1993); Donald W. Light, "Equity and Efficiency in Health Care" in *Social Science and Medicine*, 35: 4 (1992); R. Lekachman. "The Craze for Privatization: Dubious Social Results of a Reaganite Dogma" in *Dissent*, Summer (1987).

2. Arnold Relman, "An Exchange on For Profit Health Care" in Bradford Gray (ed.), *For Profit Enterprise in Health Care* (Washington DC: Institute of Medicine, National Academy Press, 1986), pp. 209–10, 217.

3. D. Himmelstein and S. Woolhandler, "Cost Without Benefit: Administrative Waste in the US Health Care System", *New England Journal of Medicine*, 314: 7 (February 13, 1986).

4. "Access to Care and Investor-Owned Providers" in Bradford Gray (ed.), *For Profit Enterprise in Health Care* (Washington DC: Institue of Medicine, National Academy Press, 1986), pp. 209–10, 217.

5. The figures for the uninsured are based on statistics cited by Jon B. Christianson, "A Supply-Side View of American Medicine: Structure, Conduct, and Performance since 1970" in Gary D. Libecap, *Advances in The Study of Entrepreneurship, Innovation, and Economic Growth*, Vol. 4 (*Health Care Issues and American Economic Growth*), Greenwich, Connecticut: JA1 Press, 1990.

6. R. Maxwell, *Health and Wealth: An International Study of Health Care Spending*, (Lexiagton, Mass: Lexington Books, 1981).

7. Donald W. Light, "Escaping the Traps of Postwar Western Medicine" in *European Journal of Public Health*, 3 (1993), pp. 284–86; Donald W. Light, "Equity and Efficiency in Health Care" in *Social Science and Medicine*, 35: 4 (1992); R. Maxwell, *Health and Wealth: An International Study of Health Care Spending* (Lexington Mass; Lexington Books, 1981).

8. Norman Daniels, *Just Health Care* (Cambridge University Press, 1985); Paul T. Menzel, *Medical Cost, Moral Choices: A Philosophy of Health Care Economics in America* (New Haven & London: Yale University Press, 1983); Larry R. Churchill, *Rationaing Health Care In America: Perceptions and Principles of Justice* (Notre Dame: University of Notre Dame Press, c1987); *Securing Access to Health Care*. Volumes 1 and 2, President's Commission for the Study of Ethical Problems in Medicine and Biomedical and Behavioural Research, 1993.

9. *Securing Access to Health Care*, Vol. 1, chapter 1.

10. Allen Buchanan, *Ethics, Efficiency and the Market* (Totowa New Jersey: Rowman and Allanheld, 1985); G.A. Cohen, "Robert Nozick and Wilt Chamberlain: How Patterns Preserve Liberty" in J. Arthus and W.H. Shaw, *Justice and Economic Distribution* (Englewood Cliffs New Jersey: Preintice-Hall, 1978).

11. Paul Billings, Mel A. Kohn, Margaret de Cuevas, Jonathan Beckwith, Joseph S. Alper & Marvin R. Natowicz, "Discrimination as a Consequence of Genetic Testing" in *American Journal of Human Genetics*, 50: 3 (1992).

12. Robert J. Pokorski, "Use of Genetic Information by Private Insurers" in Timothy F. Murphy & Marc A. Lappe (ed.), *Justice and the Human Genome Project* (Berkeley: University of California Press, 1994), pp. 101–02.

13. *Securing Access to Health Care*, Vol. 1, pp. 26–29.

14. *Securing Access to Health Care*, Vol. 1, p. 31.

15. Dennis Mueller, *Public Choice II* (Cambridge: Cambridge University Press, 1989), pp. 235–8 and 261.

16. Daniel Wikler, "Privatization and Human Rights in Health Care: Notes from the American Experience", in Kathleen E. Mahoney and Paul Mahoney (eds.), *Human Rights in the Twenty-first Century* (Dordrecht: Martinus Nijhoff Publishers, 1993), pp. 497–98; L. Uzych, "Patient Dumping", *Journal of the Florida Medical Association*, 77 (1990); Donald W. Light, "Escaping the Traps of Postwar Western Medicine" in *European Journal of Public Health*, 3 (1993), pp. 286–87; R. Lekachman, "The Craze for Privatization: Dubious Social Results of a Reaganite Dogma" in *Dissent*, Summer (1987).

17. Heidi Vernon-Wortzel and Lawrence H. Wortzel, "Privatization: Not the Only Answer" in *World Development*, 17: 5 (1989); Nicholas Van de Walle, "Privatization in Developing Countries: A Review of the Issues" in *World Development*, 17: 5 (1989); Henry Bienen and John Waterbury, "The Political Economy of Privatization in Developing Countries" in *World Development*, 17: 5 (1989); Ezra Suleiman and John Waterbury, "Introduction: Analyzing Privatization in Industrial and Developing Countries" in Ezra Suleiman and John Waterbury, *The Political Economy of Public Sector Reform and Privatization* (Boulder: Westview Press, 1990); Richard Janssen and Jan van der Made, "Privatization in Health Care: Concepts, Motives and Policies" in *Health Policy*, 14 (1990); T. Kowalik, "The Costs of 'Shock Therapy'" in *Dissent*, Fall (1991); Joel I, Nelson, "Social Welfare and the Market Economy" in *Social Science Quarterly*, 73: December (1992); Harvey B. Feigenbaum and Jeffrey R. Henig, "The Political Underpinnings of Privatization" in *World Politics*, January (1994).

18. *World Development Report: Investing in Health* (New York: World Bank, Oxford University Press, 1993), see chapter 3.

19. Paul Starr, *The Social Transformation of American Medicine* (New York: Basic Books, 1982); Donald W. Light, "Equity and Efficiency in Health Care" in *Social Science and Medicine*, 35: 4 (1992); Allen Buchanan and Daniel Wikler, "Is There a Medical Profession in the House" in David Schimm, Roy Spece, Allen Buchanan (eds.), *Conflict of Interest in Clinical Practice and Medical Research* (Oxford University Press, forthcoming).

20. Arnold S. Relman, "The New Medical-Industrial Complex" in *New England Journal of Medicine*, 303 (1980), pp. 963–70.

21. C.D. Naylor, "Privatization of South African Health Services—Are the Underlying Assumptions Correct?" in *South African Medical Journal*, 72 (21 November 1987); Max Price,

"The Consequences of Health Service Privatization for Equality and Equity in Health Care in South Africa" in *Social Science Medicine*, 27: 7 (1988); Joseph L. Scarpaci, "Dismantling Public Health Services in Authoritarian Chile" in Joseph L. Scarpaci (ed.), *Health Services Privatization in Industrial Societies* (New Brunswick: Rutgers University Press, 1989); Paul Sigmund, "Chile: Privatization, Preprivatization, Hyperprivatization" in Ezra Suleiman and John Waterbury, *The Political Economy of Public Sector Reform and Privalization* (Boulder: Westview Press, 1990).

22. Daniel Wikler and Allen Buchanan, "Health Care Reform: Who Pays for Whom?," unpublished.

23. Joseph L. Scarpaci, "Dismantling Public health Services in Authoritarian Chile" In Joseph L. Scarpaci (ed.), *Health Services Privatization in Industrial Societies* (New Brunswick: Rutgers University Press, 1989); Paul Sigmund, "Chile: Privatization, Preprivatization, Hyperprivatization" in Ezra Suleiman and John Waterbury, *The Political Economy of Public Sector Reform and Privatization* (Boulder: Westview Press, 1990); Max Price, "The Consequence of Health Service Privatization for Equality and Equity in Health Care in South Africa" in *Social Science Medicine*, 27: 7 (1988).

24. Joseph L. Scarpaci, "Introduction: The Theory and Practice of Health Services Privatization" in Joseph L. Scarpaci (ed.), *Health Services Privatization in Industrial Societies* (New Brunswick: Rutgers University Press, 1989); Dennis Mueller, *Public Choice II* (Cambridge: Cambridge University Press, 1989); David B. Johnson, *Public Choice: An Introduction to the New Political Economy* (London: Bristlecone Books, 1991).

Chapter 5

1. While the number of investor-owned, as opposed to independent for-profit hospitals has risen, hospital ownership, classified by broad categories—federal, state, and local government, nonprofit and for-profit—has changed little in the past decade. Gray, B. H. (1984) Overview: origins and trends. Keynote address, Annual Health Conference, The New Entrepeneurialism in Health Care, held by the Committee on Medicine in Society of the New York Academy of Medicine, *Bulletin of The New York Academy of Medicine*, second series, 61: 1, pp. 7–22.

2. *Securing Access to Health Care*, Report of the President's Commission for the Study of Ethical Problems in Medicine and Biomedical and Behavioral Research (Washington, D.C.: U.S. Government Printing Office, 1983) Vol. 1, pp. 92–101.

3. This statement is based on a preliminary draft of the report of the Institute of Medicine Committee on For-Profit Health Care. Additional data may be included in the final report.

4. Ibid.

5. Ibid.

6. Brown, Kathryn J., and Richard E. Klosterman. Hospital acquisitions and their effects: Florida, 1979–1982. This volume.

7. Hansmann, Henry D., The Role of Nonprofit Enterprise. *Yale Law Journal* 89:5 (1980), pp. 835–901.

8. Robert M. Veatch seems to take this position in Ethical dilemmas of for-profit enterprise in health care, *The New Health Care For Profit*, B. H. Gray (ed.) (Washington, D.C.: National Academy Press, 1983), p. 143. Cf. also Outka, Gene, Social Justice and Equal Access to Health Care in *Ethics and Health Policy*, R. Veatch and R. Branson (eds.) (Cambridge: Ballinger Publishing Co.)

9. See, for example, Guttman, Amy, For and Against Equal Access to Health Care, and Brock (1983), Dan W. Distribution of Health Care and Individual Liberty, both in *Securing Access to Health Care, Volume Two: Appendices. Sociocultural and Philosophical Studies*, Report of the President's Commission for the Study of Ethical Problems in Medicine and Biomedical and Behavioral Research (Washington, D.C.: U.S. Government Printing Office).

10. Daniels, Norman, *Just Health Care* (New York: Cambridge University Press, 1985).

11. Starr, P., *The Social Transformation of American Medicine* (New York: Basic Books, 1982).

12. Menzel, P., *Medical Costs, Moral Choices* (New Haven: Yale University Press, 1983), p. 17.

13. Veatch, R., Ethical Dilemmas of For-profit Enterprise in Health Care, B. H. Gray (ed.), *The New Health Care for Profit* (Washington, D.C.: National Academy Press, 1983), pp. 145–46.

14. Starr, P. *The Social Transformation of American Medicine* (New York: Basic Books, 1982).

15. Jonson, A. Watching the doctor, Sounding Board, *New England Journal of Medicine*, 303: 25,(1983), pp. 1531–35.

16. *American College of Physicians Ethics Manual* (1984), p. 7.

17. The term "medical-industrial complex" is borrowed from an article by Relman, A., The New Medical-Industrial Complex, *The New England Journal of Medicine*, 303:17 (1980), pp. 963–70. Relman expresses a number of the concerns about for-profits analyzed in the present essay, including the fear that large for-profit corporations may exert undue influence on public policy.

Chapter 6

1. *Privatization* is used to refer to a broad range of initiatives, including the following: (1) selling public health-care facilities and delivery organizations to private enterprises; (2) contracting out publicly provided services to private enterprises through competitive bidding; (3) using government policies to encourage the growth of for-profit health care entities (hospitals, nursing homes, and outpatient facilities); (4) using government policies to encourage greater reliance on private health insurance (including combination insurer provider organizations such as HMOs); and (5) implementing de insurance practices, such as the introduction or escalation of out-of-pocket payment for health-care services (co-payments, deductibles, and charges for prescription drugs).

2. Of course, a mixed system is only one way to achieve access to an adequate level or decent minimum of care for all. A purely public system could also achieve this. The topic of

the present article, however, is the ethical status of rationing in managed care, which exists in a mixed system.

3. Of course, some contend that there would be no access gap in an unencumbered, competitive market for health-care insurance—all would receive what they are entitled to, according to their preferences and ability to pay, if they were free to purchase from among the full range of leaner to more generous benefit packages which such a market would offer. This free-market view of just health care rests on either of two assumptions: (1) that there is no market independent health care entitlement—just health care is whatever the free market delivers; or (2) that there is an independent entitlement, but as a matter of fact an unencumbered, competitive market for health-care insurance would ensure that this entitlement was available to all. The former assumption weds the free-market theory of just health care to a larger free-market theory of justice, according to which the outcomes of competitive markets, whatever they turn out to be, are just. Virtually no one has actually espoused this view, since it is very implausible to argue that market outcomes are just regardless of the initial distribution of assets people bring to the market. Once it is admitted that the justice or injustice of the initial distribution of assets is relevant to the justice of the outcomes of market processes, the first assumption must be abandoned. The second assumption is equally implausible, in my view, because there are some individuals, including those unable to work (such as children and the severely disabled) who would not be able to get the "decent minimum" of services (under any reasonable description of the latter) at affordable prices in a competitive insurance market. However, for my purposes, it is not necessary to show that this is so; all that is necessary is to point out that in order to know whether or not the second assumption is true, we need first to settle the issue of what counts as a "decent minimum" (or "adequate level") of care. Until we know what this is, we cannot establish that a competitive market does (as assumption 2 contends) deliver it to all (Brock and Buchanan 1986: 224–49; Buchanan 1987).

4. For a prominent instance of the "essentialist" view that rationing care is incompatible with being an ethical physician, see Pellegrino and Thomasma [1988, pp. 172–73].

Chapter 7

For many helpful comments I am indebted to David Mechanic, Martin Bunzel, Doug Husak, and other participants of a seminar at which an earlier version of this paper was presented at the Rutgers University Institute for Health Care, Health Policy, and Aging, as well as to Henry Richardson of the Georgetown Philosophy Department and to participants in a Greenwall Fellows seminar at the Kennedy Institute of Ethics, including, especially, Ruth Faden.

1. For a thoughtful discussion of the conflicts of interest attendant on various forms of risk-sharing, see Rodwin (1993, pp. 135–75). For a collection of diverse critical views on conflicts of interest in medicine, see Spece, Shimm, and Buchanan (1996).

2. My analysis in this article is concerned exclusively with the role of trust in managed care. I make no assumption that the basis for well-founded trust in physicians is the same in managed care and other forms of health-care delivery. Nor do I assume that managed care is the best form of health-care delivery for our society. I am only assuming that managed

care or something very similar to it will play an important role in U.S. health care for the foreseeable future. I am indebted to Tom L. Beauchamp for emphasizing to me the importance of making this limitation of my discussion explicit.

3. This presumption of trust is not absolute, of course. If a member of a status group is seen to behave in clearly untrustworthy ways, the presumption will be withdrawn.

4. Robert Veatch (personal communication) has emphasized that technical competence and a commitment to patient's well-being, though necessary, are not sufficient for well-founded trust in one's physician. In addition, the physician must know what is in the patient's best interest if she is to strive effectively to promote the patient's good, and the physician's technical competence is not sufficient for this. Knowledge of the patient's values and priorities are also required.

5. Primary merit trust may be either direct or indirect: A patient may trust a physician because of beliefs about the competence and commitment of the physician based on perceptions of the physician's behavior, though these beliefs may be based on the reports of other patients rather than her own experience.

6. "Cost" here is to be interpreted broadly; the assumption is not that rationing means valuing dollars over lives. For one thing, most rationing is not a matter of life or death. But more importantly, managed care organizations are responsible for providing care for a population of patients and to do so it is sometimes necessary to restrict utilization of care. Dollars are means of measuring opportunity costs.

7. Triage in the emergency situation is the exception to the general denial of scarcity that is essential to the traditional medical ethics.

8. Norman Daniels (personal communication) refers to this condition as "accountability for reasons."

9. This point was raised to me by Ruth Faden.

10. It should not be assumed that the costs of criticizing should be zero. Requiring would-be critics to incur some costs—for example, in documenting the factual basis of their criticisms—may be beneficial.

11. By "commercial organizations" in the broad sense, I mean those in which the profit motive, again broadly construed, plays a significant role in setting organizational priorities. "Commercial organizations" in this broad sense include, but are not limited to, those that have "for-profit" legal status.

12. I am indebted to Robert Veatch, who emphasized the importance of this requirement to me.

13. Discussions of the ethics of managed care often proceed, quite unfairly, as if the only moral agents involved are the patient and the physician. The account of legitimacy offered in this article can be used to provide guidance for other key moral agents: the medical director and other administrators in managed care. Thus it could be argued that these agents are only morally justified in developing and implementing rationing policies if the organization is legitimate or seriously approximates legitimacy.

14. The transfer of trust can go in the other direction, of course. The extent to which a patient trusts the organization may be determined in part by the extent of her direct merit trust in her physician. I am indebted to David Mechanic for emphasizing this point to me.

15. I wish to thank David Mechanic for raising this important point.

Chapter 8

1. Examples of incentives for underutilization include pressures hospitals put on physicians (including the threat of revocation of hospital admitting privileges) to conform to the Diagnostic Related Groups (DRG) system for Medicare-reimbursed hospital charges and year-end "hold back" or bonus arrangements in which HMOs or other forms of managed care use financial penalties or rewards to discourage utilization.

2. For example, a financial interest in amortizing the debt on an expensive piece of diagnostic equipment, or an interest in a laboratory or dialysis center of which the physician is an owner, can encourage overutilization.

3. In some cases, the hospital's attempt to stay within DRG reimbursement ceilings can cause patients to be discharged from the hospital before they are able to care for themselves adequately. If family support is lacking when the patient is discharged, there may be a serious risk of injury or illness. Similarly, if, in order to stay within the utilization constraints of the HMO, a physician forgoes a test that would have detected a serious but treatable condition, the consequences for the patient may be grave.

4. Edmund Pellegrino, Trust and Distrust in Professional Ethics, in *Ethics, Trust, and the Professions: Philosophical and Cultural Aspects* (Edmund Pellegrino et al., eds., 1991), pp. 69–89.

5. An example of one who assumes that trust is unique to professionalism is Edmund Pellegrino. Id., at 72–76.

6. *See* Robert Sokolowski, The Fiduciary Relationship and the Nature of Professions, in *Ethics, Trust, and the Professions,* supra note 4, pp. 23–39 and citations therein. Note that there are other, less formal uses of the term "professional." Sometimes we refer to someone as a professional to indicate that he or she is not an amateur, meaning only that the person performs the activity in question to earn a living, not as a mere hobby or pastime.

7. Some analysts, such as Eliot Friedson, include the requirement that the special knowledge in question be formal. Eliot Friedson, Nourishing Professionalism, in *Ethics, Trust, and the Professions,* supra note 4, pp. 193–220, 194–95.

8. Some analysts distinguish an additional element in the ideal conception of a profession: a commitment to serve the public interest, as distinct from, and sometimes in opposition to, the interests of their clients or patients. *See*, for example, Chapter 4 by Hazard in this volume, at "Civic Reponsibility". Although it may be true, as Hazard says, that professionals as such are liable to experience a conflict between their obligations to their patients or clients and their obligations to society, it is not so clear that the obligations of professionals to society are different from the obligations of other persons to society. For example, a physician may experience a conflict between his obligation to his patient (John Wilkes Booth) and his obligation to the public or the state as the agent of the public concerning the apprehension of a dangerous fugitive. But from this it would not follow that the obligation to the public good (as opposed to the conflict between this obligation and the professional's obligation to his or her client or patient) is peculiar to professions. In this chapter I will not take a stand on the issue of whether professionals as such have a peculiar obligation to the public, or to serve the public good, over and

above their obligations to particular members of the public who are their clients or patients and over and above their obligations to preserve the distinctive knowledge of the profession, to maintain high standards, and so on.

9. I am indebted to Christine Korsgaard for clarifying this point.

10. *See*, for example, Uwe Rheinhardt in Arnold Relman and Uwe Rheinhardt, An Exchange on For-Profit Health Care, in *For-Profit Enterprise in Health Care* (Bradford Gray, ed., 1986), pp. 212–13.

11. In his excellent book, Marc Rodwin documents in detail the medical profession's relative lack of external regulation compared with other professions, including lawyers, financial advisers, and government officials. Especially important is his observation that the law of fiduciary obligations, which is well developed for other professions, is almost nonexistent for physician. (Rodwin, *Medicine, Money, and Morals: Physicians' Conflicts of Interest*, chapter 7 [1993]).

12. There is a looser sense of the term "professional" according to which anyone who engages in an activity to earn a living is a professional. Moreover, sometimes we say that a particular task or job was "professional," meaning only that it was done according to high standards of performance.

13. There is little doubt that organized medicine, and many individual physicians, exaggerate both the objectivity and the certainty of medical expertise, as well as its inaccessibility to layper-sons. One important aspect of a comprehensive critique of the myth of medical professionalism would be to define the pervasiveness of uncertainty and subjectivity in the exercise of clinical judgment. That task is, however, beyond the scope of this chapter.

14. For a concise explanation of the most basic concepts of principal–agent theory, see Allen Buchanan, Principal/Agent Theory And Decision-Making in Health Care, 2 *Bioethics* 317 (1988).

15. There is a growing literature, including public testimony before governmental groups, reports by health insurance groups, and scholarly articles, documenting not only the prevalence of self-referral but also the fact that ownership biases clinical judgment regarding referral. The following is a selection of sources cited in Marc Rodwin, *Medicine, Money, and Morals Physicians' Conflicts of Interest* (1993).

Issues Related to Physician "Self-Referrals": Hearings Before the Subcommittee on Health and the Subcommittee on Oversight of the Committee on Ways and Means, House of Representatives, 101st Congress, 1st Session, on H.R. 939. testimony of Richard P. Kusserow, March 2 and June 1, 1989. (Serial No. 101–58), at 124–1440.

State of Florida Health Care Cost Containment Board and Department of Economics and Department of Finance, Florida State University, *Joint Ventures Among Health Care Providers in Florida*, Vols. I–III (1990).

Jean Mitchell and Elton Scott, New Evidence on the Prevalence and Scope Physician Joint Ventures, 268 *JAMA* 80 (1992).

Jean Mitchel and Elton Scott, Evidence on Complex Structures of Physician Joint Ventures Under Existing Regulation, 9 *Yale L.J.* 489 (1992).

David Hemenway et al., Physicians' Response to Financial Incentives from For-Profit Ambulatory Care Center, 322 *N. Engl. J. Med.* 1059 (1990).

Bruce Hillman et al., Frequency and Costs of Diagnostic Imaging in Office Practice—A Comparison of Self-Referring and Radiologist-Referring Physicians, 323 *N. Engl. J. Med.* 1604 (1990).

Inspector General, U.S. Government, *Financial Arrangements Between Physicians and Health Care Business: Report to Congress* (0AI-12-88-01410) (1991).

Medical Affairs Division, Blue Cross and Blue Shield of Michigan, *A Comparison of Laboratory Utilization and Payout to Ownership* (1984).

Department of Health and Human Services, Health Care Financing Administration, Division of Health Standards and Quality, Region V. *Diagnostic Clinical Laboratory Services in Region V* (No. 2-05-2004-11) (1983).

Medical Services Administration, State of Michigan, *Utilization of Medicaid Laboratory Services by Physicians with/without Ownership Interest in Clinical Laboratories: A Comparative Analysis of Six Selected Laboratories* (1981).

Alfred Childs and E. Diane Hunter, Non-Medical Factors Influencing Use of Diagnostic X-ray by Physicians, 10 *Medical Care* 323 (1972).

Alfred Childs and D. W. Hunter, *Patterns of Primary Medical Care—Use of Diagnostic X-Rays by Physicians* (1972). *See also* chapter 13 by Jean Mitchell in this volume.

16. It would be difficult to argue that legal regulation, when it has existed in this area, resulted from a request or demand from a united medical profession.

17. There is one situation in which something like the exchange model would be literally true: when the profession as an already organized corporate entity enters into negotiations with government concerning the conditions of practice (e.g., political bargaining between leaders of organized medicine and the leadership of Congress over ceilings for physicians' fees). The difficulty with extending the model beyond this particular situation is that the model cannot explain the creation of the profession if it assumes that a profession already exists as one of the parties to the exchange.

18. Eliot Friedson, note 7, supra, at 197.

19. Bernard Shaw, *The Doctor's Dilemma* (1954).

20. The average (mean) pre-tax, after-expenses income of U.S. physicians in 1991 was $170,600, while the median was $139,000. American Medical Association Center for Health Policy Research, *Socioeconomic Character of Medical Practice* (1993).

21. See, for example, Paul Feldstein, *Health Associations and the Demand for Legislation: The Political Economy of Health Care* (1977), and *Health Economics* (1979). See also Paul Starr, The *Social Transformation of Medicine in America* (1982).

22. Very recently, several medical specialties have begun to take steps to devise significant procedures for ensuring that their members continue to possess technical competence. However, it is worth noting that even with these continuing competence requirements, those who fail to meet them are still able to practice medicine so long as they do not represent themselves as recertified specialists.

23. Russell Localio et al., Relation Between Malpractice Claims and Adverse Events Due to Negligence, Results of the Harvard Medical Practice Study III, 325 *N. Engl. J. Med.* 245 (1991).

24. In many locales, state medical associations suppressed HMOs by blacklisting HMO doctors from specialty organizations and revoking their admitting privileges in hospitals

owned or controlled by association members. In some cases, medical associations have lobbied to make midwifery illegal; in others, they have succeeded in placing so many restrictions on the practice of midwifery as to make it economically unfeasible.

25. Rodwin, *Medicine, Morals, and Money*, especially chapter 2.

26. Id., chapter 2.

27. Id., chapter 2.

28. See, for example, AMA Rules Against Self-Referrals, *Chicago Tribune*, N20 (December 9, 1992).

29. It is far from clear that organized medicine in the United States could take effective measures to ensure a reasonable level of compliance with substantive standards concerning conflicts of interest even if it did a much better job of articulating such standards than it hitherto has. Since only about one-half of practicing physicians in the United States even belong to the AMA, the threat of expulsion is somewhat less than devastating. Moreover, the AMA only has the power to recommend policies to state medical associations, which may or may not ratify them. Finally, it can be argued that antitrust laws in particular, as well as the general emphasis in our legal system on individual freedom of contract, greatly restrict the feasible range of alternatives for ensuring compliance.

30. Uwe Rheinhardt makes this point in Arnold Relman and Rheinhardt, An Exchange on For-Profit Health Care, supra note 10, at 213.

31. Dan Brock and Allen Buchanan, Ethical Issues in For-Profit Health Care, in *For-Profit Enterprise in Health Care* 242 (1987).

32. See *Socioeconomic Characteristics of Medical Practice*, Table 48 (Martin Gonzalez, ed., 1992).

33. See Rheinhardt in Relman and Rheinhardt, An Exchange on For-Profit Health Care, pp. 209, 211, 212, 213. See also, Brock and Buchanan, supra note 31, at 241.

34. Rheinhardt in Relman and Rheinhardt. An Exchange on For-Profit Health Care, at 212.

35. For two discussions of data showing that the higher the average income of a given specialty the more applicants there are for residency positions in that specialty, see letters to the editor by Mark Ebell and by David Shulkin, 262 *JAMA*, 1630 (1989). The former analyzes data from the National Residency Match Program (1988); the latter uses data from that source and from the Medical Economics Earnings Survey (1988).

36. Paul Feldstein, *Health Associations and the Demand for Legislation: The Political Economy of Health* (1977), pp. 480–553.

37. Daniel Fox, *The Politics of Trust in American Health Care,* supra note 4, pp. 10–13.

38. Charles Beitz, *Political Equality* (1989); Joshua Cohen, Deliberation and Democratic Legitimacy, in *The Good Polity* (Alan Hamlin and Philip Pettit, eds., 1989), pp. 17–34; and Thomas Christiano, Freedom, Consensus, and Equality in Collective Decision Making, 10 *Ethics* 151 (1990).

39. Richard Zaner, The Phenomenon of Trust and the Physician–Patient Relationship in *Ethics, Trust, and the Professions: Philosophical and Cultural Aspects,* supra note 4, p. 480.

40. I am not aware of empirical studies on this phenomenon, but can report from my own experience as a patient that it certainly does occur. For example, when I asked a urolo-

gist whether there were any risks of infection from the cystoscopy he had just ordered for me (without asking my permission and without explaining the costs and benefits), he was astonished at my impudence. When, after his reluctant admission that there was such a risk. I declined his recommendation, he terminated the relationship.

41. The strongest case presently available for this approach is found in Marc Rodwin's book. See note 16, supra. See also the discussions of fiduciary duty by Morreim in chapter 11 and by Shimm and Spece in chapters 3 and 14, respectively.

42. This alternative for legal control of conflicts of interest is considered, but not endorsed by Rodwin, note 15 supra.

43. See chapter 10 by Mark Hall in this volume. See also supra note 14.

44. Supra note 14, pp. 317–33.

45. See, for example, Ian MacNeil, *The New Social Contract: An Inquiry into Modern Contractual Relations* (1980).

46. I am indebted to the following people, who generously supplied astute comments on earlier versions of this paper: Thomas Christiano, Christine Korsgaard, Jean Hampton, Thom Hudson, John Rawls, Tim Scanlon, and Roy Spece. I also have benefited from the perceptive comments of several members of the audience at a colloquium of the Center for Ethics and the Professions at Harvard University, where I presented this paper.

Chapter 9

1. See, for example, Audrey Chapman's "Introduction" in Chapman [1994, p. 9]: "Clearly there are areas of the world in which the most valuable steps toward improvement of health care are not medical services but public health protection. Poor countries with limited resources would better improve health standards by investing scarce resources in clean water and environmental cleanup rather than by offering curative health care to a small fraction of the population. Moreover, even within an advanced industrialized country, health status will continue to deteriorate and health care costs will continue to escalate unless there is greater attention to promoting more favorable health conditions."

2. The World Bank divides public health into three categories: population-based services, like immunizations; efforts to promote healthy behaviors, like antismoking campaigns; and efforts to provide healthy environments, including adequate public sanitation and clean water supplies (see World Bank [1993, p. 72], and more generally chapter 4, "Public Health").

3. For example, see the World Bank's correlation between fertility rates and life expectancy in sub-Saharan Africa and Latin America and the Caribbean (World Bank 1993, p. 30); and charts relating national income with fertility, infant mortality, and life expectancy (p. 236).

4. International Covenant on Economic, Social and Cultural Rights, G.A. res. 2200A (XXI), 21 U.N. GAOR Supp. (No. 16) at 49, U.N. Doc. A/6316 (1966), 993 U.N.T.S. 3, entered into force January 3, 1976. Article 12.

5. Universal Declaration of Human Rights, Article 25.

6. For extended treatment of this point, see Holmes and Sunstein [1999].

7. The Human Rights Committee is responsible for monitoring the implementation of civil and political rights within nations.

8. We do not discuss Norman Daniel's account of the importance of health care for preserving equality of opportunity. Although this important account may be suitable for grounding a human right to health care, the account was not explicitly developed in these terms. Because it would take a lengthy analysis to ascertain the implications of Daniels's account for the human right to health care, and then to assess its adequacy in that regard, we leave this analysis for another day. (See Daniels [1985].)

9. Ozar is guilty in this particular study of narrowly focusing on medical care and avoiding the issue of public-health needs.

10. We assume here that we cannot have rights to things that are impossible to guarantee. (In contrast, there is no problem asserting rights that, for contingent reasons, cannot currently be honored but that could plausibly be honored in the future. Such rights are ones to be progressively realized.) Probably the best that can be guaranteed is an equal or fair chance at receiving a heart transplant.

11. Ozar's account is probably also too narrow. We might believe it is possible that a right to health care includes the right to a cure for painful conditions that limit the extent to which sufferers can take advantage of important opportunities (along the lines of Norman Daniels's account of the importance of health care. See Daniels [1985]). Ozar's account seems to rule out this possibility on principle, because curing such conditions is not necessary for continued survival.

Chapter 10

The authors are grateful for research support for this paper from Duke University's Center for Genome Ethics, Law, & Policy, part of the Duke Institute for Genome Sciences & Policy.

1. "International organization" here means an organization in which states are the primary participants. "Transnational organization" refers to an organization that encompasses individuals or groups across state borders and in which states may not be the primary participants.

2. A cosmopolitan ethical perspective is one that takes individual human beings—regardless of where they happen to reside and independently of what national or ethnic group they are members of—as the fundamental objects of moral concern. Of course, the cosmopolitan perspective may not be the only possible normative basis for taking global health to be an important moral issue. On its most plausible reconstruction, however, the contemporary conception of human rights is a cosmopolitan conception.

3. Bradford Gray, ed., *For-Profit Enterprise in Health Care* (Washington, DC: National Academy Press, 1986), pp. 187–89. For a further account of why for-profit health-care organizations do not have determinate obligations to provide access to the indigent, see Dan W. Brock and Allen Buchanan, "Ethical Issues in For-Profit Health Care," in this volume, pp. 224–49.

4. Allen Buchanan, *Justice, Legitimacy, and Self-Determination: Moral Foundations for International Law* (New York: Oxford University Press, 2003), pp. 85–98.

5. Onora O'Neill argues against states as the primary agents of global justice; her view is at least partly based on the failure of states to accomplish justice beyond their borders in the past. This does not necessarily mean that states do not have, or are ill suited to carry out, at least some of the determinate responsibilities we describe. See Onora O'Neill, "Global Justice: Whose Obligations?," in *The Ethics of Assistance: Morality and the Distant Needy*, Deen K. Chatterjee (ed.) (New York: Cambridge University Press, 2004), pp. 242–59.

6. Allen Buchanan, "The Right to a Decent Minimum of Health Care," *Philosophy & Public Affairs*, 13 (1984), pp. 55–78.

7. Gopal Sreenivasan, "International Justice and Health: A Proposal," *Ethics & International Affairs*, 16 (2002), pp. 81–90.

8. Thomas Pogge has rightly emphasized the role that the recognition of these two rights plays in global poverty. Thomas Pogge, *World Poverty and Human Rights* (Cambridge, UK: Polity Press, 2002), pp. 22–23, 223–25, 117, 153, 162–66, 238, 258, 264, and 266.

9. A. Buchanan, *Justice, Legitimacy, and Self-Determination: Moral Foundations for International Law*, pp. 261–65.

10. International Commission on Intervention and State Sovereignty, The Responsibility to Protect (Ottawa: International Development Research Centre, 2001), pp. 12–18.

11. Marc Lacey, "Beyond Bullets and Blades," *The New York Times* (March 20, 2005).

12. James Nickel, *Making Sense of Human Rights* (Berkeley: University of California Press, 1987), pp. 41–43.

13. For a lucid articulation and defense of this "entitlements plus" conception of human rights, see Nickel, cited in no. 9, above, chapters 1 and 2. For the view that there are certain rights that are preconditions for the enjoyment of all other rights, see Henry Shue, *Basic Rights: Subsistence, Affluence, and U.S. Foreign Policy*, 2nd edition, (Princeton, NJ: Princeton University Press, 1980), pp. 22–34.

14. For a valuable contribution to the solution of this problem, see Kristen Hessler, "A Theory of Interpretation for Human Rights," Ph.D. dissertation, University of Arizona, 2001. See also, Kristen Hessler and Allen Buchanan, "Specifying the Content of the Human Right to Health Care," in *Medicine and Social Justice: Essays on the Distribution of Health Care*, Rosamond Rhodes, Margaret Battin and Anita Silvers (eds.) (New York: Oxford University Press, 2002), pp. 84–96.

15. Anne-Marie Slaughter, *A New World Order* (Princeton, NJ: Princeton University Press, 2004), pp. 1–35.

16. World Trade Organization, *The WTO in Brief* (Geneva: World Trade Organization, 2003), p. 2.

17. World Health Organization and World Trade Organization Secretariat, *WTO Agreements and Public Health* (Geneva: World Trade Organization, 2002), pp. 11, 15, 31, 84.

18. World Trade Organization, *Agreement on Trade-Related Aspects of Intellectual Property Rights* (Geneva: World Trade Organization, 1994). Available at: http://www.wto.org/english/docs_e/legal_e/27-trips.pdf. Accessed March 25, 2005.

BIBLIOGRAPHY

Aaron, H. and Schwarz, R. (1984). *The Painful Prescription: Rationing Hospital Care.* Washington, DC: The Brookings Institution.

Baily, M. A. (1986). "Rationing Health: Defining the Adequate Level." In George Agich and Charles Begeley, eds., *What Price Health*? Dordrecht, Holland: D. Reidel.

Brock, D. W. (1973). "Recent Work in Utilitarianism." *Am Philos Q* 10:8, 15.

———. (1988). "Ethical Issues in Recipient Selection for Organ Transplantation." In D. R. Mathieu, ed., *Organ Substitution Technology: Ethical, Legal, and Public Policy Issues.* Boulder, CO: Westview Press, 86–99.

Brock, D. W. and Allen Buchanan. (1986). "Ethical Issues in For-Profit Health Care." In Bradford H. Gray, ed., *For Profit Enterprise in Health Care.* Washington, DC: National Academy, 224–49.

Buchanan, A. E. (1981). "Justice: A Philosophical Review." In E. E. Shelp, ed., *Justice and Health Care.* Dordrecht, Holland: D. Reidel, 3–21.

———. (1983). "The Right to a 'Decent Minimum' of Health Care". *Philosophy and Public Affairs* 13(2):55–78.

———. (1984a). "The Right to a 'Decent Minimum' of Health Care." *Philos Pub Aff* 13, 55–78.

———. (1984b). "What's So Special About Rights?" *Soc Philos Policy* 2, 63.

———. (1985). *Ethics, Efficiency, and the Market.* Totowa, NJ: Rowman & Allanheld.

———. (1987). "Justice and Charity." *Ethics* 97, 558–75.

———. (1992). "Private and Public Responsibilities in the U.S. Health Care System." In Robert P. Huefner and Margaret P. Battin, eds., *Changing to National Health Care.* Salt Lake City: University of Utah Press.

———. (1996a). "Health Care Delivery and Resource Allocation." In Robert M. Veatch, ed., *Medical Ethics*, 2d. Boston: Bartlett and Jones.

———. (1996b). "Is There a Medical Profession in the House?" In Roy Spece, Jr., David Shimm, and Allen Buchanan, eds., *Conflict of Interest in Clinical Practice and Research.* New York: Oxford University Press, 105–36.

———. (1996c). "Toward a Theory of the Ethics of Bureaucratic Organizations." *Business Ethics Quarterly* 6:419–40.

———. (1998). "Managed Care: Rationing Without Justice, But Not Unjustly". *Journal of Health Politics, Policy and Law* 23:617–34.

Buchanan, A. E. (2003). *Justice Legitimacy, and Self-Determination: Moral Foundations for International Law*. New York: Oxford University Press.

Chapman, A. (1994). *Health Care Reform: A Human Rights Approach*. Washington, DC: Georgetown University Press.

Childress, J. F. (1982). "Priorities in the Allocation of Health Care Resources." In T. L. Beauchamp and L. Walter, eds., *Contemporary Issues in Bioethics*, 2nd ed. Belmont, CA: Wadsworth, 417–23.

Christiano, T. (1994). *Rule of the Many*. Boulder, CO: Westview Press.

Cohen, G. A. (1978). "Robert Nozick and Wilt Chamberlain: How Patterns Preserve Liberty." In J. Arthur and W. H. Shaw, eds., *Justice and Economic Distribution*. Englewood Cliffs, NJ: Prentice Hall, 246–62.

Council on Ethical and Judicial Affairs, American Medical Association. (1995). "Ethical Issues in Managed Care." *Journal of the American Medical Association* 273:4, 330–35.

Cranston, M. (1973). *What Are Human Rights?* New York: Taplinger Publishing.

Daniels, N. (1985). *Just Health Care*. Cambridge: Cambridge University Press.

———. (1986). "Why Saying No to Patients in the United States Is So Hard," *New England Journal of Medicine* 314:21, 1380–83.

———. (1993). "Rationing Fairly: Programmatic Considerations." *Bioethics* 7:2–3, 224–33.

———. (1996). *Justice and Justification*. Cambridge: Cambridge University Press.

Daniels, N., and Sabin James. (1998). Last Chance Therapies and Managed Care: Pluralism, Fair Procedures, and Legitimacy. *Hastings Center Report* 28:2, 27–41.

Department of Health, Education and Welfare (1986). *Report of the Task Force on Organ Transplantation*. Washington, DC: U.S. Department of Health and Human Services.

Donnelly, J. (1985). *The Concept of Human Rights*. London: Croom Helm.

———. (1989). *Universal Human Rights in Theory and Practice*. Ithaca, NY: Cornell University Press.

Dworkin, R. (1977). *Taking Rights Seriously*. Cambridge: Harvard University Press.

Emanuel, Ezekiel J. and Nancy Neveloff Dubler. (1995). "Preserving the Physician Patient Relationship in the Era of Managed Care." *Journal of the American Medical Association* 273:4, 323–29.

Feinberg, J. (1979). "The Nature and Value of Rights." In D. Lyons, ed., *Rights*. Belmont, CA: Wadsworth, 143–58.

———. (1980). "The Nature and Value of Rights." In *Rights, Justice, and the Bounds of Liberty*. Princeton, NJ: Princeton University Press, 143–58.

Gibbard, A. (1983). "The Prospective Pareto Principle and Equity of Access to Health Care." President's Commission, *Securing Access to Health Care, Vol. 2: Appendices: Sociocultural and Philosophical Studies*. Washington, DC: U.S. Government Printing Office, 153–78.

Gray, Bradford, ed. (1986). *For-Profit Enterprise in Health Care*. Washington, DC: National Academy Press.

Gutman, A. (1983). "A Principle of Equal Access." President's Commission, *Securing Access to Health Care, Vol. 2: Appendices: Sociocultural and Philosophical Studies*. Washington, DC: U.S. Government Printing Office, 51–66.

Health Care Study Group. (1994). "Understanding the Choices in Health Care Reform." *Journal of Health Politics, Policy and Law* 19:3, 499–541.

Hessler, K. (2001). "A Theory of Interpretation for Human Rights." Ph.D. dissertation, University of Arizona.

Hessler, K. and A Buchanan. (2002). "Specifying the Content of the Human Right to Health Care." In R. Rhodes, M. Battin and A. Silvers, eds., *Medicine and Social Justice: Essays on the Distribution of Health Care*. New York: Oxford University Press.

Hirshman, Albert O. (1970). *Exit, Voice, and Loyalty*. Cambridge, MA: Harvard University Press.

Holmes, S. and Sunstein, C. (1999). *The Cost of Rights: Why Liberty Depends on Taxes*. New York: Norton.

International Commission on Intervention and State Sovereignty. (2001). *The Responsibility to Protect*. Ottawa: International Development Research Centre.

Kohn, L., Corrigan, Janet, and Donaldson, Molla. (2000). *To Err Is Human: Building a Safer Health System*. Committee on Quality of Health Care in America, Institute of Medicine. Washington DC: National Academy Press.

Lacey, M. "Beyond Bullets and Blades." *The New York Times*. March 20, 2005.

Mathieu, D. R., ed. (1988). *Organ Substitution Technology: Ethical, Legal, and Public Policy Issues*. Boulder, CO: Westview Press.

McBride, J. (1997). "Reservations and the capacity to implement human rights treaties." In J. P. Gardner, ed., *Human Rights as General Norms and a State's Right to Opt Out: Reservations and Objections to Human Rights Conventions*. London: The British Institute of International and Comparative Law.

Mechanic, D. (1998). "The Functions and Limitations of Trust in the Provision of Medical Care". *Journal of Health Politics, Policy and Law* 23, 661–86.

———. and Meyer, Sharon. (2000). Concepts of Trust Among Patients with Serious Illness. *Social Science & Medicine* 51:5, 657–68.

Menzel, P. T. (1983). *Medical Costs, Moral Choices*. New Haven: Yale University Press.

Nickel, J. (1987). *Making Sense of Human Rights*. Berkeley: University of California Press.

Norman, R. (1999). Equality, Priority and Social Justice. *Ratio* (new series) XII (June), 178–94.

Nozick, R. (1974). *Anarchy, State, and Utopia*. New York: Basic Books.

O'Neill, O. (2004). "Global Justice: Whose Obligations?" In D. K. Chatterjee, ed., *The Ethics of Assistance: Morality and the Distant Needy*. New York: Cambridge University Press, 242–59.

Ozar, D. (1983). "What should count as basic health care?" *Theoretical Medicine* 4, 129–41. Reprinted in P. Werhane, A. R. Gini, and D. T. Ozar, eds., *Philosophical Issues in Human Rights*. New York: Random House, 1986.

Parfit, D. (1997). Equality and Priority. *Ratio* (new series) X (December), 202–21.

Pellegrino, E., and David Thomasma. (1988). *For the Patient's Good: The Restoration of Beneficence in Health Care*. New York: Oxford University Press.

Pogge, T. (2002). *World Poverty and Human Rights*. Cambridge UK: Polity Press.

President's Commission. (1983). *Securing Access to Health Care, Vol. 2: Appendices: Sociocultural and Philosophical Studies*. Washington, DC: U.S. Government Printing Office.

President's Commission for the Study of Ethical Problems in Medicine and Biomedical and Behavioral Research. (1983). *Securing Access to Health Care, Vol. 1: Report.*

President's Commission for the Study of Ethical Problems in Medicine and Biomedical and Behavioral Research. (1983). *Securing Access to Health Care*, vol. 2. Washington, DC: U.S. Government Printing Office.

Rawls, J. A. (1971). *Theory of Justice*. Cambridge: Harvard University Press.

Rescher, N. (1976). "The Allocation of Scarce Exotic Livesaving Therapy." In S. Gorovitz et al., eds., *Moral Problems in Medicine*. Englewood Cliffs, NJ: Prentice Hall, 522–35.

Rodwin, M. (1993). *Medicine, Money, and Morals: Physicians' Conflicts of Interest* New York: Oxford University Press.

Roter, D. and Hall, Judith. (1995). *Doctors Talking With Patients/Patients Talking With Doctors: Improving Communication in Medical Visits*. Westport, CT: Greenwood Publishing Group, Inc.

Sartorius, R. E. (1975). *Individual Conduct and Social Norms*. Belmont, CA: Dickenson.

Shue, H. (1980). *Basic Rights: Subsistence Affluence, and U.S. Foreign Policy* (2nd ed.). Princeton, NJ: Princeton University Press.

———. (1996). *Basic Rights*, 2nd ed. Princeton, NJ: Princeton University Press.

Slaughter, Anne-Marie. (2004). *A New World Order*. Princeton NJ: Princeton University Press.

Spece, Roy G., Jr., David S. Shimm, and Allen Buchanan, eds. (1996). *Conflicts of Interest in Clinical Practice and Research*. New York: Oxford University Press.

Sreenivasan, G. (2002). "International Justice and Health: A Proposal." *Ethics & International Affairs* 16, 81–90.

Starr, P. (1982). *The Social Transformation of American Medicine*. New York: Basic Books.

Thomasma, D. (1997). "Bioethics and International Human Rights." *Journal of Law, Medicine and Ethics* 25, 295–306.

Toebes, B. (1999). *The Right to Health as a Human Right in International Law*. Amsterdam: Hart/Intersentia.

Veatch, R. M. (1981). *A Theory of Medical Ethics*. New York: Basic Books.

Weinstein, M. and Stason, W. (1977). "Foundations of Cost-Effectiveness Analysis for Health and Medical Practices." *N Engl J Med* 296, 716–21.

White, J. (1995). Competing Solutions: American Health Care Proposals and International Experience. Washington, DC: Brookings Institution.World Bank (1993). *World Development Report 1993: Investing in Health*. New York: Oxford University Press.

World Health Organization World Trade Organization Secretariat. (2002). *WTO Agreements and Public Health*. Geneva: World Trade Organization.

World Trade Organization. (1994). Agreement on Trade-Related Aspects of Intellectual Property Rights. Geneva: World Trade Organization. Available at: http://www.wto.org/english/docs_e/legal_e/27-trips.pdf. Accessed March 25, 2005.

World Trade Organization. (2003). *The WTO in Brief*. Geneva: World Trade Organization.

INDEX

www.ingramcontent.com/pod-product-compliance
Ingram Content Group UK Ltd.
Pitfield, Milton Keynes, MK11 3LW, UK
UKHW040919150926
475595UK00001B/8

9 780195 394061